BEYOND
common
Ground

ALDEN THOMPSON

BEYOND

Why liberals and conservatives need each other

common Ground

Pacific Press® Publishing Association
Nampa, Idaho
Oshawa, Ontario, Canada
www.pacificpress.com

Cover design by Gerald Lee Monks
Cover design resources from iStockphoto.com and dreamstime.com
Inside design by Aaron Troia

You can obtain additional copies of this book by calling toll-free 1-800-765-6955 or by visiting www.adventistbookcenter.com.

Library of Congress Cataloging-in-Publication Data:

Thompson, Alden L. (Alden Lloyd)
  Beyond common ground : why Liberals and Conservatives need each other / Alden Thompson.
    p. cm.
  Includes bibliographical references and index.
  ISBN 13: 978-0-8163-2340-1 (pbk. : alk. paper)
  ISBN 10: 0-8163-2340-2 (pbk. : alk. paper)
  1. Christianity and politics—Seventh-day Adventists. 2. Seventh-day Adventists—Doctrines.
  3. Adventists—Doctrines. 4. Liberalism—Religious aspects—Seventh-day Adventists.
  5. Conservatism—Religious aspects—Seventh-day Adventists. I. Title.
  BR115.P7T53 2009
  286.7'32—dc22

                                                                          2009000028

09 10 11 12 13 • 5 4 3 2 1

Contents

Preface

Writing this book has been an exciting event. Scary, but exciting.
Why?

Because this is the kind of stuff that can bring a church together. Not always. But when the Spirit is at work, it happens. And that's exciting.

The broad vision for this book is captured in the following lines, drawn from the opening paragraphs of Ellen White's *Patriarchs and Prophets:*

"God is love." 1 John 4:16. His nature, His law, is love. It ever has been; it ever will be. . . .

Every manifestation of creative power is an expression of infinite love. The sovereignty of God involves fullness of blessing to all created beings. . . .

The history of the great conflict between good and evil, from the time it first began in heaven to the final overthrow of rebellion and the total eradication of sin, is also a demonstration of God's unchanging love. . . .

The law of love being the foundation of the government of God, the happiness of all intelligent beings depends upon their perfect accord with its great principles of righteousness. God desires from all His creatures the service of love—service that springs from an appreciation of His character. He takes no pleasure in a forced obedience; and to all

He grants freedom of will, that they may render Him voluntary service.[1]

That's the vision. So, like Jesus' early followers, let's talk it through, pray it through, until it seems "good to the Holy Spirit and to us."[2]

---

1. Ellen White, *Patriarchs and Prophets* (Mountain View, Calif.: Pacific Press® Publishing Association, 1958), 33, 34.
2. Acts 15:28.

Part 1

Simplicity, Certainty, and Stability: Three Anchors

The Bible says, "For my thoughts are not your thoughts,
    nor are your ways my ways, says the LORD.
For as the heavens are higher than the earth,
    so are my ways higher than your ways
and my thoughts than your thoughts."[1]

Others say, "The really important stuff in Scripture is embarrassingly clear."[2] —Gordon Balharrie

Others say, "If we know that we don't have to know everything, then the things that we can know, we can know with greater certainty."[3] —Alden Thompson

The three chapters in part 1 present three different ways of focusing on what really matters in Scripture, the important stuff—three anchors, if you please. That needs to be perfectly clear before we go on.

Don't the details matter? Of course. And if liberals and conservatives are actually going to live and work together as the body of Christ, we'll need to look at some important details, specifics that may look different depending on whether one sees them as a liberal or as a conservative.

But many of us will resist looking at potentially troubling details unless we are quite sure that it is "safe." We don't want to look stupid; we don't want people to think we are wicked when we are just trying to be honest; and we don't want to get angry at God. Not all of us will be troubled by each of those issues to the same extent, and we don't have to be. Some of us won't be troubled at all. That's good, too—maybe even crucial.

In general, however, for conservatives, it is terribly important to sense that God's steadying hand is on the wheel of history and that He is active in our lives. For the conservative side of me, that is very important. *Precious* is not too strong a word.

For liberals, it is terribly important to look at all the evidence and to be honest with it. For the liberal side of me, that is very important. *Precious* is not too strong a word.

My own conviction that both perspectives can live together energetically and harmoniously, has been shaped by my own experience, reinforced in particular and forever by my History of Adventism class in the spring of 1979 at Walla Walla College—the first time I taught the class. I tell the story briefly in my earlier book, *Escape From the Flames: How Ellen White Grew From Fear to Joy—and Helped Me Do It Too.* I quote three paragraphs from that story below, but first, a brief introduction.

Studying the Bible in Scotland transformed my view of the way God works with people. Because I was away from home, out of my comfort zone in the United States, I saw things I had never seen before. But when I finished my doctoral studies in Scotland in 1974, I knew that I would have to immerse myself in my Adventist heritage if I was going to share my insights with my church. With the basic conviction firmly in place that the Bible, Ellen White, and believers in general—each in our own way—move from an emphasis on God's power (fear) to an emphasis on His goodness (joy), I decided to read through the full nine volumes of Ellen White's *Testimonies for the Church.* Excerpting from my book, *Escape From the Flames,* here's part of the story:

> With that fear-to-joy model firmly in place from my study of Scripture and with my study of Scripture stabilized by the writings of Ellen White, I immersed myself in the *Testimonies* and was amazed. Because the first five volumes of the *Testimonies* simply follow chronological order (covering the years from 1855 through 1889), I saw Ellen White

10

grow and change. I watched her traverse the Sinai-Golgotha road, step by step. I saw the frown of Christ disappear and joy in the Lord break forth. It was exhilarating.

On March 21, 1979, the very day on which the new term began, I finished the last of the more than 4,800 pages in the *Testimonies.* I had taken copious notes. I was on a roll and ready to roll. If any of you reading this book were in that "History of Adventism" class, spring term, 1979, you may remember it as well as I do. It was one of the most exciting classes I have ever taught.

The short version is: The class of eighty students, spread all the way across the Adventist spectrum, came together on common ground. The devout conservatives on the right rejoiced because they sensed that God's hand was clearly leading in Ellen White's growing experience. The left-leaning liberals with their inclination to cynicism also came on board, for here was a model that allowed them to be absolutely honest with all the evidence. In that class, I glimpsed something that I sensed could work for the entire Adventist family. The dream that took on flesh and blood in that classroom has been a driving force in my life ever since. That is the experience I want for my church. And in a very real sense, that's why I'm writing this book.[4]

And that's why I am writing *this* book, too, urged on by a host of people who share my vision for the church. But the form of the first three chapters of this book has been shaped by a recent encounter with a forceful Ellen White quote. Written in 1872, it was originally addressed to J. N. Andrews, one of our most gifted early scholars—he could read the Bible in seven languages, for example, and could reproduce the entire New Testament from memory.[5]

Andrews was such a thorough and conscientious scholar, however, that he was sorely tempted to multiply arguments to the point that ordinary people simply lost interest. "Plain, pointed arguments, standing out as mileposts," Ellen White wrote to him, "will do more toward convincing minds generally than will a large array of arguments which cover a great deal of ground, but which none but investigating minds will have the interest to follow."[6] Get your *History of the Sabbath* before the public, she urged, "even if not in all that perfection you could desire."[7] Later, she observed that Andrews "was seeking too hard to arrive at perfection." He should have gotten the book out, making improvements in later editions.[8]

So here I am exploring the implications of that line about "plain, pointed arguments, standing out as mileposts." In short, I have discovered that different people find different ways of sorting out and holding on to that which is most important. What concerns me—driven now by many years of teaching—is that dreaded feeling that I find so often among devout people, that if someone or something were to dislodge even a small piece from their belief structure, the whole thing could collapse. Indeed, the rhetoric driving that feeling lurks everywhere in our culture: if you find even one error in the Bible, you can toss the whole thing out. That "logic" is believed at a deep level, both by devout conservatives, who are fearful of losing their faith, and by cynical liberals, who have already lost their faith. Neither side easily sees the middle ground that I believe is so crucial. So, in these first three chapters, I simply want to remind us of the mileposts that stand out so clearly, which will make it safe to explore the details that confirm the middle ground.

In my collection of quotations I rarely save anything I have composed myself, but on the day before Christmas in 2005, I worked out a few lines that summarize my concerns about knowledge and certainty and help explain the shape of the first three chapters. I still think both the quotes are true. The first one appears at the beginning of this introduction to part 1. Here is the other one:

> If we are certain that we don't have to be certain about everything, then we can be certain about those things which really are certain. But if we are certain that we have to be certain about everything, we will have great difficulty being certain about anything else.

Survival in the real world of everyday life requires us to sort out what is urgent, what is important, what has to be done today, and what can wait. Inevitably, some things never get done, even things that we once thought were urgent or important. But life continues. The famous Serenity Prayer of Alcoholics Anonymous points in that direction:

God grant me the serenity to
accept the things I cannot change;
courage to change the things I can;
and wisdom to know the difference.

I am convinced that the life of faith is like that too. We don't have to sort out everything. We build on what we know really matters and keep on going. But our preferred structures for sorting out the basics will vary from person to person. In these first three chapters, I explore three ways of simplifying and ordering our lives—three anchors that overlap and augment each other. I have found all three to be helpful, sometimes one more than the others. They are as follows:

1. Anchor 1: The Landmarks
2. Anchor 2: The Law of Love
3. Anchor 3: Jesus

The message is nearly identical in each case and is of crucial importance: Hold on to that which is clear. The world won't fall apart if you can't sort out everything. The things that really matter in Scripture, in faith, in life are "embarrassingly clear."

If we can have that kind of certainty, then it will be safe to look more closely at the details that fill out the rest of the picture. If you want potato soup, you'll need potatoes. The rest of the ingredients are important too. But if you have only the potatoes, you'll probably survive.

---

1. Isaiah 55:8, 9.

2. Gordon Balharrie, dean of the School of Theology, Walla Walla College from 1961 to 1977. Balharrie was dean when I was a student at Walla Walla College and when I returned as a teacher.

3. Alden Thompson, professor of Biblical Studies at Walla Walla University and author of this book.

4. Alden Thompson, *Escape From the Flames: How Ellen White Grew From Fear to Joy—and Helped Me Do It Too* (Nampa, Idaho: Pacific Press®, 2005), 30, 31.

5. See *Seventh-day Adventist Encyclopedia,* 2nd rev. ed., ed. Don F. Neufeld and others (Hagerstown, Md.: Review and Herald® Publishing Association, 1996), s.v. "Andrews, John Nevins."

6. Ellen White, *Testimonies for the Church* (Mountain View, Calif.: Pacific Press®,

1948), 3:39. As published in the *Testimonies,* Ellen White's statement is given a general application: "The world needs labor now. Calls are coming in from every direction like the Macedonian cry: 'Come over and help us.' " But to J. N. Andrews, probably the original recipient of the message, the lead-in is more specific: "Your Sabbath history should be given to the public, if not in all that perfection you could desire. Souls need the work now." Ellen White, *Manuscript Releases* (Silver Spring, Md.: E. G. White Estate, 1993), 13:345.

    7. White, *Manuscript Releases,* 13:345.

    8. Ellen White, *Selected Messages* (Washington, D.C.: Review and Herald®, 1958), 3:97.

Chapter 1

Anchor 1: The Landmarks

The Sabbath and the Advent (the Second Coming)—they are the glue that bond Seventh-day Adventists together around the world. They are in our name. Adventists everywhere cherish the day God has blessed and live in hope of Jesus' return.

In 1861, early Adventists also began signing a simple covenant whenever a local church was organized. The last words of that covenant are the last words in the three angels' messages, affirming that Adventists "keep the commandments of God, and the faith of Jesus Christ."[1]

We may differ on many points and puzzle over even more, but our common ground is clear: Sabbath, the Second Coming, the keeping of God's commandments, and the faith of Jesus Christ. Hold on. It will mean simplicity, certainty, and stability.

Now let's look at the details.

> We, the undersigned, hereby associate ourselves together, as a church, taking the name, Seventh-day Adventists, covenanting to keep the commandments of God, and the faith of Jesus Christ.[2]

Count them. Just twenty-nine words. That's all. Sign off, and you could be an official Adventist in Michigan, where our first churches were organized in 1861.

Being Adventist has always meant much more, to be sure. And by the time another decade had passed, our spiritual forebears fleshed out the picture with a published list of twenty-five beliefs. Still, they didn't want to push anyone around. The second sentence of the 1872 Fundamental Principles Taught and Practiced by Seventh-day Adventists is to the point: "We do not put forth this as having any authority with our people, nor is it designed to secure uniformity among them." It was merely a description of what Adventists had believed "with great unanimity."[3] How they put those pieces together is part of our story here.

The covenant cited above is a good place to start: Adventists cherish the commandments of God and the faith of Jesus Christ. Period. But we can be even more specific, more simple. It's in our name: Sabbath and the Advent. In that connection, an early comment by James White is revealing. Responding to an inquiry from a Seventh Day Baptist in 1853, ten years before our own General Conference was organized, White explained that "as a people we are brought together from divisions of the Advent body [the Millerites], and from the various denominations."

Before saying even one word about common beliefs, White notes that this diverse group of people holds "different views on some subjects." In short, there was diversity from the start. But then he turns to common ground: "Yet, thank Heaven," he exclaims, "the Sabbath is a mighty platform on which we can all stand united. . . . [We] have no other creed than the Word of God. . . . We are united in these great subjects: Christ's immediate, personal second Advent, and the observance of all of the commandments of God, and the faith of his Son Jesus Christ, as necessary to a readiness for his Advent."[4]

James White's list is simple: Sabbath, Word of God, Second Advent, commandments of God, and the faith of Jesus Christ. Wherever one travels in the wide world today, that is still the glue that holds Adventism together. However much we might argue about various aspects of our faith, we are still Seventh-day Adventists—Sabbath and the Advent are in our name and come first in James White's explanation to his Seventh Day Baptist brother.

But note, also, how terribly important the Bible is for these core beliefs. Without the Word of God, we would know nothing about Sabbath, nothing about the Second Coming, and nothing about Jesus. Nothing. Certain aspects of our faith, to be sure, link us with the world's great religions, the world's great thinkers, and even with the convictions of devout heathen. There is great value in knowing how close others come to the commandments of God and the faith of Jesus Christ. That was the basis of Paul's appeal to the philosophers in Athens (Acts 17) and the basis of his comments in Romans 2 about the Gentiles who don't have the law but who "do instinctively what the law requires."[5]

But Paul didn't just talk soothingly about the beliefs he shared with others. Common ground was his starting point, but he boldly moved to the distinctives of his faith. In Athens, for example, he brought the Resurrection to center stage, a radical departure from anything the Athenians had ever heard before. Did any of the New Testament writers waffle on Jesus' resurrection? Never. Some believers raised questions about the Resurrection, to be sure, and that explains Paul's strong defense of the Resurrection hope in 1 Corinthians 15. But the New Testament writers never questioned the Resurrection. They debated many issues among themselves, but not the fact of the Resurrection. If Jesus was the heart of their faith, His resurrection was its foundation.

We could ask the same question of the Second Advent: Did any New Testament writer ever waffle on the Second Coming? Never. Some believers raised questions, to be sure, even claiming that "all things continue as they were from the beginning of creation!"[6] But Peter emphatically refuted them, pointing clearly to the Christian conviction that the second coming of Jesus would mark the end of this present world. It's clear that the New Testament writers were already tussling with questions of delay, even in their day. Matthew 24 and 25 are evidence enough for that. But question the Second Advent itself? Not the New Testament writers. Never.

Right here, in connection with the Seventh-day Adventist message and mission, it is appropriate to ask why Adventists emphasize the Sabbath when the New Testament never does, at least not in the way that it emphasizes the Resurrection and Second Coming.

What Seventh-day Adventists have done is to point to the fact that the Seventh-day Sabbath was also a solid part of the early Christian faith, a truth that was nearly lost during the many centuries of Christian history. The New Testament writers did not present forceful arguments in favor of the Sabbath because the earliest Christians were all Sabbath-keeping Jews. Indeed, Jesus' attitude toward the Sabbath suggests that God's people had become too rigid in their attitudes toward the Sabbath. Mark's Gospel records Jesus as saying, "The sabbath was made for humankind, and not humankind for the sabbath; so the Son of Man is lord even of the sabbath."[7] Similarly, the events recorded in Matthew 12 suggest that the early Christians needed a more humane attitude toward the Sabbath. In light of that Jewish experience, no one in the New Testament would have dreamed of arguing for the Sabbath. Everyone already knew that the Sabbath was the day God had blessed.

In the course of time, perhaps even by the end of the first century, some who came from a non-Jewish background began to raise questions about the Sabbath. That's when the arguments for and against the Sabbath begin to show up. But they are not found in the New Testament itself.

So Adventists pick up the gospel story, the faith of Jesus Christ, with its essential teachings about the incarnation, death, resurrection, and return of Jesus. Our voices have joined the chorus of general Christian voices in affirming those great teachings. But the Sabbath needed a fresh voice, and we sought to be faithful to God's calling in that respect. Actually, even the conviction that the world would soon end with Jesus' return also became obscured. Adventists brought back that message, too, with vigor and enthusiasm, even before we began to preach the Sabbath.

How much diversity? Three simple steps

Spotting the common ground in the New Testament is easy: the Resurrection and Second Coming crop up everywhere. And once we understand something of the history of the Sabbath, it, too, is perfectly clear in the New Testament. But the early Christians faced the same challenge that Adventists struggle with today: how much diversity does our common ground allow?

In facing that question the church constantly battles the two extremes—a rigidity that snuffs out diversity and a laxity that erodes unity. Or to use more concrete images, the danger of walls that are too high and thick versus the danger of no walls at all. But we don't have to choose between boundaries that are too rigid and no boundaries at all. We can find the middle ground.

How do we find it? Surprise! Contrary to popular opinion, turmoil helps us find it, especially the turmoil in the New Testament. That turmoil is not a sign of weakness; it is a sign of life and strength! Paul could challenge Peter to his face,[8] and Peter could claim that Paul was hard to understand.[9] Without that give-and-take, we would have no idea how to handle issues in the church today. Paul soundly rebuked the believers in Corinth for choosing up sides between their favorite preachers.[10] But the record of their tussles is terribly important for us today. Why should the church in our day experience any less turmoil? Turmoil in the church is normal. Indeed, without it, spiritual life could be at risk.

In Adventist history, Ellen White highlighted that very issue in the 1888 debate over righteousness by faith. Opposing those who simply wanted an easy unanimity in the church, Ellen White forcefully argued for room to disagree:

> As real spiritual life declines, it has ever been the tendency to cease to advance in the knowledge of the truth. Men rest satisfied with the light already received from God's word and discourage any further investigation of the Scriptures. They become conservative and seek to avoid discussion. . . .
>
> When no new questions are started by investigation of the Scriptures, when no difference of opinion arises which will set men to searching the Bible for themselves to make sure that they have the truth, there will be many now, as in ancient times, who will hold to tradition and worship they know not what.[11]

Alright, let's have diversity, and the liberals will say, "Amen." But where are the boundaries? That's what the conservatives want to know. And they are absolutely right to raise that question. Both concerns are terribly important for the life of the church. We run the risk of having no boundaries at all if the liberals "win," or boundaries that are too rigid if the conservatives "win." That is precisely why Jesus needs both liberals and conservatives! If we kill off one side or the other, the church will be greatly impoverished.

I would like to propose three simple steps that will help us find and hold that middle ground between no boundaries and boundaries that are too rigid:

1. Remember our common ground. If we are going to be Adventists, then let's make sure that we remember what we all hold in common—Sabbath, the Second Coming, the Bible as our only creed, the commandments of God, and the

faith of Jesus Christ. All of that is found in James White's one paragraph response to a Seventh Day Baptist in 1853 as noted above.

But even if we celebrate our common ground, we should never simply toss
the rest. A very helpful procedure, for example, is to compare all three of our
full statements of belief—the unofficial one from 1872, the first official one
from 1931, and the first one to be discussed and voted at a full General Conference Session from 1980. In my view, these three statements provide the outer
boundaries, so to speak, of what is allowable within Adventism. For example,
our current Trinitarian statement contrasts with the non-Trinitarian position
of the 1872 statement. Should we exclude someone from the church who happens to prefer James White's non-Trinitarian position to our current Trinitarian one? Personally, I would not object if a believer were to hold such a view
privately. But if he or she became belligerent and began to attack the church's
current position on the Trinity, that would be quite unacceptable.

Another feature of the early Adventist experience that is frequently over-
looked by both liberals and conservatives in the church is the key role that the
sanctuary doctrine played in the early Adventist discovery of the Sabbath and
the binding nature of the Ten Commandments. Note how Ellen White linked
the sanctuary experience and the landmarks with Revelation 11:19, "Then
God's temple in heaven was opened, and the ark of his covenant was seen
within his temple." Commenting on that early experience, she wrote,

> The passing of the time in 1844 was a period of great events, open-
> ing to our astonished eyes the cleansing of the sanctuary transpiring in
> heaven. . . . One of the landmarks under this message was the temple
> of God, seen by His truth-loving people in heaven, and the ark con-
> taining the law of God. The light of the Sabbath of the fourth com-
> mandment flashed its strong rays in the pathway of the transgressors of
> God's law. The nonimmortality of the wicked is an old landmark. I
> can call to mind nothing more that can come under the head of the old
> landmarks.[12]

We could spend many hours debating how all the parts fit together. But my
point here is that regardless of how we deal with some of the details, we can still

claim our simple and secure common ground. That is an anchor that does not move. The rest is still very important. But if we can celebrate our common ground, we will find ways of seeing how the rest points to the landmarks. Understanding how all the pieces fit together, however, is where we are most likely to hold "different views on some subjects," to borrow James White's words.[13]

2. Treat others as we would want to be treated if we were in their place. In Matthew 7:12, Jesus says this principle is the law and the prophets. In Romans 13:8–10, Paul declares that love fulfills the law, in other words, fills it clear full. Galatians 5:14 uses the same word, translated by the New Revised Standard Version as "summed up." "The whole law is summed up in a single commandment, 'You shall love your neighbor as yourself.' " In Matthew 22:35–40, this principle is Jesus' second great command, following the command to love God wholeheartedly. Jesus' wording is crucial: "On these two commandments hang all the law and the prophets" (verse 40). In short, everything we say or do should be tested by these two great commands. *Everything.*

Part of what we want to do in this book is explore why it is so easy for us to forget this clear command when we discuss doctrine and the Christian life. Is any doctrine worth defending if we destroy a brother or sister for whom Christ died? Indeed, Paul warned precisely of that danger after quoting the "single" commandment: "If, however, you bite and devour one another, take care that you are not consumed by one another."[14]

Ellen White applied that command to our day when she observed that "a jealous regard for what is termed theological truth often accompanies a hatred of genuine truth as made manifest in life. . . . Men may profess faith in the truth; but if it does not make them sincere, kind, patient, forbearing, heavenly-minded, it is a curse to its possessors, and through their influence it is a curse to the world."[15]

3. Remember that the whole Bible is our only creed. Note the addition of the word *whole* in this third step. Protestants are fond of saying "the Bible only." I am convinced that Adventists are in a wonderful position to emphasize the *whole* Bible as our only creed. And I am not thinking just about our defense of the Sabbath, as important as that is. I am more concerned here about those differences in the Bible writers that will enable us to address the tensions between liberals and conservatives in our day.

By paying attention to *all* the Bible, we can learn why there is so much more to the Old Testament than just the Ten Commandments, even though the Ten Commandments clearly stand head and shoulders above the rest. By paying attention to *all* the Bible, we can learn why there is so much more in the New Testament, even though Jesus' two great commands clearly summarize it all. The additional bits and pieces fill out the story, revealing how one Bible writer sees it one way, while another has a different perspective.

Ellen White applies this principle of diversity to the modern Bible classroom. Students should not have the same teacher "term after term," she argues. "Different teachers should have a part in the work, even though they may not all have so full an understanding of the Scriptures. . . . Why do we need a Matthew, a Mark, a Luke, a John, a Paul, and all the writers who have borne testimony in regard to the life and ministry of the Saviour?" she asks. Because the minds of human beings "differ." God gives to "some Bible students views of truth that others do not grasp. It is possible for the most learned teacher to fall far short of teaching all that should be taught."[16]

Understanding this diversity is a crucial link between this third step and the second. If we can't see how the differences in our perspectives reflect the differences in the Bible writers, we can all too easily consider the views of our brothers and sisters to be dangerous rather than helpful. And when we consider their views as dangerous, it's not as easy to be kind.

Some differences are inappropriate, to be sure, and the church must address those. We must preserve our common ground from any and all attacks. But in defending the truth, we must follow the ways and methods of Jesus. One of my favorite Ellen White quotations in this respect—words that I have to repeat to myself when I am overly agitated about the prospect of heresy in the church—is this one, spoken to a brother who was having some difficulty following the ways of Jesus: "If you would always manifest kindness, respect, noble love and generosity, toward even wicked men, you might render effectual service to Christ."[17]

A simple nucleus—but singing in harmony, not just in unison

The central features of Adventism are like a bugle call—clear, focused, even piercing. But in real life, as in music, harmony is more likely to carry the day than unison. A full orchestra introduces even more diversity. But harmony is always the goal. There will be the occasional solo and touch of unison, but perpetual unison is not the best way to make good music.

The music metaphor can tell us more about diversity. Where there is a theme with variations, for example, the variations must not overpower the theme. Somehow, the church must preserve the theme while nurturing the variations. If it feels as though we have to play in unison all the time, no one will come to the concert; the players won't even show up for rehearsals!

My impression is that many Adventists feel oppressed by our long statement of beliefs, now a total of twenty-eight. As I have listened to the conversations, I have sensed that the concern is often more about the *feeling* of oppression than dislike for particular Adventist beliefs. Can we simplify our message so that the theme is preserved while allowing for variations? How can we make the church feel like it is singing in harmony, not just in unison?

A suggestion: Let's return to the simple covenant that Adventists used when we first began to organize as a church. From a merely human point of view, of course, that's an unlikely move. As churches "mature," they tend to multiply rules and regulations, not simplify them. Handbooks easily turn into encyclopedias. Actually, the early Adventist rhetoric against any creed except the Bible reflects the conviction that we should not attempt to define every point of doctrine with precision.

Interestingly enough, even though our current statement of belief is long compared to that simple original covenant, the preamble to our current (1980) statement actually contains a provision that would allow us to make that kind of change—placing the covenant at the head of our beliefs, signifying more clearly the common ground to which the rest is commentary. In its current form, the preamble reads,

> Seventh-day Adventists accept the Bible as their only creed and hold certain fundamental beliefs to be the teaching of the Holy Scriptures. These beliefs, as set forth here, constitute the church's understanding and expression of the teaching of Scripture. Revision of these statements may be expected at a General Conference session when the church is led by the Holy Spirit to a fuller understanding of Bible truth or finds better language in which to express the teachings of God's Holy Word.[18]

The preamble makes two major points: the Bible is our only creed, and revision may be expected. But what the preamble does not spell out is the common ground that binds all Adventists together: Sabbath, the Advent, the commandments, and the faith of Jesus Christ. Along with the Bible as our "only creed," those are the core convictions that make us what we are. And somehow we need to say more clearly that Jesus is at the heart of who we are. The very last words in the covenant are "the faith of Jesus Christ." We have saved the best until last. Maybe we should put it at the beginning as well. When we are fully committed to Jesus, then, when any of us are inclined to go astray, we can call each other to account, in the name of Jesus, for His sake, and by following His methods.

We will talk further about the relationship between Jesus and our Adventist essentials. But we also need to address the nagging fear that if we say too loudly that some things are more important than others, we are tossing out the lesser things completely. That sounds scary and feels scary, at least to some. But let's remember that we have a solid foundation, common ground on which we all stand. If we can celebrate that common ground, we will find simplicity, certainty, and stability. And we will discover that we don't all have to agree on everything. Our early Adventist pioneers could say a hearty "Amen" to that, and so can we.

Anchor 1? A good one. Very good.

---

1. Revelation 14:12, KJV.

2. Original church covenant used to organize Adventist churches when organization first began to happen in 1861. Published in "Doings of the Battle Creek Conference, Oct. 5 & 6, 1861," *Review and Herald,* October 8, 1861. See *Seventh-day Adventist Encyclopedia,* 2nd rev. ed., s.v. "Covenant, Church."

3. The 1872 statement, along with the 1931 and 1980 statements, are published in appendix 1 of Gary Land, ed., *Adventism in America* (Grand Rapids, Mich.: Wm. B. Eerdmans, 1996), 231–250. All three statements are laid out in synoptic format in Rolf Pöhler's *Continuity and Change in Adventist Teaching* (New York: Peter Lang, 2000).

4. James White, "Resolution of the Seventh-day Baptist Central Association," *Review and Herald,* August 11, 1853. See also *Seventh-day Adventist Encyclopedia,* 2nd rev. ed., s.v. "Doctrinal Statements, Seventh-day Adventist."

5. Romans 2:14.

6. 2 Peter 3:1–13.

7. Mark 2:27, 28.

8. See Galatians 2:11.

9. See 2 Peter 3:15, 16.

10. See 1 Corinthians 1:10–17.

11. Ellen White, *Testimonies for the Church,* 5:706, 707.

12. Ellen White, *Counsels to Writers and Editors* (Nashville, Tenn.: Southern Publishing Association, 1946), 30, 31.

13. James White, *Review and Herald,* August 11, 1853.

14. Galatians 5:15.

15. Ellen White, *The Desire of Ages* (Mountain View, Calif.: Pacific Press®, 1940), 309, 310.

16. Ellen White, *Counsels to Parents, Teachers, and Students* (Mountain View, Calif.: Pacific Press®, 1943), 432, 433.

17. Ellen White, *Testimonies for the Church,* 4:331.

18. Preamble of the 1980 Fundamental Beliefs of Seventh-day Adventists, voted at the Dallas, Texas, General Conference Session. General Conference of Seventh-day Adventists, "Fundamental Beliefs," General Conference of Seventh-day Adventists, http://www.adventist.org/beliefs/fundamental/index.html.

Chapter 2

Anchor 2: The Law of Love

Jesus quoted them.[1] So did Paul and James.[2] It's all about love, the Bible tells us, a love that hates to see anyone get hurt.[3] That's why God rattled Mount Sinai with fire and smoke and gave the Ten Commandments.[4] The people were terrified but delighted—God had shown them how to live! Moses was right, they said: No other nation ever had a god like that. Their neighbors agreed.[5]

Years later, Jesus, the same God in human flesh, came to live on earth.[6] He came to save us from sin,[7] show us how to live,[8] and show us what God is like.[9] He lived, died, and rose again to make it all happen.[10] It's all about love, He said, loving God and loving people.[11] And the best way to love God is to love people. In fact, God asks just one question in the judgment: Have you been helpful to others? It's that simple.[12]

But there's a catch. The God who saves us loves all His children so much that He does startling things in order to reach them, even things that look shocking to us. But it's only because He loves them just like He loves us.[13] The Bible, especially the Old Testament, is full of tough stuff like that.[14] But don't let it throw you. If we could see through God's eyes and through the eyes of the people He was trying to reach, it would make perfectly good sense.

In the meantime, hang on to the clear things, the things that never change and that apply to all of us, all the time: the *one* great law of love, the *two* great commands, and the *Ten* Commandments, the law God carved in stone with His own finger.[15] It's simple. It's certain. It's an anchor that never moves.

Now let's look at the details.

Don't Burn This Book

or

Don't Give Up Too Soon—It's Not as Scary as It Sounds

Ellen White says, "Edson, please read this carefully. Do not cast it aside or burn it."[16]

Ellen White says, " 'Why, mother!' cried I, in astonishment, 'this is strange talk for you! If you believe this strange theory, do not let anyone know of it; for I fear that sinners would gather security from this belief, and never desire to seek the Lord.' "[17]

These two quotes from Ellen White reflect two opposite fears: the fear that someone won't listen and the fear that someone will! To a certain extent, we all struggle with those same two fears. How they affect us in the church is my concern here.

My original title for this chapter, "Don't Burn This Book!" plays off Ellen White's urgent plea to her wayward son Edson in a handwritten comment across the top of a letter she wrote to him: "Please read this carefully. Do not cast it aside or burn it." Every week brought Edson a long letter from his mother, and not just long, but pointed and tedious. And all of the letters were remarkably similar. As one Adventist historian quipped, "It's not hard to see why Edson would want to burn the letter."

Like Edson's mother, I want to break through initial resistance to something very important. I want Adventist liberals and conservatives—hang on until we define these terms more carefully in part 3—to talk with each other and help each other and thus strengthen the work of the church. In short, I want them to listen. So don't burn the book!

But the other quote is just as crucial—Ellen White's astonishing alarm that her mother might jettison belief in an eternally burning hell. Now the fear of losing hell, in and of itself, is not at all surprising. Millions would heartily affirm young Ellen's alarm. They believe God wouldn't be God without the fires of an eternal hell. What is astonishing is that this same Ellen White changed sides—and did it with passion. In her later years, for example, she exclaimed that the doctrine of hell can so "outrage [our] sense of justice, mercy, and benevolence" that it drives some people into skepticism.[18] In short, that which Ellen White once greatly feared she later wholeheartedly embraced!

Now I realize that the argument can cut both ways. Most of us know people who have rejected truth for error. That's often a reason why some conservatives don't want to talk. They're tempted to believe that conversations with liberals could be a demonic plot to destroy faith. My point here is only to raise the possibility that such conversations are not necessarily a curse—they could be a great blessing. They need not result in dangerous compromise.

And let me emphasize that this book is not a call for compromise. I don't want strong convictions to melt down into flabbiness. What I do want is for us to see how apparently conflicting convictions can be seen as complementary rather than contradictory. The result will be cooperation rather than compromise. But it will take time to make that point clear. In the meantime, don't burn the book!

As I seek to make the case that Jesus needs both liberals and conservatives and so do we, the following three practical concerns need to be clear from the outset.

1. The writers of the Bible include both liberals and conservatives. I never tire of arguing that diversity among the Bible writers is not the problem, but the solution. Both liberals and conservatives speak for God, but from differing perspectives. Yet conservatives are often so unsettled by the fear of contradiction that they have difficulty accepting the liberal need to hold several positions in tension. Thus conservatives resist the very differences that liberals celebrate. Meanwhile, liberals are often too easily exasperated when their more exploratory ideas are met with resistance.

Ellen White did not hesitate to argue that diversity enhances the perfection of the Bible. On a tree, no "two leaves [are] just alike," she noted. "This variety adds to the perfection of the tree as a whole." All the Bible writers have their own "individuality." "Each has an experience of his own, and this diversity broadens and deepens the knowledge that is brought out to meet the necessities of varied minds."[19]

Most nonspecialists are not aware of the subtle tensions that often exist between biblical scholars and systematic theologians, to use their more technical labels. Biblical scholars focus on individual texts and passages, while systematic theologians seek for a larger and consistent unity to the whole. Biblical scholars make it their business to trace the precise nuances of a particular text, regardless of how their conclusions mesh with the interpretation of other texts. We—as a biblical scholar, I include myself here—revel in differences, tensions, and paradoxes, not only between writers but also within a document written by a single author. Systematic theologians are not likely to be enthusiastic at my exclamation, "The problems are the solution!" Yet from a practical point of view, as Ellen White so forcefully argues, we need that diversity.

2. I want to win only one argument. The only argument I really want to win is the argument that both liberals and conservatives belong in the church and urgently need each other if the church is going to be successful in its mission. Admittedly, since my competitive side secretly wants to win every argument, I am exaggerating a bit when I say that I really want to win only one. But it's true. For the health of the church, the discussion must stay alive.

As we look at the issues over which liberals and conservatives quarrel, I often favor one perspective over another—sometimes on the liberal side, sometimes on the conservative. But whether or not I make my own position clear, I would be deeply troubled if I were to win any of those arguments to the point where the alternative position withers and dies, and those who support it go off by themselves. And that leads to the next point.

3. This book is the beginning of the discussion, not the end. If I can make the case persuasively, then Adventism can be a vibrant, dynamic community, exploring the tension between that which never changes (landmarks) and the growing edge that does change (present truth). If either side "wins" to the point where it vanquishes the other side, the church will be greatly weakened. By preserving the creative tensions among us, we enable the church to address new questions and new situations in ways that will enhance our mission.

The challenge for Adventism is that we have a regrettable and tenacious history of wanting to be right, completely right. And when people know that they have always been right, they have absolutely no interest in change. In the heat of the 1888 battle, for example, G. I. Butler, the General Conference president, exclaimed that Adventists have "never taken a stand upon Bible exegesis which they have been compelled to surrender."[20] And after encouraging A. T. Jones to do further research on the identity of the ten kingdoms in Daniel, Uriah Smith suddenly changed his tune when Jones decided that the tenth kingdom was the Alemanni rather than the Huns. You are "ten percent short" of the truth, declared Smith, arguing that Jones would simply "unsettle minds" and "create confusion."[21]

Interestingly enough, it was the 1888 debate that seems to have opened Ellen White's eyes to the importance of allowing diverse views on the interpretation of Scripture. In an 1892 manuscript, she argues that when someone presents one perspective on a passage of Scripture and another person sees a different point, "both may be of the highest value." And if somebody makes a mistake, should this be divisive? "God forbid," she exclaimed. "We cannot then take a position that the unity of the church consists in viewing every text of Scripture in the very same light." Even if the church passes "resolution upon resolution" in an attempt to quell disagreement, "these resolutions may conceal the discord, but they cannot quench it and establish perfect agreement."

Then she tells us how we can disagree, but still live in harmony: "The great truths of the Word of God are so clearly stated that none need make a mistake in understanding them. When as individual members of the church, you love God supremely and your neighbor as yourself, there will be no need of labored efforts to be in unity, for there will be oneness in Christ as a natural result."[22]

Love wins where arguments lose

What Ellen White is doing is shifting the focus from argument and doctrine to attitude and spirit. Sometimes, she is so forceful that I use the label *prophetic overstatement,* a phrase I use for passionate words by prophets or apostles when they want to make sure they are heard. "Don't ever forgive their terrible crimes," Jeremiah cries to God. "Drive out the wicked person from among you," thunders Paul to the Corinthians.[23]

For Ellen White, the hot passion came when the brethren quarreled over the meaning of passages in the Bible. One night after a particularly heated discussion over Galatians 3, she returned to her room deeply troubled. "Many hours that night were spent in prayer," she wrote. The specific issue under discussion she described as "a mere mote." But then this prophetic overstatement: "Whichever way was in accordance with a 'Thus saith the Lord,' my soul would say, Amen, and Amen. But the spirit that was controlling our brethren was so unlike the spirit of Jesus, so contrary to the spirit that should be exercised toward each other, it filled my soul with anguish."[24]

In her more sober moments, would Ellen White really want to say that the interpretation of a particular passage was "a mere mote" of little significance? Probably not. But when she saw the devastating results of overzealous theological arguments, she spoke with a passion that made her point perfectly clear.

In the course of this book, I want to lay out clear guidelines that will provide a kind of safety net within which it is safe for us to disagree with one another while still remaining faithful to Scripture and to our Adventist heritage. But underlying the whole issue is the conviction that our views of Scripture, indeed, even the way we see certain doctrines, are shaped by our differing temperaments and experiences. Nowhere have I seen this point made more forcefully than by Ellen White in *The Ministry of Healing,* in the opening lines of the chapter, "In Contact With Others." "We differ so widely," Ellen White asserts, that "our understanding of truth, our ideas in regard to the conduct of life are not in all respects the same." Thus, "the duties that one finds light are to another most difficult and perplexing."[25]

Treating people right, of course, was Jesus' point when He gave us that marvelous one-sentence summary of the Old Testament: "In everything do to others as you would have them do to you; for this is the law and the prophets."[26] That means allowing others room to think, feel, and follow God in ways that bring joy to their hearts, not just to our own.

But isn't a one- or two-command summary (as in Matthew 7 and 22) too general? Too short on the kind of muscle needed to craft a community or a church? Quite right. That's why God hasn't left us with only these one- or two-command summaries. He's given us a host of examples to illustrate what love means in a host of different circumstances. For Jesus and His disciples, that illustration was the whole Old Testament. Paul refers to these stories as examples written for our benefit.[27]

These examples are essential for illuminating larger principles. Ellen White makes that point when describing the purpose of the Mosaic laws. The motley crowd of ex-slaves was not only incapable of appreciating the two great commands, they couldn't even grasp the crucial implications of the Ten Commandments. So God graciously gave the people more help. "That the obligations of the Decalogue might be more fully understood and enforced, additional precepts were given, illustrating and applying the principles of the Ten Commandments."[28]

And right here is where the Adventist "advantage" kicks in; for if the two great commands are too general to be adequate for sinful humans, the additional legislation is often so detailed and so far removed from where we are, that we are easily tempted simply to lay it aside. But in the middle, between the two and the many, stands the Decalogue, the Ten, God's amazing gift to His people to keep them out of trouble.

Just how crucial those Ten are, was brought forcibly to my attention a number of years ago when I was chatting with a well-known Old Testament professor during a brief visit to Scotland.

As we talked about our various projects, he asked me what I was doing. I frankly told him that I was writing a book to help my students see more clearly what never changes in Scripture. I said I was sick and tired of seeing my students lose their faith when they discovered things in the Bible they didn't think were supposed to be there. In summary form, my argument went like this: The unchanging anchor in Scripture consists of the great principle of love, its more specific definition through Jesus' two great commands—love to God and love to your neighbor—and their even more specific application in the Ten Commandments. You can draw a double line around those laws, I said, marking them off from everything else, for they never change. The rest of Scripture simply illustrates and applies them in particular times and places, an interpretation suggested by Jesus' summary comment on the two great commandments: "On these two commandments hang all the law and the prophets."[29]

While the two great commands are certainly enduring, I noted that the Ten Commandments represent an additional layer of stability. They, too, hang on the two great commands, but they never change. Draw your double line after the Ten. Everything else in Scripture—all the laws and stories—hang on the two, illustrating how we are to understand and apply the fundamental principle of love, the two great commands, and the Ten Commandments in many and varied circumstances.

So, I thought to myself, *that's my good Adventist Bible study on the law.*

To my amazement, the Scottish professor replied without hesitation, "Of course, that's where the Bible draws the double line. Look at Deuteronomy four, verses thirteen and fourteen."

Incredibly, our next few moments together still sounded like an old-fashioned Adventist Bible study on the law!

"Note the difference between verses thirteen and fourteen," he said. "In verse thirteen, God is addressing Israel directly, not speaking through Moses. According to this text, God gave the people 'his covenant' and described what He gave them as 'ten commandments.' Furthermore, the text states that God Himself wrote the commandments on two stone tablets."

"But," my professor friend continued, "note the changes in verse fourteen. First, God is addressing Moses, not the people. Second, to Moses, He gave 'statutes and ordinances,' not 'his covenant' or the 'ten commandments.'"

"In short," he concluded, "you're quite right. The double line comes after the Ten Commandments. That's where the Bible itself puts it."

I was astounded that he would respond so spontaneously and so quickly with that solid "Adventist" exposition of the Bible. Of course, it's not just Adventist. It's just a simple and straightforward reading of the Bible, a reading that should be evident to any honest person.

To make the Bible study complete, we would simply need to add two additional points. First, that the "statutes and ordinances" were written down by Moses in a book and placed beside the ark, not in the ark,[30] and second, that the penalties for breaking the Ten Commandments are not included in the Decalogue itself but in the additional legislation, thus giving the Decalogue a more enduring quality.

I might note that penalties are much more likely to be shaped by time, place, and culture, and thus vary considerably, even in the Bible. In the Old Testament, for example, the additional Mosaic legislation assigns the death penalty to every one of the Ten Commandments except the last one (don't covet), an application matching the more rigorous needs of the undisciplined ex-slaves who had come out of Egypt.

Jesus, of course, coming to earth as God in the flesh, points us toward the nonviolent ideal, with the story of the woman taken in adultery being the most famous example: "Neither do I condemn you. Go your way, and from now on do not sin again."[31] Thus, in striking instances, Jesus could omit the penalty while still affirming the command as enduring.

Summary

In conclusion, I say with passion: some things never change. God has spelled them out in Scripture with remarkable clarity—the *one* great principle of love, Jesus' *two* great commands, and the *Ten* Commandments. Everything else, all the "cases" He has ever given through inspiration and revelation, simply illustrate and apply these great principles, these great commands.

The capstone to this whole process of helping us know God's will is found in the revelation of God in Jesus Christ. He is the embodiment of God's law of love, the law pyramid (one-two-ten) in human flesh, so to speak. Through Him and through His example, we learn best of all how we are to live.

But what is most important is the realization that all our good efforts to live out the law of love can never earn salvation. That is God's gift. And it is always a gift, never something that we earn by our efforts. Indeed, if we are really serious about living out God's law of love, we will discover the painful truth of the paradox noted by Ellen White: "The closer you come to Jesus, the more faulty you will appear in your own eyes; for your vision will be clearer, and your imperfections will be seen in broad and distinct contrast to His perfect nature."[32]

That is when we stand side by side with Brother Paul, and for all our talk about the "good news" version of the law, we cry out with him: "Wretched man that I am! Who will rescue me from this body of death?"[33]

But Paul didn't stop with wretchedness, nor should we. We must move on with him from the anguish of Romans 7 to the exuberance of Romans 8: "There is therefore now no condemnation for those who are in Christ Jesus."[34]

Yes, the law is good news. It is our anchor, protecting us from a host of evils and helping us to know what is good. But if you will pardon the mixed metaphor, we will never go anywhere at all if all we have is an anchor. The law is indeed our anchor, but Jesus is the wind in our sails. He is our Strength, our Power, and our Motivation. And it is because of Jesus that we can say with Paul that "neither death, nor life, nor angels, nor rulers, nor things present, nor things to come, nor powers, nor height, nor depth, nor anything else in all creation, will be able to separate us from the love of God in Christ Jesus our Lord."[35]

So, with a secure anchor, the law, and with the wind in our sails, Jesus, we can explore more thoroughly what it means for liberals and conservatives to be faithful to God within a community that provides a secure home for them both.

In the next chapter, we will take a closer look at Jesus, the third way of finding simplicity, certainty, and stability. Even though He is the wind in our sails, Jesus is also an anchor. And we will consider more carefully how all three ways of organizing our faith relate to each other. They overlap, but are not quite the same. In chapter 1, the emphasis was on Adventist common ground—Sabbath, the Advent, the Bible, the commandments, and the faith of Jesus. This chapter has focused on the stabilizing structure of the law pyramid, the things that never change in Scripture—the *one* principle of love, the *two* great commands, and the *Ten* Commandments. The third way of organizing our faith puts Jesus at the center. His story lurks in every corner of the first two chapters. But in our next chapter, He will be at the center of the stage as we explore more carefully how Jesus relates to the key elements of our Adventist common ground and to the stabilizing structure of the law pyramid.

---

1. See Matthew 19:16–21; Mark 10:17–21; Luke 18:18–30.

2. See Romans 13:8–10; James 2:8–12.

3. See Psalm 19:7–13; Matthew 25:31–46; Galatians 5:13–15; 1 John 2:3–11; 3:10–18, 23; 4:7–12, 16–21; 5:1–3.

4. See Exodus 19; 20; Deuteronomy 5:6–21.

5. See Exodus 20:18–21; Deuteronomy 4:5–8.

6. See Matthew 1:21–23; John 1:1–3, 14.

7. See Matthew 1:21; John 3:16; Acts 4:12; 5:31.

8. See Matthew 5–7; 20:20–28.

9. See John 14:8, 9.

10. See Philippians 2:1–11.

11. See Matthew 7:12; 19:16–21; 22:35–40; Mark 10:17–21; 12:28–31; Luke 10:25–28; 18:18–22; John 13:34, 35; 15:12, 17.

12. See Matthew 25:31–46. Note Ellen White's comment on Jesus' judgment parable: "Christ on the Mount of Olives pictured to His disciples the scene of the great judgment day. And He represented its decision as turning upon one point. When the nations are gathered before Him, there will be but two classes, and their eternal destiny will be determined by what they have done or have neglected to do for Him in the person of the poor and the suffering." *The Desire of Ages*, 637.

13. Paul's description of his own approach is one of the best ways to understand some of God's strange acts: "I have become all things to all people, that I might by all means save some" (1 Corinthians 9:22).

14. The biblical narrative from Joshua through the books of 1 and 2 Samuel and 1 and 2 Kings relates some vivid and startling incidents; some of the laws in the Pentateuch seem very strange to us, even shocking. For example, see Deuteronomy 13.

15. See Deuteronomy 4:13, 14.

16. Ellen White to Edson White, June 21, 1893. Letter 123, 1893. (W-123-1893).

17. White, *Testimonies for the Church,* 1:39.

18. Ellen White, *The Great Controversy* (Mountain View, Calif.: Pacific Press®, 1950), 525. The full quote reads, "The errors of popular theology have driven many a soul to skepticism who might otherwise have been a believer in the Scriptures. It is impossible for him to accept doctrines which outrage his sense of justice, mercy, and benevolence; and since these are represented as the teaching of the Bible, he refuses to receive it as the word of God." That she had in mind the doctrine of an everlasting hell seems clear from her statement in ibid., 535: "How repugnant to every emotion of love and mercy, and even to our sense of justice, is the doctrine that the wicked dead are tormented with fire and brimstone in an eternally burning hell; that for the sins of a brief earthly life they are to suffer torture as long as God shall live."

19. White, *Selected Messages,* 1:21, 22.

20. Quoted in George R. Knight, *Angry Saints: Tensions and Possibilities in the Adventist Struggle Over Righteousness by Faith* (Washington, D.C.: Review and Herald®, 1989), 15.

21. Uriah Smith to A. T. Jones, November 8, 1886, quoted in Knight, *Angry Saints,* 20.

22. Ellen White, *The Ellen G. White 1888 Materials* (Washington, D.C.: Ellen G. White Estate, 1987), 3:1092, 1093.

23. Jeremiah 18:23, CEV; 1 Corinthians 5:13, NRSV.

24. White, *The Ellen G. White 1888 Materials,* 1:223.

25. Ellen White, *The Ministry of Healing* (Boise, Idaho: Pacific Press®, 1942), 483.

26. Matthew 7:12.

27. See 1 Corinthians 10:11.

28. White, *Patriarchs and Prophets,* 310.

29. Matthew 22:40.

30. See Deuteronomy 31:24–26.

31. John 8:11.

32. Ellen White, *Steps to Christ* (Boise, Idaho: Pacific Press®, 1990), 64.

33. Romans 7:24.

34. Romans 8:1.

35. Romans 8:38, 39.

Chapter 3

Anchor 3: Jesus

If you want to know what God is like, look at Jesus.[1] He was always gentle and encouraging with any struggling soul who wanted to be a better person, with anyone who wanted to make the world a better place. Often He was nearly mobbed by the poor, the sick, and the outcasts of the world.[2] Children came running to Him, even when He was angry with evil adults.[3]

And Jesus could get angry. He never killed anyone, never even struck anyone. But He was no pushover; many of His stories end with judgment and strong words.[4] And He was very blunt with bad people who tried to make themselves look good.[5] Jesus was never soft on sin, because sin is anything that hurts God's creation, especially His children.[6] The tantalizing truth is that Jesus came to earth because of sin—to destroy sin while saving sinners.[7]

Jesus said that His salvation would come through serving, suffering, and dying.[8] But no one believed it until after the Resurrection.[9] What the people really wanted was a warrior messiah to drive out their oppressors and restore the kingdom. And they stoked their angry enthusiasm with passages of Scripture.

Jesus simply ignored those warrior passages without ever explaining why.[10] Indeed, He never tried to explain any of the "problems" of the Old Testament, even though He often quoted from it and clearly cherished it as God's Word. The New Testament clearly establishes these three truths: (1) the Old Testament was Jesus' Bible; (2) the God of the Old Testament was Jesus' God; and (3) Jesus Himself was the Yahweh God of the Old Testament, Yahweh in human form. They tried to stone Him for that.[11]

But if Jesus was the Yahweh God of the Old Testament in human flesh, and if God is like Jesus, then only one conclusion fits all the evidence: the tough stuff in the Old Testament is simply the story of an incredibly patient God—patient like Jesus—who knows the horrifying effects of sin on the human heart and mind. His goal? To bring His lost and wandering children as quickly as possible to the peaceable kingdom where no one will hurt or destroy in all God's holy mountain and where even the animals are vegetarians.[12]

But that can't happen all at once. En route to the peaceable kingdom, God has to reach people where they are and speak a language they can understand.[13] That can be troubling for us until we realize that it was exactly what those people needed, so that they, too, could take a step closer to God's new earth.

Jesus came to earth to make that new world possible. And His wonderful example of gentle love is the one we need to follow. You don't have to understand all the shocking stuff. Maybe you should be aware of it, but you don't need to dwell on it. Jesus Himself just ignored it, drawing from His Bible the good news that made Him who He was. According to the book of Hebrews, the revelation of God in Jesus Christ is better than anything God had ever done before.[14]

So whenever you wonder what God is like, just look at Jesus. And keep it up. Now the details.

The Bible says, "In the beginning was the Word, and the Word was with God, and the Word was God. He was in the beginning with God. . . . And the Word became flesh and lived among us, and we have seen his glory, the glory as of a father's only son, full of grace and truth."[15]

The Bible says, "We declare to you what was from the beginning, what we have heard, what we have seen with our eyes, what we have looked at and touched with our hands, concerning the word of life—this life was revealed, and we have seen it and testify to it, and declare to you the eternal life that was with the Father and was revealed to us."[16]

The Bible says, "Whoever has seen me has seen the Father."[17]

Ellen White says, "Good news! Good news! ring throughout the world! 'For God so loved the world, that He gave His only-begotten Son, that whosoever believeth in Him should not perish, but have everlasting life.' This lesson is one of the greatest importance to every soul that lives; for the terms of salvation are here laid out in distinct lines. If one had no other text in the Bible, this alone would be a guide for the soul."[18]

Of the three anchors for bringing certainty, simplicity, and stability into our lives, Jesus is the most tantalizing and probably the most popular. He may also be the most effective. To see, to hear, and to touch a real person can be a powerful experience. That's what John testifies to in the first lines of his first epistle: "We declare to you . . . what we have heard, what we have seen . . . , what we have . . . touched."[19] In our day, of course, we cannot see, hear, or touch Jesus as the apostles did, but we do have their testimony and can be blessed by the knowledge of their hands-on experience with the Lord.

The way of Jesus is solidly linked with the other two ways of finding certainty, simplicity, and stability. If we look at the foundational truths on which Adventism is built—for example, the common ground approach—faith in Jesus Christ is right there. Whatever theological shortcomings our Adventist forebears may have had, here they had it right: Jesus is the way, the Cornerstone in the foundation of their faith.

The law pyramid (the *one,* the *two,* the *ten*), the law of love, is an even closer matchup with Jesus. Jesus Himself, His disciples, and all early Christians, understood Jesus to be the incarnation of the law of love. The *one,* the *two,* and the *Ten* Commandments spell out the truth in words. Jesus makes them come alive in the flesh.

But whichever of the three anchors a person may find most helpful, each in its own way highlights one of the great strengths of Adventism, namely, the simplicity of its basic message. It's a turnkey operation. One doesn't have to be a mechanical or electrical genius or know all the whys and wherefores—just turn the key. When the church gets it right, it will be home for the simplest child as well as for the most brilliant genius.

Even those who love the slogan, "The Bible says it. I believe it. That settles it," rarely make a serious effort to practice what they preach. At a practical level, the vast majority of believers live their lives based on certain broad principles. Inevitably, however, a smattering of specifics, understood to have been commanded by God, are integrated into daily life. Yet these specifics vary widely from one person to another.

For example, when I was a pastor, I was grateful for those members who attended services regularly, assisted in the programs of the church, and supported the work of the church through tithes and offerings. Some members, however, attended services regularly, but seldom returned tithes and offerings; others almost never attended, but would occasionally send in a tithe check. How did each person decide which specifics to adopt? I simply do not know.

Sabbath keeping habits may offer the richest variety of specifics. When I was the guest of an Adventist woman in Germany, she simply would not allow the use of a frying pan in her kitchen on Sabbath. Yet she did not hesitate to do a little shopping on her way home from church. Again, I simply do not know how she made her choices.

The challenge comes when a curious soul like me attempts to move beyond the elementary level and begins to analyze some of the "differences" in the biblical stories and in the writings of Ellen White. All of a sudden, sleeping dogs begin to bark. Sometimes, they even bite. For some people, differences turn into contradictions, and the authority of the prophetic Word seems to be at risk.

I sometimes have to put on the brakes lest I write only for "investigating minds."[20] I love to explore parallel biblical passages, especially those in the Old Testament. I find it very helpful to know the differences between the two editions of the Decalogue: Exodus 20 and Deuteronomy 5. And the comparisons between 1 and 2 Samuel, 1 and 2 Kings, and 1 and 2 Chronicles are absolutely intriguing—in my view, that is. But recently, I was brought back down to earth by the editors of a recently published book of Old Testament parallels. "Only the most diligent students," wrote the editors, have compared the two editions of the Decalogue; and "only the most curious" read Chronicles along with 1 and 2 Samuel and 1 and 2 Kings.[21] Do Adventists love the Bible enough to prove the editors wrong? That's probably the wrong question. Ellen White would likely remind me that some ways of studying the Bible may appeal only to "investigating minds"!

The real question is how to make the Bible "safe" for ordinary people to read and explore. Any way you look at it, it takes time. But any one or all three of the anchors described in these first three chapters can be helpful. One needs to find a way to affirm that which is really important. Then, with one or more anchors solidly in place to preserve our certainty and to provide stability, we can explore the rest of Scripture to see how even the small pieces might fit in. We can even puzzle over the things that don't seem to make sense. But our faith will not be at risk, because our anchor holds.

And dealing with the smaller pieces can be a real challenge. One pastor, who was struggling with the issues, told me that at one point in his experience he had felt a keen disappointment with God for not providing a preface on how to read the Bible. "After all, it is His Word to us," he commented. "How else was I meant to read it but as inerrant and unchanging? It would have been disrespectful of me to start sorting out which proverbs—let alone laws—were applicable to my immediate situation and which weren't. You don't question professors and policemen. They are above, and I am down here."

For him, the story of Jesus ended up being most helpful. It was "the discovery that the Almighty God is also the One who graciously dwells and 'speaks' among the lowly and in their context. And that is best illustrated in Jesus."

Recently, another friend of mine quoted lines from a well-known evangelist that he found helpful, "Jesus is God with skin on."[22] For him, that line was the key to knowing what God is like. Having a clear focus like that can be crucial if one happens to be reading from some of the more vivid parts of the Old Testament.

I was once speaking with a devout Christian woman who had decided to go back and read the Old Testament. The experience horrified her. "I can't read it anymore," she said. "It's so gruesome. How could a good God command such terrible things? What is God like anyway?"

After a few moments of reflection, I simply said, "Look to Jesus—God with skin on."

She paused briefly and then said, "OK, I can live with that."

I hadn't really answered her questions. But the story of Jesus made the difference. Knowing how Jesus dealt with hurting people, people in trouble and deep need, opened enough of a window so that she could see God.

In what follows, we will look more closely at Jesus as He is presented in the New Testament, especially in connection with what we find in the Old Testament. Since the Old Testament was Jesus' Bible, we have every reason to take it seriously. Then, in light of some general comparisons, we will look more specifically at Jesus' life, ministry, and teachings to see how He dealt with the people of His day, both friends and foes.

Jesus and the Old Testament

The question of how the God revealed in Jesus compares with the God of the Old Testament is a crucial one. Jesus claimed the God of the Old Testament as His God; indeed, He claimed to *be* the God of the Old Testament.[23] Nevertheless, to our way of thinking, a great gulf seems fixed between the gentle Jesus, who invited the children to sit on his lap, and the Almighty, who thundered from Sinai that if even an animal came too close it must be killed. Put bluntly, in the Old Testament, God comes to kill; in the New Testament, God comes to die. Yet, it is the same God.

Against the backdrop of that stark contrast, the following points are significant:

1. Jesus sharply contrasted His way with that of the Old Testament, claiming His way to be better, while fully affirming the Old Testament as God's Word. Matthew 5 is the crucial chapter here. Jesus says that He didn't come to destroy the law, but to fulfill it; that is, He came to fill it full of new meaning (verse 17). The six contrasts that follow point to the full internalization of the law: The Old Testament prohibits murder; Jesus goes one better and condemns murderous anger (verses 21, 22). The Old Testament prohibits adulterous acts; Jesus condemns lustful thoughts (verses 27, 28). Instead of an eye for an eye, Jesus calls for going the second mile (verses 38–42). Instead of hating your enemies, Jesus says we should love them (verses 43–48).

The startling conclusion to all that is the recognition that we can honestly speak of the newer revelation as being better, without denying the validity of the older. New and old are both fully inspired and fully authoritative.

2. In defining His own mission, Jesus drew on the Old Testament selectively, focusing on the suffering and serving Messiah, but ignoring the warrior passages.

42

Jesus' visit to the synagogue in Nazareth strikingly illustrates His selective use of a Messianic passage. Reading from Isaiah 61, Jesus quotes the lines describing a ministry to the poor, the captives, the blind, and the oppressed. But He stops short of the line, "the day of vengeance of our God" (verse 2). He did not explain why. He simply ignored the day of vengeance.

The keynote of Jesus' ministry was Isaiah 53, the song of the Suffering Servant. Why did Jesus choose that passage of Scripture? We don't know. Before the Resurrection, no one wanted to hear that message of suffering and death. No one. Still, Jesus chose it as the theme of His ministry. And after the Resurrection, the message spread like wildfire. Today, it still has the potential to transform the world.

3. Jesus never attempted to explain the "problems" of the Old Testament. Jesus frequently quoted from the Old Testament. But all those issues which trouble us He simply ignored. I'm still pondering the implications of that one.[24]

Jesus in conflict with people: How does He measure up?

Jesus was a person of high moral vision who came to call sinners to repentance. In doing so, He also challenged the religious status quo. That adds up to high potential for conflict. Jesus' additional claim to be God on earth led to another whole level of conflict with the religious leaders of His own community. That is a special issue that we will address more specifically below. But here I want to summarize key aspects of Jesus' message, His methods of presenting it, and His response to the conflict that followed.

If Jesus was God incarnate as He claimed to be, what might that mean for our expectations of Him based on the revelation of God in the Old Testament? This is the backdrop against which the summary below should be seen. Based on the Gospels' records, here is what we know:

1. While He was on earth, Jesus never killed anyone and never struck anyone. In the Old Testament, God racks up an impressive death toll. So do some of his prophets. Elijah, for example, killed 450 prophets of Baal during the reign of Ahab and Jezebel, and two groups of fifty soldiers sent by King Ahaziah.[25] Jesus killed no one and struck no one. Even when He cleansed the temple, He attacked the furniture, not the people.[26] When Jesus' anger flashed forth, evil people fled, but the children, the blind, and the lame all came running to

Him.[27] In the Gospels, the only destructive miracles attributed to Jesus involved pigs and figs.[28]

2. Not only did Jesus teach us that we should love our enemies, He practiced what He preached, praying while He hung on the cross for God to forgive those who were crucifying Him.[29] Whether His enemies tried to stone Him or simply insulted Him, Jesus never responded in kind.

3. Jesus never defended His own authority, never commanded anyone to worship Him. In the Gospels, the closest Jesus came to defending Himself was when one of the temple police struck Him the face for His answer to the high priest. "If I have spoken wrongly, testify to the wrong," Jesus told him. "But if I have spoken rightly, why do you strike me?"[30] When James and John asked for the top places in the kingdom, Jesus simply noted that He did not come to be served but to serve and that He expected the same of them.[31]

4. In Jesus' stories, strong punishments are meted out to evil people. Although Jesus Himself was always gentle in dealing with the wayward, He did not hesitate to use strong language in His stories to describe the dire consequences of doing evil.[32] The implications are tantalizing and sobering.

Jesus and people

After that general survey, we can look more specifically at several groups of people with whom Jesus had significant contact during His ministry. Right at the outset, we could say that Jesus didn't seem to worry much about reputation. He associated freely with "tax collectors and sinners,"[33] to use terms of derision tossed at Jesus by His detractors. In contrast to John the Baptist, a determined ascetic, Jesus was a party person, "eating and drinking," to use the Gospel phrase.[34] Yet Jesus had words of praise for His self-denying forerunner.[35] There is no trace of any inappropriate behavior on Jesus' part, but He was not afraid to associate with people of low reputation.

In Galatians 3:28, Paul envisions an ideal world "in Christ" where all the major inequalities that have haunted the human family are banished—racial (Jew/Gentile), economic (slave/free), and sexual (male/female). The New Testament reveals that the early followers of Jesus grappled seriously with only one of these three, namely, the racial one (Jew/Greek). But given the culture of the time and some strong inequalities sanctioned in the Old Testament, Jesus' way of relating to all classes of people is astonishing. Here is a summary:

1. The poor, sick, and oppressed. Helping hurting people was first on Jesus' agenda. In the synagogue at Nazareth, He read the list from Isaiah 61—the poor, the captives, the blind, and the oppressed.[36] When John the Baptist sent messengers to ask about Jesus' ministry, Jesus told them to go back and give John the list—the blind, the lame, the lepers, the deaf, the dead, and the poor.[37] Time and again, Jesus healed the sick and fed the hungry. He was never too busy to take time for a person in need.

2. The ritually unclean. As recorded in each of the first three Gospels, one of Jesus' earliest miracles was the healing of a leper. All three Gospels say that Jesus "touched him," breaking all the rules of ritual cleanliness.[38] Jesus was a hands-on kind of Person. He took Peter's feverish mother-in-law by the hand and raised her up; en route to the raising of Jairus's daughter, He allowed a hemorrhaging woman to touch Him and be healed. When He got to Jairus's home, He took his daughter by the hand and raised her up.[39] Luke even says in one passage that Jesus "laid his hands" on each of the sick people He had cured.[40] Any way you look at it, Jesus simply had great compassion for people in need. No germs or rituals could get in His way.

3. Children. Jesus had a way with children. Even as He angrily drove the money changers out of the temple, the children came running to Him.[41] When eager parents brought their children to Jesus to be blessed, they got a scolding from the disciples. Mark's account is especially vivid: Jesus was "indignant," says Mark. Calling the children to Him, Jesus didn't just touch them; He "took them up in his arms."[42]

4. Women. Jesus began to open windows and doors for women. In Orthodox Judaism, a synagogue quorum (*minyan*) still requires ten males; women don't count. A famous Jewish prayer thanks God that the male doing the praying was not created a slave, a Gentile, or a woman. Jesus began to change all that. Some of the most striking events in Jesus' life were with women and for women: He raised a widow's son, healed a crippled daughter of Abraham in a synagogue on Sabbath, talked at length with the Samaritan woman at the well, and gave hope to the woman taken in adultery.[43] Women supported Jesus' ministry financially and traveled with Him and His disciples;[44] they were among His closest friends and were the first at the tomb on Resurrection morning.[45]

Even Jesus' seemingly hard-line on divorce[46] is seen by scholars as a coup for women since in that time and culture only men had the right to divorce and could request one for the most frivolous reasons. Jesus came to change all that.

5. *Foreigners.* As noted above, of the three great inequalities mentioned in Galatians 3:28 (Gentiles, slaves, and women), the Jew/Gentile inequality was the only one addressed effectively in the New Testament. Even here, God was incredibly patient, waiting several years after the Resurrection before sending Peter to Cornelius in Caesarea. Peter was so unnerved by the command that he took no less than six Jewish men along as witnesses. When these Jews saw that the Holy Spirit was being poured out on the Gentiles, they were "astounded."[47]

The reluctance of the first Christians to grant full acceptance to foreigners is surprising in view of the teachings and example of Jesus. It is true that when Jesus sent out the Twelve disciples on their first missionary trip, He told them not to go to Gentiles or Samaritans: "Go rather to the lost sheep of the house of Israel."[48] That blunt tactical advice may have been necessary because of everything else Jesus was doing to open the way for non-Jews to accept Him—He made special forays into Gentile territory, healing the Gadarene demoniacs[49] and the daughter of a Syro-Phoenician woman.[50] Jesus also took His disciples north of the Sea of Galilee to the Greco-Roman city of Caesarea Philippi. It was in the shadow of that largely pagan city that Peter gave his famous confession of faith in Jesus as the Messiah.[51]

Perhaps even more memorable were Jesus' efforts on behalf of the beleaguered Samaritans. Most pointed in that respect was His parable of the good Samaritan. A priest and Levite both ignored the needs of their Jewish compatriot who had been beaten and robbed on the road to Jericho. But a despised Samaritan came by and willingly cared for the man's broken body.[52] Not surprisingly, perhaps, that story is found only in Luke, a Gospel that most scholars agree was written for non-Jews. Luke also tells the story of the ten lepers who were healed, only one of which came back to thank Jesus. Noting that the man was a Samaritan, Luke records Jesus' poignant question: "Was none of them found to return and give praise to God except this foreigner?"[53] Jesus' conversation with the Samaritan woman at Jacob's well also belongs on Jesus' pro-Samaritan list.

Finally, we should note some important bridges between Jesus' more open attitude toward foreigners and the attitudes found in the Old Testament. It's not hard to make a list of "exclusive" statements from the Old Testament, especially when dealing with the "original" inhabitants of Canaan.[54] But note what Matthew does with his genealogy, breaking all the rules of Jewish genealogies by including four women in Jesus' royal lineage, all of them notable: (1) Tamar, the Canaanite, who committed incest with her father-in-law; (2) Rahab, a Canaanite prostitute; (3) Ruth, the Moabite; and (4) Bathsheba, who committed adultery with King David. Ruth is the only "good" girl in the list, and she was a Moabite, seemingly barred from the community by Mosaic law.[55]

But perhaps, even more amazing is the passage in Isaiah 19 that promises to Egypt and Assyria/Babylon, Israel's great historic enemies, an equal share with Israel in God's future kingdom: "Israel will be the third with Egypt and Assyria," declares the prophet, "whom the LORD of hosts has blessed, saying, 'Blessed be Egypt my people, and Assyria the work of my hands, and Israel my heritage.' "[56] Jesus built on that visionary foundation.

6. The wealthy. The rich take their lumps from Jesus, especially in Luke's Gospel: "Sell all that you own," He counsels the rich young ruler.[57] Matthew, Mark, and Luke all tell the story, but only Luke uses the word *all*. Each of the Gospels, however, follows the story with Jesus' comment on how difficult it is for the rich to be saved.[58] Both Mark and Luke tell the story in which Jesus affirms the widow who gave all that she had—two small copper coins—over against the rich who gave "out of their abundance."[59] Luke also includes the story of the foolish rich man who built bigger barns, only to face death and final accountability that very night. In the Sermon on the Mount, of course, Jesus says that it is better to store up treasure in heaven than on earth.[60]

But in spite of all that grim news for the rich, Jesus offers some subtle affirmations of wealthy people. Jesus commanded the rich young ruler to sell everything, but when he went to the home of Zacchaeus, the wealthy tax collector from Jericho, Jesus welcomed him into the kingdom for promising to give just half his goods to the poor (not all) and to restore fourfold to anyone whom he had defrauded. Apparently, Joseph of Arimathea and Nicodemus were also men of some means. Indeed, Matthew describes Joseph as "rich,"[61] and the handsome quantity of spices that they provided for Jesus' burial in Joseph's new tomb would also point toward significant wealth.[62] Yet the Gospels never criticize them for their wealth.

In summary, Jesus in the Gospels clearly saw wealth as something that could easily compromise one's commitment to God. Yet He was at ease with people of means and rebuked those who had grumbled at Mary's extravagant gift of ointment when she washed His feet. That gift was worth a full year's wages for a working person. Yet Jesus reveled in the gift and commended the one who gave it.[63]

7. Religious leaders. On the surface, based on what we have in our four Gospels, Jesus' attitude toward the religious leaders of His day appears to be stark and sobering. His woes against the Pharisees in Matthew 23 include strong words. It is hard to see how "hypocrites," "blind guides," "blind fools," and "brood of vipers"[64] can be turned into gentle language.

In this connection, it is worth pondering Ellen White's famous line about Jesus' strong words: "He fearlessly denounced hypocrisy, unbelief, and iniquity, but tears were in His voice as He uttered His scathing rebukes." First published in 1884, these words have been immortalized in *Steps to Christ* and *The Desire of Ages.*[65] Perhaps Ellen White was doing what Jesus did with the Old Testament, that is, simply ignoring the really hard statements.

Yet when innocent people are hurt by those who are evil or careless, would it not be dangerous just to shrug? Here, another famous Ellen White quote needs to be part of the story—her commentary on the "wrath of the Lamb" (Revelation 6:16). Initially, she imagines a father and mother whose child has been lost in a winter storm and who have discovered that someone had passed by their child without helping. How would they react? "Would they not be terribly grieved, wildly indignant?" she exclaims. "Would they not denounce those murderers with wrath hot as their tears, intense as their love? The sufferings of [each person] are the sufferings of God's child," she declares, "and those who reach out no helping hand to their perishing fellow beings provoke His righteous anger. This is the wrath of the Lamb."[66]

Yet those who take it upon themselves to rebuke others are on dangerous ground. To those who claimed they were following her example in rebuking others, Ellen White had pointed words: "God has not given my brethren the work that He has given me," she wrote. "It has been urged that my manner of giving reproof in public has led others to be sharp and critical and severe. If so, they must settle that matter with the Lord." She urged that only God could lay a heavy burden on the heart. "If they," she continued, "disregard the instructions He has given them again and again through the humble instrument of His choice, to be kind, patient, and forbearing, they alone must answer for the results."[67]

In 1901, Ellen White applied that principle even more specifically in writing to a brother who apparently had become very belligerent in his relationship to church leadership. "The influence of your teaching would be tenfold greater if you were careful of your words," wrote Ellen White. "Words that should be a savor of life unto life may by the spirit which accompanies them be made a savor of death unto death. And remember that if by your spirit or your words you close the door to even one soul, that soul will confront you in the judgment. . . . Every sermon you preach, every article you write, may be all true," she observed, "but one drop of gall in it will be poison to the hearer or the reader. Because of that drop of poison, one will discard all your good and acceptable words. Another will feed on the poison; for he loves such harsh words; he follows your example, and talks just as you talk. Thus the evil is multiplied. . . . The truth is to be spoken in love," she urged. "Then the Lord Jesus by His Spirit will supply the force and the power. That is His work."[68]

Because the work of rebuking a brother or sister is such delicate work, I suspect Ellen White was simply falling back on Jesus' words in the Sermon on the Mount and His example on the cross. When we take it upon ourselves to call a brother or sister to account, especially if it is someone who has hurt us, we are at great risk spiritually. If we are certain that there are tears of love in our voice, it may be safe to deliver a rebuke. But who among us has the insight to be certain?

On balance, I find that guiding my life by the story of Jesus is an amazing way to simplify the issues that I face day by day. He is truly the embodiment of God's law—God's law in the flesh, indeed, God with skin on. The first verses of John's first epistle are to the point: Jesus was Someone the disciples "heard," Someone they had "seen," Someone they had "touched with [their] hands."[69] The news was so wonderful they couldn't resist sharing the message with the world and with us.

Do you want certainty, simplicity, and stability? Keep your eyes on Jesus. You can't find a better anchor than that.

1. See John 14:8, 9.

2. For an example, see Luke 4:38–41.

3. See Matthew 21:12–16.

4. See Matthew 21:33–44; 22:1–14; 24:45–51; 25:14–46.

5. See Matthew 23.

6. See Matthew 18:6, 7.

7. See John 3:16.

8. See Matthew 20:25–28; Mark 8:31–33.

9. See Luke 24:21.

10. For examples of warrior passages, see Isaiah 11:4; 61:2.

11. See Matthew 5:17–19; 7:12; 22:35–40; John 8:48–59.

12. See Isaiah 11:6–9.

13. See Matthew 19:8; Mark 10:4–6. These passages on divorce, given because the people were so " 'hard-hearted,' " are the only instances I know of where Jesus explicitly endorses the idea of radical divine accommodation.

14. See Hebrews 1; 2; especially 1:1–4.

15. John 1:1, 2, 14.

16. 1 John 1:1, 2.

17. John 14:9.

18. Ellen White, *Testimonies to Ministers and Gospel Workers* (Mountain View, Calif.: Pacific Press®, 1962), 370.

19. 1 John 1:1, 2.

20. White, *Testimonies for the Church,* 3:39. See page 13, note 6.

21. John C. Endres, William R. Millar, and John Barclay Burns, eds., *Chronicles and Its Synoptic Parallels in Samuel, Kings, and Related Biblical Texts* (Collegeville, Minn.: Liturgical Press, 1998), ix, x.

22. The quote was attributed to the British evangelist Bernard Kinman.

23. See John 8:58.

24. The fact that Jesus attempted no explanations of Bible problems should not be taken to mean that we should never ask questions. Abraham and Moses are notable examples of biblical questioners (see Genesis 18:22–33; Exodus 32:11–14). In a famous passage in Isaiah (1:18), God, through the prophet, invites the readers to come and "reason together" (KJV); the NRSV has "argue it out." In the New Testament, Paul attempted apologetics in Athens (see Acts 17:16–34). In Romans 9:6–18, he also attempts (rather unconvincingly) to explain the hard words of Malachi 1:2, "I have loved Jacob but I have hated Esau." The point is that there are times when one should simply ignore the problems. But there are times when we should do our best to meet them.

25. See 1 Kings 18:22, 40; 2 Kings 1:10, 12.

26. Reynolds Price, *Three Gospels* (New York: Simon & Schuster, 1996), 42, 43.

27. See Matthew 21:12–16.

28. See Mark 5:11–13; 11:12–14, 20, 21.

29. See Matthew 5:44; Luke 23:34.

30. John 18:23.

31. See Matthew 20:25–28.

32. See Matthew 21:33–44; 22:1–14; 24:45–51; 25:14–46.

33. Mark 2:13–17.

34. Matthew 11:19.

35. See Matthew 11:7–19.

36. See Luke 4:18.

37. See Luke 7:18–23.

38. Matthew 8:3; Mark 1:41; Luke 5:13.

39. See Matthew 9:18–25.

40. Luke 4:40.

41. See Matthew 21:12–17.

42. Mark 10:13–16.

43. See Luke 7:11–15; 13:11–16; John 4:1–42; 7:53–8:11.

44. See Luke 8:1–3.

45. Mary and Martha of Bethany were especially close to Jesus (see John 11); Mark 16:1 lists three women as being first at the tomb: Mary Magdalene, out of whom Jesus had cast seven demons (see Luke 8:2), Mary the mother of James, and Salome.

46. See Matthew 5:32; 19:9; Luke 16:18.

47. Acts 10:45; 11:12.

48. Matthew 10:5, 6.

49. See Matthew 8:28–34; Mark 5:1–20; Luke 8:26–39.

50. See Matthew 15:21–28; Mark 7:24–30.

51. See Matthew 16:13–20; Mark 8:27–29.

52. See Luke 10:25–37.

53. See Luke 17:11–19. Luke 17:18

54. See Exodus 23:23–33; Ezra 9; 10; Nehemiah 13:23–31.

55. See Deuteronomy 23:3–6.

56. See Isaiah 19:18–25; Isaiah 19:24, 25.

57. See Matthew 19:16–22 and Mark 10:17–22; Luke 18:22.

58. See Matthew 19:23–30; Mark 10:23–31; Luke 18:24–30.

59. See Mark 12:41–44; Luke 21:1–4; Luke 21:4.

60. Matthew 6:19–21; Luke 12:33, 34.

61. Matthew 27:57.

62. See John 19:38–42.

63. See Matthew 26:6–13; Mark 14:3–9; John 12:1–8; cf. Luke 7:36–50.

64. Matthew 23:13, 16, 17, 33.

65. White, *The Desire of Ages,* 353; cf. *Steps to Christ,* 12. The earliest use of the phrase "tears were in his voice" is found in *Review and Herald,* December 16, 1884. Interestingly enough, she strengthens the statement in *The Desire of Ages* by adding the word *fearlessly* ("fearlessly denounced"), a word that is absent from the earlier occurrences.

66. White, *The Desire of Ages,* 825.

67. White, *Testimonies for the Church,* 5:20; repeated in 677, 678.

68. White, *Testimonies for the Church,* 6:122, 123.

69. 1 John 1:1, 2.

Part 2

Practical Stuff: Keeping It Simple

The Bible says, "Then he brought them outside and said, 'Sirs, what must I do to be saved?' They answered, 'Believe on the Lord Jesus, and you will be saved, you and your household' " (Paul and Silas to the Philippian jailer).[1]

The Bible says, "Just then a lawyer stood up to test Jesus. 'Teacher,' he said, 'what must I do to inherit eternal life?' He said to him, 'What is written in the law? What do you read there?' He answered, 'You shall love the Lord your God with all your heart, and with all your soul, and with all your strength, and with all your mind; and your neighbor as yourself.' And he said to him, 'You have given the right answer; do this, and you will live' " (Jesus and the lawyer).[2]

The Bible says, "Work out your own salvation with fear and trembling; for it is God who is at work in you, enabling you both to will and to work for his good pleasure" (Paul to the Philippian believers).[3]

Ellen White says, "There are no two whose experience[s are] alike in every particular. The trials of one are not the trials of another. The duties that one finds light are to another most difficult and perplexing."[4]

If you were awake when you read the Bible texts above, the intensity of your "Amen" would likely vary from passage to passage. The first one gives the Philippian jailer's question, "How can I be saved?" along with the answer from Paul and Silas: "Believe on Jesus and you and your household will be saved." Simple: just believe.

Some believers actually take this "belief" out of human hands and give it completely to God. They are fearful that even the choice to believe could be seen as a "work" that attempts to earn salvation. For them, grace must be entirely of God.

The second passage takes quite a different approach. When the lawyer wanted to know how to inherit eternal life, Jesus asked him what was written in the law. The lawyer answered correctly according to Jesus: "Love God with all your heart, soul, strength, and mind; and your neighbor as yourself." When the rich, young ruler asked the same question, Jesus actually ticked off several of the Ten Commandments and added a bonus requirement: "Sell everything you own, give to the poor, and come follow Me."[5] Simple—but tough.

All Christians would undoubtedly agree that God is the Author of our salvation and that we should live holy lives in Christ Jesus. But those simple affirmations suddenly become complex when we try to understand just how the human will relates to the divine will. In chapter 18, I address that tension briefly in connection with last-day events, that is, from the perspective of those who see God's plans as fixed and final and from the view of those who are willing to see the human potential for disrupting God's plan (conditionalism). But that tension between those who emphasize the human will and choice and those who emphasize the divine will and rule affects many aspects of the Christian life. In part 2, I will seek to address, briefly and pointedly, some practical concerns that affect us all though in differing degrees, depending on whether your natural tendency is to emphasize the human will ("Let me do it!") or the divine will ("Carry me, Daddy!").

In other words, certain practical issues affect us all and certainly affect the life of the church. We may all be seeking the same goals, but we take different routes to get there. The Bible rarely shows us how to resolve the apparent contradictions that shape the different routes we may take. But Scripture does emphasize both sides of the paradox in such a way that we can easily recognize what is important even if we can't explain it.

In that connection, C. S. Lewis's comment on Philippians 2:12, 13 is insightful. Referring to free will Pelagianism and divine will Augustinianism, the two movements named after the great opponents, Pelagius and Augustine, who faced off against each other some four hundred years after Christ, Lewis notes that Philippians 2:12 by itself is "pure Pelagianism": "Work out your own salvation with fear and trembling." But verse 13 that immediately follows is "pure Augustinianism," telling the how and the why: "For it is God who is at work in you, enabling you both to will and to work for his good pleasure."

Lewis notes that Scripture "just sails over the problem. . . . We profanely assume," he says, unafraid to use strong language, that the human will and the divine will "exclude one another like the actions of two fellow-creatures so that 'God did this' and 'I did this' cannot both be true of the same act except in the sense that each contributed a share."[6] In short, the human will and the divine will are both essential. But human beings probably can't explain just how they relate to each other.

The huge theological systems that have grown up around these two perspectives struggle with the passages that would temper their respective emphases. In their excellent little handbook, *How to Read the Bible for All Its Worth,* Gordon Fee and Douglas Stuart note that for those in the free will tradition, the predestination passages are "something of an embarrassment,"[7] while the "Calvinists have their own ways of getting around" the free will passages.[8] And on both sides of the issue, Fee and Stuart admit rather ruefully, their students "seldom ask what these text mean; they want to know 'how to answer' these texts!"[9]

In the five chapters of this "practical" part 2, the issues are seldom directly affected by the human will/divine will issue. But knowing that the tension exists can help us understand why the practical issues are so important for the individual Christian and for the church. "There are no two whose experience[s are] alike in every particular," wrote Ellen White. "The trials of one are not the trials of another." So, as we noted earlier, "the duties that one finds light are to another most difficult and perplexing."[10] That's why the practical issues are so crucial.

1. Acts 16:30, 31.

2. Luke 10:25–28.

3. Philippians 2:12, 13.

4. White, *The Ministry of Healing,* 483.

5. See Mark 10:17–23.

6. C. S. Lewis, *Letters to Malcolm: Chiefly on Prayer* (San Diego, Calif.: Harcourt Brace, 1992), 49, 50.

7. Gordon Fee and Douglas Stuart, *How to Read the Bible for All Its Worth,* 3rd edition, (Grand Rapids, Mich.: Zondervan, 2003), 74. The key predestination passages they cite are Romans 8:30; 9:18–24; Galatians 1:15; and Ephesians 1:4, 5.

8. Ibid. The key free will passages they cite are 1 Corinthians 10:1–13; Hebrews 6:4–6; and 2 Peter 2:20–22.

9. Ibid.

10. White, *The Ministry of Healing,* 483.

Chapter 4

Leaving Things Out

The Point: Not everyone needs to hear everything all the time.

Isaiah says, "The spirit of the Lord God is upon me,
    because the Lord has anointed me;
  he has sent me to bring good news to the oppressed . . .
    and release to the prisoners;
  to proclaim the year of the Lord's favor,
    and the day of vengeance of our God."[1]

Jesus quotes Isaiah, " 'The Spirit of the Lord is upon me,
    because he has anointed me
      to bring good news to the poor . . .
      to let the oppressed go free,
    to proclaim the year of the Lord's favor.'

  And he rolled up the scroll, gave it back to the attendant, and
    sat down."[2]

Exodus says, "The Lord God, merciful and gracious, longsuffer-
  ing, and abundant in goodness and truth, keeping mercy for
  thousands, forgiving iniquity and transgression and sin, *and*

that will by no means clear the guilty; visiting the iniquity of the fathers upon the children, and upon the children's children, unto the third and to the fourth generation."[3]

Ellen White quotes Exodus, "The Lord God, merciful and gracious, long-suffering, and abundant in goodness and truth, keeping mercy for thousands, forgiving iniquity and transgression and sin."[4]

Ellen White says, "You need to educate yourself, that you may have wisdom to deal with minds. You should with some have compassion, making a difference, while others you may save with fear, pulling them out of the fire.[5] Our heavenly Father frequently leaves us in uncertainty in regard to our efforts."[6]

Ellen White says, "Yours can yet be a happy family. Your wife needs your help. She is like a clinging vine; she wants to lean upon your strength. You can help her and lead her along. You should never censure her. Never reprove her if her efforts are not what you think they should be. Rather encourage her by words of tenderness and love. You can help your wife to preserve her dignity and self-respect."[7]

When dealing with the personal needs of real human beings, experienced parents, pastors, and teachers instinctively adapt their message to the needs of the person, making sure that certain things are said forcefully and carefully, while other things are just as carefully *not* said. Do prophets treat people in the same way? Indeed they do, though the traditional, heavy-handed way of using the writings of Ellen White within Adventism can easily obscure her real-life sensitivity in this respect.

One of the more notable examples from her pen is her counsel—quoted more fully above—to a brother who was being harsh with his wife: His wife, she counseled, "wants to lean upon your strength. . . . You should never censure her. Never reprove her."[8]

"Never censure." "Never reprove." *Never.* My guess is that most Adventists would be shocked to hear that Ellen White actually said that. Why? Because of the way we have used her writings to censure and reprove!

Speaking about the larger audience, she said something similar to A. T. Jones: "The Lord wants His people to follow other methods than that of condemning wrong."[9]

Had Ellen White come to the conclusion that rebuke, censure, and condemnation of wrong were no longer useful? Not at all. And maybe it is ironic that in both instances, the counsel *not* to rebuke, censure, or condemn came as a rebuke to someone who was rebuking too much! And that is the terrible dilemma Christians face when dealing with people. We want to be positive and affirming whenever possible, but there are those painful occasions when the positive doesn't do the job.

One notable danger, of course, is that when we start being critical of those who are too critical, it doesn't take very long before we can be more critical in our attitude than the people we are criticizing for being too critical.

When dealing with the contrasts between the positive and the negative in the writings of Ellen White, it is helpful to remember that those same contrasts are at least as striking in the Bible. I never cease to marvel that 1 Corinthians chapters 5 and 13 are in the same letter. In chapter 13, Paul is extraordinarily gentle: "Love is patient and kind," he declares. But in chapter 5, he is far from gentle: "Hand this man over to Satan," he thunders, concluding the chapter with words almost as strong: "Drive out the wicked person from among you."[10]

When it comes to our use of Scripture, two examples of notable and purposeful omissions are reflected in the quotations at the head of this chapter. One of them illustrates Jesus' use of Isaiah 61, and the other, Ellen White's use of Exodus 34 in *Steps to Christ.* Jesus stopped short of quoting the phrase that we can surmise everyone was waiting to hear: "the day of vengeance of our God." Ellen White stopped short of quoting the lines that promise punishment for sin.

In both cases, references to God's heavy hand are omitted. Neither Jesus nor Ellen White explained their omissions. But from our vantage point, we can perhaps see why. While Jesus could be very pointed in condemning evil,[11] He carefully avoided quoting those Old Testament passages that might reinforce the idea of the warrior Messiah.

As for Ellen White, her intention in *Steps to Christ* is revealed by the title of the first chapter: "God's Love for Man." In seeking to affirm God's gracious character, she even states that it was Satan who led men to conceive of God as a "severe judge, a harsh, exacting creditor."[12]

Thus she quotes the affirming words from Exodus 34:6, 7, words that describe God as "merciful and gracious, long-suffering, and abundant in goodness and truth, keeping mercy for thousands, forgiving iniquity and transgression and sin." But she is careful to quote only the affirming part of the passage, stopping short of the strong words that follow: "Who will by no means clear the guilty, visiting the iniquity of the fathers upon the children and the children's children, to the third and the fourth generation."[13] In short, she is here intent on presenting a gracious picture of God and will not allow anything to detract from that purpose. Does she still believe in judgment? Of course. But that is another message for another time and another place.

One more example of a significant omission in the writings of Ellen White comes to light in her telling of the story of how God chose David to take the place of the rejected Saul. In the Bible, when God commands Samuel to go and anoint David, the prophet reacts with horror, exclaiming, "If Saul hears of it, he will kill me." Without missing a beat, the Bible records God's response: "Take a heifer with you, and say, 'I have come to sacrifice to the LORD.'"[14] To be perfectly blunt, God is telling Samuel to mislead Saul.

Now, if one wanted to explore the biblical understanding of the command against bearing false witness, this passage would be illuminating. But Ellen White does not want to raise that question here.[15] So she simply omits Samuel's exclamation, yielding this result in *Patriarchs and Prophets:* "I will send thee to Jesse the Bethlehemite: for I have provided Me a king among his sons. . . . Take an heifer with thee, and say, I am come to sacrifice to the Lord."[16]

By that simple omission, the quotation avoids drawing the attention of the reader to the fact that God was instructing Samuel to mislead Saul. I believe she did exactly the right thing.

To sum up, given the differences in people and circumstances, even a prophetic messenger such as Ellen White could be very selective in her use of Scripture, deliberately omitting words, sentences, and verses that would detract from the message she believed she was called to give. Not surprisingly, liberals and conservatives often differ in what they choose to include and omit. Given their respective conscientious concerns, they may be entirely justified in doing so. But shouldn't the church as a whole want to ensure that both sides are fully represented as we seek to work with each other and with the larger world? Jesus needs all the bits that are left out, whether by liberals or by conservatives.

My wife is a very good cook; I am not. If you expect me to bake, cook, or stew, your expectations should be very low. But I am quite willing to admit that I am a Pauline Christian who is eager to eat whatever (vegetarian) dishes my wife sets before me, asking no questions for conscience's sake. I do the shopping, she does the cooking, and we both sit down together to eat. But even with my limited abilities in the kitchen, I am quite sure that my wife has never used all the ingredients in the pantry to prepare a single dish or even a full meal. But she still needs a well-stocked pantry in order to make a variety of tasty dishes.

The Bible is like that. We don't need everything all the time. But it is important that we know what we need when we need it. There are parts of the Bible that some sensitive people should never read or read only once to know that they are there. And there are parts that intense people should probably avoid—the parts that wind them up when they really need to wind down. By God's grace, we can help each other find what we need as we grow toward the kingdom. And that applies to both liberals and conservatives. We all need lots of help.

---

1. Isaiah 61:1, 2; emphasis added.
2. Luke 4:18–20, reflecting Jesus' use of the Greek Old Testament (the Septuagint).
3. Exodus 34:6, 7, KJV; emphasis added.
4. White, quoting Exodus 34:6, 7, KJV, in *Steps to Christ,* 10.
5. Cf. Jude 22, 23, KJV.
6. White, *Testimonies for the Church,* 3:420.
7. White, *Testimonies for the Church,* 2:305.
8. Ibid.
9. White, *Testimonies for the Church,* 6:121.
10. 1 Corinthians 13:4, RSV; 5:5, 13, NRSV.
11. See, for example, the woes on the Pharisees in Matthew 23.
12. White, *Steps to Christ,* 11.
13. Exodus 34:7, RSV.
14. 1 Samuel 16:2.
15. In its narrowest meaning, the command against bearing false witness is applied in the Old Testament itself to cases in which malicious self-interest is involved. Hence, the penalty: "You shall do to the false witness just as the false witness had meant to do to the other" (Deuteronomy 19:19). In several instances in the Old Testament, an evil tyrant in

pursuit of the innocent was not told the full truth: the midwives' response to Pharaoh (see Exodus 1:15–22), Hushai's response to Absalom (see 2 Samuel 16; 17), and God's counsel to Samuel in connection with Saul, all fit into that category. See *Patriarchs and Prophets*, page 735 for Ellen White's affirmation of Hushai's misleading counsel. But the issue is hotly debated among ethicists. For that very reason, Ellen White omitted the sentence that would have raised that issue.

16. White, *Patriarchs and Prophets*, 637, quoting KJV.

Chapter 5

God Is in Heaven, and You Are on Earth

The Point: The Bible is not God, but even its tiniest scrap points to God.

The Bible says, "God is in heaven
and you are on earth,
so let your words be few."[1]

The Bible says, "For my thoughts are not your thoughts,
nor are your ways my ways, says the LORD.
For as the heavens are higher than the earth,
so are my ways higher than your ways
and my thoughts than your thoughts."[2]

The Bible says, "I have uttered what I did not understand,
things too wonderful for me, which I did not know. . . .
I had heard of you by the hearing of the ear,
but now my eye sees you;
therefore I despise myself,
and repent in dust and ashes."[3]

The Bible says, "All scripture is inspired by God."[4]

Ellen White says, "God and heaven alone are infallible."[5]

Ellen White says, "The Bible is written by inspired men, but it is not God's mode of thought and expression. It is that of humanity. God, as a writer, is not represented. Men will often say such an expression is not like God. But God has not put Himself in words, in logic, in rhetoric, on trial in the Bible. . . . It is not the words of the Bible that are inspired, but the men that were inspired."[6]

Ellen White says, "You need to educate yourself, that you may have wisdom to deal with minds. You should with some have compassion, making a difference, while others you may save with fear, pulling them out of the fire.[7] Our heavenly Father frequently leaves us in uncertainty in regard to our efforts."[8]

In some ways, this chapter is mostly a reminder, a reminder of a crucial truth that needs to become second nature, namely, that God is God, and we are mere humans, able to grasp only the faintest glimpse of heavenly realities. Given the pressures of our secular culture, that important truth will always be at risk. Yet we can take steps to preserve it. That's what this chapter is about.

As I was working on this chapter, however, I suddenly realized that if I am successful in nailing down the point of the chapter—the truth of a great gulf between God and our perceptions of Him—the very process of establishing that truth begins to subtly undermine our convictions of that other truth—that all Scripture is inspired by God.

In chapter 16, I explore more fully the apparent desire of human beings to see inspired words as eternal and everlasting, applying to all people at all times. If the Bible is shown to be something less than that, namely, *adapted* truth, in some mysterious way, the idea of adaptation begins to drain some of the power from the Word, making it somehow feel more human and less divine.

Typically, liberals are the first to jump ship, finding it easier than conservatives simply to shrug at adapted truth. Conservatives will hold on longer but may live in fear that what they really want from Scripture may not be true after all.

Given that troubling dilemma, all we can do is emphasize both sides of the equation. "We have this treasure in clay jars,"[9] declares Paul. Still, "all Scripture is inspired."[10] And *all* means *all.* We are not allowed to pick and choose. In short, we have clay, but the clay is still inspired.

The idea of incarnation is very useful here. Jesus may have looked like an ordinary man, but Christians eventually concluded that He was also God, thus fully man and fully God—not half and half, but 100 percent of each. That's bad mathematics, but good theology. Psalm 127:1 gives us a wonderful Old Testament example of that dual truth: "Unless the LORD builds the house, / those who build it labor in vain." Who builds the house? Human beings, of course. Yet the psalmist tells us that it is actually the Lord who builds the house. In some mysterious way, then, the human and the divine are united. But believers are constantly being tempted to fall off on one side of the fence or the other.

But back to the point of the chapter. The leading candidates for my title for this chapter came from Ecclesiastes ("God is in heaven and you are on earth") and Isaiah ("My thoughts are not your thoughts"). Both move in the same direction, though Isaiah is more blunt. And the truth is indeed blunt: We are mere humans and can't possibly grasp God in His pure essence. We are creatures, not the Creator.

Job was another candidate, a distant third. After significant pummeling, Job admitted that he was a long way from understanding the things of God. "I have uttered what I did not understand," he says, almost with a shudder, "things too wonderful for me, which I did not know."[11]

Our creatureliness, however, is not the only reason we cannot grasp the things of God with absolute clarity. We are just creatures, to be sure, but we are also *sinful* creatures. How could we possibly imagine that we might know pure truth as God knows it? The more I have thought about it, the more I am convinced that this double argument for our humility—creatureliness and sinfulness—should be a truth that even Calvinists ought to support. Calvinists, of all people, laud the sovereignty of God and the sinfulness of humankind. Yet the Calvinists have been the ones who have been most vocal in support of inerrancy, the teaching that Scripture is without error. Why?

I posed that question to a former student of mine, an active Seventh-day Adventist, but one who knows the Calvinist community well and is himself a firm believer in divine sovereignty. "Why is it," I asked, "that Calvinists are prepared to overthrow some of the clearest teachings of Scripture—our creature-liness and sinfulness—in support of inerrancy?" Waxing even more eloquent, I pressed the matter: "Not only does inerrancy imply that humans can grasp absolute truth, but it also denies the very nature of Scripture, as seen, for example, in the differences in parallel accounts. Why?" I asked, with increasing urgency.

"It's the slippery slope," he answered without hesitation. "If one admits a human frailty in Scripture, where will it stop?"

Now, I am quite familiar with the slippery slope and all its cousins. I am constantly working with my students as they tussle with the fear of the slippery slope or when they find themselves actually sliding down the slippery slope. It is a very real fear and something we need to address if we want to make it safe for believers to study the Bible. The slippery slope isn't really an argument, but it is a powerful psychological reality and is known by a host of other labels—"domino theory," "camel's nose under the tent," "foot in the door," and "crack in the dike," to mention some of the more prominent ones.

I am convinced that we can conquer the slippery slope by securing our faith by one or more of the three anchors suggested in the first three chapters: (1) seeking the common ground held by all Adventists—the Sabbath, the Second Advent, commandments, and the faith of Jesus; (2) recognizing the stabilizing function of the law pyramid—the *one,* the *two,* and the *ten;* and (3) focusing on Jesus as the clearest and best revelation of God.

But it will take all the king's horses and all the king's men to overcome the deep-rooted feeling that the Bible takes us directly into the courts of heaven. The Bible does, indeed, give us truth, a host of practical pointers to God, a cluster of practical truths that are embarrassingly clear, but we are always human, never God. That makes a huge difference in what we can know.

Ours is a worthy goal, I believe, seeking to establish the Bible as a safe and secure resource. Then liberals and conservatives can come together, pooling their respective strengths in the serious study of God's Word. Admittedly, the Bible can never be entirely safe—holy things are always dangerous—but surely there are enough frightening things in the world without our having to be frightened of our Bibles too!

So let us conspire together for a good cause, reviving something like that ancient Philistine cry when they heard the terrifying news that the ark had arrived in the Israelite camp. "Be strong, and quit yourselves like men," they cried.[12] Good idea! Let us be strong, bringing our sisters in Christ on board, too, quitting ourselves like true children of God.

When we are firmly anchored in our faith, three great benefits come our way. And here I am speaking from my own experience:

1. Honesty without fear. I don't have to be haunted by the fear that my house of faith will collapse if I look too closely at one of the bricks. I can look at anything and everything in Scripture and in nature. If everything in Scripture points to God but is never confused with God Himself, then it is safe to look under every stone, bush, and tree, in our efforts to understand Scripture and apply it to our lives. Unless you are afflicted with the same powerful sense of curiosity as I am, you will have no idea how liberating that concept is. But it truly is liberating, a wonderful gift of God.

If the old fears threaten, we can go to some of the quotes noted at the beginning of this chapter and remind ourselves that God's thoughts are not our thoughts. We can reassure ourselves with Ellen White's candid admission that "God and heaven alone are infallible," and that certain things in Scripture are "not like God." And she put all that in print. What a gift!

If the critics start to crow about errors and contradictions, we can simply remind them that the Bible belongs to believers, not to critics. It's our book, not theirs. All the astonishing diversity in Scripture—indeed, the contradictions—is just what we need if the book is to be a practical guide in the things of God.

2. Confidence with humility. Confidence and humility are usually enemies, not friends. Most of us all too easily slide off one side of the fence into arrogance or off the other side into timidity. But our confidence can be rooted in the conviction that our major resource (Scripture) is secure. And our humility comes from the recognition that Scripture itself does not tell us exactly how to apply God's Word in all the particular circumstances of our life. Ellen White was insightful when she urged a brother to educate himself so that he would have wisdom to deal with different kinds of minds. "You should with some have compassion," she urged, "while others you may save with fear." But the sentence that follows is the crucial one: "Our heavenly Father frequently leaves us in uncertainty in regard to our efforts."

3. Practicality. Once we make peace with the diversity in Scripture, we don't need to be haunted or frozen in place by that imaginary anchor: "The Bible says it. I believe it. That settles it." We can recognize what the Bible actually says. We can believe it. But we can know that what is fixed and settled in Scripture consists of a host of secure illustrations that can guide us in the practical business of daily living. We can begin to build bridges between some of the strange laws and events of the past, exploring ways in which the principles they illustrate can be applied in fresh situations today. Ellen White was on to something when she said, "The Bible was given for practical purposes."[13]

So let us be strong, coming together in confident humility. The rewards will be rich and enduring.

---

1. Ecclesiastes 5:2, TNIV.

2. Isaiah 55:8, 9.

3. Job 42:3–6.

4. 2 Timothy 3:16.

5. Ellen White, "Search the Scriptures," *Review and Herald,* July 26, 1892; *Selected Messages,* 1:37.

6. White, *Selected Messages,* 1:21.

7. Cf. Jude 22, 23, KJV.

8. White, *Testimonies for the Church,* 3:420.

9. 2 Corinthians 4:7.

10. 2 Timothy 3:16.

11. Job 42:3.

12. 1 Samuel 4:9, KJV.

13. White, *Selected Messages,* 1:20.

Chapter 6

Motivation, Not Just Information

The Point: Motivation, not mere information, changes the world.

The Bible says, "Through love become slaves to one another. For the whole law is summed up in a single commandment, 'You shall love your neighbor as yourself' " (Paul to the Galatian believers).[1]

Ellen White says, "Why do we need a Matthew, a Mark, a Luke, a John, a Paul, and all the writers who have borne testimony in regard to the life and ministry of the Saviour? . . . Because the minds of [people] differ. . . . [The Lord] gives to some Bible students views of truth that others do not grasp. It is possible for the most learned teacher to fall far short of teaching all that should be taught."[2]

Ellen White says, "Every sermon you preach, every article you write, may be all true; but one drop of gall in it will be poison to the hearer or the reader."[3]

Others say, "The earliest converts were converted by a single

historical fact (the Resurrection) and a single theological doctrine (the Redemption) operating on a sense of sin which they
already had."[4]—C. S. Lewis

When Jesus and Paul summarize the law in one sentence, they're telling
liberals and conservatives that we have no real choice but to work together. If
our goal—based on God's command and God's goal—is to treat others the
way we would want to be treated if we were in their place, then we have to ask
the question: "What works?" The focal point becomes motivation, not just information. Not just right doctrine, but how the doctrine makes us right.

A story may have all the facts right and still fall flat. The textbook may have
all the right information and still fall flat. A page of music may have all the right
notes and still fall flat. A teacher may say all the right words but leave the students unmoved, maybe even angry. A musician may perform in a way that is
technically correct but does not touch the heart. In some cases, good information doesn't just stay neutral—it can actually turn deadly. "Every article you
write, may be all true," Ellen White told A. T. Jones, "but one drop of gall in
it will be poison to the . . . reader."[5]

C. S. Lewis makes the audacious claim that the earliest Christian converts
were won "by a single historical fact (the Resurrection) and a single theological
doctrine (the Redemption)."[6] So getting the information right can be crucial.
Yet without the right circumstances, the right voice, and the right setting, good
information just remains dormant; it can even turn deadly.

As I reflected on how to make this chapter come alive, I reviewed key moments in my own life, moments when the vision throbbed with new life, but
also moments when the vision almost died.

When I was in seminary, for example, I was electrified by the discovery from
John's Gospel that Jesus was God in the flesh. I thought I knew that already.
But when the truth actually struck home, it was a life-changing moment.

Also at the seminary, however, I remember a withering moment in class
when we asked a teacher about the facts involving the Sermon on the Mount.
I still remember the caustic effect of his response. "I wish I could believe like
you guys do," he said. "But what can you do when you have tasted of the waters
of truth, and they are bitter?" Many years later, that teacher more than re-

deemed himself, but at the time, his comment was a body blow to an idealistic, young seminarian.

When I was a young pastor, to cite another example, I vividly remember being touched to the depths of my soul when the choir of La Sierra College—now La Sierra University—sang two anthems for us at a meeting for pastors. I could have gone home and worked for days on the power of that music. But right on the heels of that powerful music, one of our brothers stood before us and scolded us for not having enough baptisms. Instead of going home with a life-giving song in my heart, I went home that day and wept.

I could multiply stories of highs and lows, moments when God's plan for me was so very clear and His presence in my life so real, but also moments when the sun seemed to have disappeared forever and life seemed nearly hopeless. But what we live for are those moments that give us life, hope, and joy.

In that connection, a liberal-conservative story is to the point of this chapter and this book. It happened in the spring of 1981 on the campus of Marienhöhe Seminary in Darmstadt in what was at that time West Germany. The participants in a conference on ecumenism painfully illustrated what happens when liberals and conservatives are divided. Whenever a speaker argued for greater cooperation with other Christians, enthusiastic applause broke out from one segment of the audience. Similarly, whenever a speaker argued for keeping our distance from other organizations, enthusiastic applause broke out from another segment of the audience. I found the experience painful and exhausting. Unity in the church seemed so far away.

But then Dieter Leutert, a teacher at Friedensau Seminary in what was then East Germany, gave his presentation on a Sabbath afternoon. Because the Berlin wall still separated the two Germanys at that time, Leutert was only able to attend the conference in West Germany by special permission of the Communist government. What happened when he spoke has left an indelible impression on my soul. As he told the story of believers behind the iron curtain, he noted that Adventists were still Adventists, Catholics were still Catholics, Baptists were still Baptists, but over against the atheistic Communist government, they were all one in Christ Jesus.

For the first and only time during that entire weekend, no applause divided the audience. Instead, there were tears in our eyes and lumps in our throats as we caught a brief glimpse of a world we all wanted. A marvelous sense of common faith bonded us together—only briefly, as it turned out. The divisive applause soon returned. But the motivating power of that experience is still bringing positive results in my life.

I would hope there could be more moments like that in the church. Liberals and conservatives don't worry about the same things, nor are we always energized by the same things. But if we are sensitive to each other's needs, the results will only be positive for us as individuals and for the church as a whole.

As I am writing this chapter, more recent experiences have proven to be a powerful source of motivation. A woman who witnessed the results of the Rwandan genocide of 1994—an event that took the lives of at least a half million people, maybe a million, no one really knows—was quoted in a *Newsweek* column in a way that lit a fire in my soul. Rakiya Omaar noted that education was no cure for the madness in that country. Doctors, politicians, and teachers contributed to the mayhem as much as anyone else. Those who shielded their neighbors from violence "at huge personal risk," to quote the *Newsweek* article, "were 'almost universally peasants,' " said Omaar. " 'It was very shocking to me that education isn't, in the way you want it to be, the answer.' " The column concluded on this sobering note: "The ultimate, and disheartening, lesson of Rwanda may be that there is no foolproof antidote to genocidal madness—short of creating a universe in which all human life is equally revered."[7] Amen. Christians live in hope of just such a universe.

Triggering similar concerns, a book that details the events of the Holocaust experience in Belgium has galvanized strong convictions in my soul recently. Marion Schreiber's *The Twentieth Train*[8] vividly recounts the horrific story of how human beings coldly snuffed out the lives and hopes of other human beings—babies, the elderly, the sick, it made no difference. The Nazi machine moved mercilessly forward in its plan to exterminate every last European Jew.

But what I found so inspiring was the story of ordinary people who did what they could to help. In many cases, helpful Belgians could not do much to stop the deadly juggernaut. But they did what they could. I am finding that enormously inspiring and motivating. I, too, want to do what I can to make a difference for good in the world. It may not be much, but I want to follow the example of my Lord and the example of many of my fellow human beings and do what I can to make this earth more like the new one that Jesus has promised us.

So let's pay close attention to what motivates our brothers and sisters in Christ and what motivates those who do not yet know our Lord. By God's grace, His Spirit will be able to light a fire in the hearts of His people that no earthly power can ever quench.

---

1. Galatians 5:13, 14.

2. White, *Counsels to Parents, Teachers, and Students,* 432, 433.

3. White, *Testimonies for the Church,* 6:123.

4. C. S. Lewis, *The Screwtape Letters* With *Screwtape Proposes a Toast* (New York: HarperCollins, 2001), 126.

5. White, *Testimonies for the Church,* 6:123.

6. Lewis, *The Screwtape Letters,* 126.

7. Ellis Cose, "The Lessons of Rwanda," *Newsweek,* April 21, 2008, 33.

8. Marion Schreiber, *The Twentieth Train: The True Story of the Ambush of the Death Train to Auschwitz,* trans. Shaun Whiteside (New York: Grove Press, 2004).

Chapter 7

Jesus' Most Difficult Command

The Point: Jesus' command to treat others as we would want to be treated if we were in their place is His most difficult command and the one we try hardest to avoid.

Jesus says, "In everything do to others as you would have them do to you; for this is the law and the prophets."[1]

Ellen White says, "Even among the heathen are those who have cherished the spirit of kindness. . . . Among the heathen are those who worship God ignorantly, those to whom the light is never brought by human instrumentality, yet they will not perish. Though ignorant of the written law of God, they have heard His voice speaking to them in nature, and have done the things that the law required. Their works are evidence that the Holy Spirit has touched their hearts, and they are recognized as the children of God."[2]

Others say, "One of the remarkable experiences for we who measure goodness by the person of Jesus Christ is that we see it displayed in people who do not follow him. Our Lord once met a Samaritan, whose belief was condemned by Judaism.

Jesus so admired the man's tenderhearted action that he held him up as a model of compassion. Jesus didn't become a Samaritan, and he didn't give up his passion for the Jewish vision of God's reign. But when he met goodness, he simply rejoiced in it."[3]—Kari Sandhaas

Others say, "I have come to suspect that when people complain about 'organized' religion what they are really saying is that they can't stand other people."[4]—Kathleen Norris

Others say, "The months of seesawing between the two worlds had finally ended for me this night with nothing but an awareness of how deep the separating chasm really was and how impossible it seemed to bridge it—unless you were . . . rooted deeply enough in one world to enable you to be concerned only about the people of the other and not about their ideas."[5]—Reuven Malter in Chaim Potok's *The Promise*

Others say, "We have quite removed from men's minds what that pestilent fellow Paul used to teach about food and other unessentials—namely, that the human without scruples should always give in to the human with scruples. You would think they could not fail to see the application. You would expect to find the 'low' churchman genuflecting and crossing himself lest the weak conscience of his 'high' brother should be moved to irreverence, and the 'high' one refraining from these exercises lest he should betray his 'low' brother into idolatry. And so it would have been but for our ceaseless labour. Without that the variety of usage within the Church of England might have become a positive hotbed of charity and humility."[6]—Screwtape to Wormwood in C. S. Lewis's *The Screwtape Letters*

Others say, "The Christian way is different: harder, and easier. Christ says 'Give me All. I don't want so much of your time and so much of your money and so much of your work: I want You. I have not come to torment your natural self, but to kill it. No half-measures are any good. I don't want to cut off a branch here and a branch there, I want to have the whole tree down. I don't want to drill the tooth, or crown it, or stop it, but to have it out. Hand over the whole natural self, all the desires which you think innocent as well as the ones you think wicked—the whole outfit. I will give you a new self instead. In fact, I will give you Myself: my own will shall become yours.' "[7]—C. S. Lewis

Treating people right is what matters most to God. The cluster of quotations at the beginning of this chapter all point in that direction even though they vary dramatically in their starting points.

And what does "treating people right" mean? Treating them the way we would want to be treated if we were in their place. And if that's what matters most to God, it should matter most to us, too, for we are God's children. But judging by our track record, that ideal is elusive. In the words of G. K. Chesterton, "The Christian ideal has not been tried and found wanting. It has been found difficult; and left untried."[8]

But let's not give up. How can it happen? The clue is in the last quotation above, the one from C. S. Lewis on the new self, an echo of Jesus' words to Nicodemus that one must be "born of the Spirit."[9] Lewis paraphrases: " 'I have not come to torment your natural self, but to kill it.' "[10]

After the new birth experience, the world looks like a new place and people look like new creatures. In the words of Paul, "Everything old has passed away; see, everything has become new!"[11]

Typically, the new birth experience is described in religious terms, as having to do with a person's relationship with God. But 1 John 2:29 surprisingly describes the new birth in ethical and moral terms, declaring that "everyone who does right has been born of him." That reference to right behavior ties in with Ellen White's commentary on the parable of the sheep and the goats in Matthew 25: "When the nations are gathered before Him," she says, "there will be but two classes, and their eternal destiny will be determined by what they have done or have neglected to do for Him in the person of the poor and the suffering."[12]

That link between human responsibility and the kingdom is likely to be troubling to those of a Calvinist bent, for it begins to sound like salvation by works. But note that in the parable of the sheep and the goats, none of the good deeds are done in order to impress God or to earn His favor. The Lord's commendation comes as a surprise.

For those who argue that the so-called golden rule is not unique to Christianity, we can readily agree. As one of my colleagues reminds me from time to time, "Morality is pretty much the same around the world. The difference is in the motivation."[13] The difference in the Christian story is the astonishing claim that our *God* took human flesh and came among us to model unselfish service in life and in death. He also promised us His Spirit as an ongoing presence to help us follow His example. That's the difference in motivation. We worship a God who gave all for us.

Thus, when Paul admonishes us to become slaves to one another "through love,"[14] he is simply asking us to follow the divine example. Against the backdrop of all other religions, that is revolutionary.

Now, my argument in this chapter is that we have our greatest difficulty with Jesus' command to love one another, given as *the* summary of the law and the prophets in Matthew 7:12 and as the second great command in Matthew 22:35–40. With some notable exceptions, liberals are inclined to put their energies into the horizontal dimension of humanitarian service, thus affirming the second command to love one another. By contrast, conservatives are inclined to put their energies into the vertical dimension of serving God, thus fulfilling the first command to love God wholeheartedly. Bluntly put, liberals want to save the body; conservatives seek to save the soul!

The 9/11 attacks illustrate with horrible clarity an extreme conservative impulse to serve God wholeheartedly—human life means absolutely nothing. The liberal neglect of the divine can be almost as striking, though without obvious bloodshed.

Two of the quotations above directly address the liberal/conservative divide, one from a Christian context, the other from a Jewish perspective. C. S. Lewis's comment about the "pestilent fellow Paul," is from *The Screwtape Letters* and focuses on the "high church" liberals and the "low church" conservatives. Those distinctions are not likely to be very meaningful in an Adventist setting, but I really like the final line that emphasizes diversity as a source of Christian charity. Without the ceaseless efforts of the demonic forces, Screwtape argues, "the variety of usage within the Church of England might have become a positive hotbed of charity and humility."[15] What a wonderful concept! Our diversity forces us to recognize the need to be caring and charitable! I think Jesus would like that.

The other quotation is from Chaim Potok's masterpiece, *The Promise,* a book that vividly illustrates how liberals and conservatives divide over issues relating to their sacred texts. Through the narrative voice of the moderate Reuven Malter, Potok describes the tension between the extreme Hasidic Jews and the rest of the world. Danny Saunders—a secular psychologist in real life—has brought his liberal Jewish bride, Rachel, into his conservative Hasidic community. Saunders himself has made peace with the radical differences between his secular existence and his devout Hasidic community. How? As Potok puts it, by being "rooted deeply enough in one world to enable you to be concerned only about the people of the other and not about their ideas."[16]

I believe that God calls us, as Christians, to always be concerned about people first and foremost. Ideas, of course, can be a powerful transforming force for good or for evil. But our first concern must always be to treat people as we would want to be treated if we were in their place. Jesus shows us how. His relations with the poor, the rich, foreigners, women, and social outcasts point the way to God's kingdom.

Finally, a suggestion on how liberals and conservatives can merge their respective agendas. As noted above, liberals typically are more interested in the horizontal (human relations), while conservatives are more interested in the vertical (obedience to God). Through the example and teachings of Jesus, we can learn that the best way to serve God is by loving people. "Love [for people] is the earthward manifestation of the love of God," wrote Ellen White. "When we love the world as He has loved it, then for us His mission is accomplished. We are fitted for heaven; for we have heaven in our hearts."[17]

In short, whether we are liberal or conservative, nothing is so important as people. Every person on earth is one of God's children. Our calling is to treat people like the royal offspring that they truly are.

1. Matthew 7:12.

2. White, *The Desire of Ages,* 638.

3. Kari Sandhaas, Context, quoted in "Rejoice," Signs of the Times®, July 1993, 6.

4. Kathleen Norris, *Amazing Grace: A Vocabulary of Faith* (New York: Penguin Putnam, 1998), 258.

5. Chaim Potok, *The Promise* (New York: Fawcett Crest, 1970), 369.

6. C. S. Lewis, *The Screwtape Letters,* 84, 85.

7. C. S. Lewis, *Mere Christianity* (New York: HarperCollins, 2001), 196, 197.

8. G. K. Chesterton, *What's Wrong With the World* (New York: Dodd, Mead and Co., 1910), 48, quoted in "Reflections: Classic and Contemporary Excerpts," *Christianity Today,* January 9, 1995, 36.

9. John 3:8.

10. Lewis, *Mere Christianity,* 196.

11. 2 Corinthians 5:17.

12. White, *The Desire of Ages,* 637.

13. Jon Dybdahl, professor emeritus of theology and former president of Walla Walla University.

14. Galatians 5:13.

15. Lewis, *The Screwtape Letters,* 85.

16. Chaim Potok, *The Promise,* 369.

17. White, *The Desire of Ages,* 641.

Chapter 8

The Devotional Life

The Point: Diversity makes prayer more crucial but less visible.

Jesus says, "Whenever you pray, do not be like the hypocrites; for they love to stand and pray in the synagogues and at the street corners, so that they may be seen by others. Truly I tell you, they have received their reward. But whenever you pray, go into your room and shut the door and pray to your Father who is in secret; and your Father who sees in secret will reward you"[1] (from the Sermon on the Mount).

Jesus says, "When you are praying, do not heap up empty phrases as the Gentiles do; for they think that they will be heard because of their many words. Do not be like them, for your Father knows what you need before you ask him"[2] (from the Sermon on the Mount).

The Bible says, "In the morning, while it was still very dark, he got up and went out to a deserted place, and there he prayed"[3] (Mark, on Jesus' prayer life).

Ellen White says, "Those who do not learn every day in the school of Christ, who do not spend much time in earnest prayer, are not fit to handle the work of God in any of its branches; for if they do, human depravity will surely overcome them and they will lift up their souls unto vanity."[4]

Ellen White says, "When men cease to depend upon men, when they make God their efficiency, then there will be more confidence manifested in one another. Our faith in God is altogether too feeble and our confidence in one another altogether too meager."[5]

Others say, "I am certainly unfit to advise anyone else on the devotional life. My own rules are (1) To make sure that, wherever else they may be placed, the main prayers should *not* be put 'last thing at night.' (2) To avoid introspection in prayer— I mean not to watch one's own mind to see if it is in the right frame, but always to turn the attention outwards to God. (3) Never, never to try to generate an emotion by will power. (4) To pray without words when I am able, but to fall back on words when tired or otherwise below par. With renewed thanks. Perhaps *you* will sometimes pray for *me?*"[6]—C. S. Lewis to Mrs. Ursula Roberts

This is an awkward chapter for me. The topic of prayer sets off several warning bells in my head. First, in at least two places, the Gospels warn of the dangers of advertising our prayer life. In the Sermon on the Mount, Jesus bluntly advises a private prayer life behind closed doors.[7] And Jesus' story of the Pharisee and the publican is hardly a ringing call to convene a prayer conference.[8]

I have always been intrigued by the fact that the Gospels tell us almost nothing about Jesus' own prayer life. Mark tells us that Jesus got up very early, went to a private place, and prayed. But Mark doesn't tell us anything about what actually happened when Jesus prayed. When the disciples asked Jesus to help them with their praying, "as John taught his disciples,"[9] our Greek New Testament puts Jesus' answer into a thirty-eight-word prayer. That's all. Hardly the stuff to take you through a full night of prayer. The similar prayer in the Sermon on the Mount is a bit longer: fifty-seven words plus the later addition of the fifteen-word doxology.

Coming down to my own day, I remember the wry comment of Gordon Balharrie, dean of the School of Theology when I enrolled at Walla Walla College as a first-year theology student. "Young theology students are sorely tempted to preach their first sermon on the topic of prayer," he said. "Don't do it. You don't know enough about the topic to preach on it."

Finally, I remember the comments of two devout young women who attended a prayer conference led by a well-known Evangelical. In the course of the conference, the leader presumed to specify how much time one should spend in prayer each day. "I was making good progress in my prayer life—until I went to the conference," one of girls told me. "The conference put my prayer life into reverse!"

All that almost adds up to a convincing argument *against* saying anything about prayer! But not quite.

In fear and trembling, I do want to share a few insights that I have found beneficial—ones that are directly connected with my discovery of the diversity to be found in Scripture and in the church. To be quite candid, in my earlier years, my devotional life was quite ordinary. I had been following the basic plan popularized by a number of speakers and writers—the "big three" of the devotional life: pray, study, and share.

The plan is a solid one. My problem was that, for me, it was mostly external, a checklist rather than an internalized process. Pray? Check. Study? Check. Share? (The toughest one.) Check. I imagined God to be something like a giant Scoutmaster with a chart. If I could tick off my big three for the day, God would be pleased, and I could get on with life. I didn't want to admit it, but with that kind of external, checklist approach, I could miss my devotions and not even miss them. It was embarrassing, troubling, and discouraging.

But when I began to realize the significance of the diversity in Scripture—matching the diversity in the church—a transformation was underway. I will simply lay out my conclusions under the heading of the three conversation partners.

Three conversation partners: Scripture, reason, and the Holy Spirit

In my more traditional approach to prayer, my conversation partners in prayer found it easy to quarrel with each other and for two reasons. First, if my reason told me that a particular passage of Scripture didn't apply to me, I felt guilty for rejecting the authority of Scripture in favor of my own reason. Second, I had been programmed as a child, probably as an adult, too, to turn to prayer as a last resort. Lost keys, for example? Turn the house upside down, exhausting all merely *human* resources, then pray. That's prayer as a last resort.

The new plan is revolutionary and peace-loving. My conversation partners never quarrel anymore. Each has a clear-cut task to bring to the table, and we work it through. It's a wonderful plan. Let me explain.

1. Scripture. Once I was able to say out loud that Scripture is more like a casebook than a codebook, then I could be perfectly honest with what Scripture can and cannot do. What became clear to me is the difference between a visit from a live prophet and a visit to the written record of the prophet's work in Scripture. A great gulf is fixed between the two. If a prophet were to confront me, for example, as Nathan did David with his bony finger and an announcement— "You are the man!"[10]—how could I possibly claim that the prophetic message did not apply to me but should simply be added to the casebook? To quote an Old Testament exclamation: " 'Such a thing is not done in Israel!' "[11]

But when the confrontation is over and all we have is the written record, then the event does, indeed, simply become part of an expanded casebook. In David's case, of course, his guilt was clearly evident. There's absolutely no question about that. But where the casebook would come in for Nathan, for example, is in the question of how to deal with David. Heavy-handed or gentle? Sermon, story, or straight rebuke? In our day, the question might revolve around e-mail, voice mail, regular mail, or a personal visit. Which one and when? From among the cases open to him, Nathan chose to open with the parable of the rich man who stole the poor man's sheep.

So, to be perfectly blunt, Scripture can never tell me exactly what I should teach my students. The "cases" in Scripture can inform questions of content, as well as questions of when and how. But nowhere in Scripture can I find a clear "Thus saith the Lord" to guide me in all my decisions day by day. Nor will

Scripture tell me what I should include in this book. It provides me with a host of examples. But the decisions do not simply jump from my Bible into the manuscript. And that brings me to the next conversation partner—reason.

2. Reason. Several thoughtful voices have suggested that my approach to Scripture exalts reason over revelation. That is a serious matter, to be sure. But if Scripture does not self-apply in my daily life (as noted above), just how are applications to be made? The hard truth is that my head (or heart, I use the terms almost interchangeably) is the only part of my body suitable to the task. I cannot use my elbow, my chin, or my knee. I have to use my head.

But one of the truths that is abundantly clear in a host of passages throughout Scripture—could I say a host of "cases"?—is that my reason (heart) is suspect, seriously suspect. "The heart is deceitful above all things, and desperately wicked," exclaims Jeremiah.[12] The NRSV says it is "devious" and "perverse."

So, what does one do with a deceitful, devious, wicked, and perverse heart?

Our only choice is to bring it to God and plead, as David did, for cleansing and renewal. In Psalm 51, for example, the cries rise heavenward again and again: "Wash me." "Cleanse me." "Purge me." "Create in me a clean heart, O God, / and put a new and right spirit within me."[13]

My head, my heart, is the only part of me capable of evaluating and applying the cases I find in Scripture. Yet my heart is thoroughly incapable unless I come to God in brokenness and humility. The bitter truth of that necessity is vividly portrayed in these lines from W. H. Auden:

O stand, stand at the window
    As the tears scald and start;
You must love your crooked neighbor
    With your crooked heart.[14]

A crooked heart is all I have. So I come to God for cleansing and for healing. Unless I do, I am in great danger of twisting Scripture, misusing it in my life and in the lives of others, wreaking havoc wherever I might turn, and greatly dishonoring my Savior. God's Spirit is quite capable of working through good people who do not even know Him.[15] But for those of us who claim to know Him and claim to be acting on His behalf, the expectations are infinitely higher.

These stinging words from Ellen White are ones that I rarely share, and for several reasons which you might surmise. But this is where they fit: "Those who do not learn every day in the school of Christ," she says, "who do not spend much time in earnest prayer, are not fit to handle the work of God in any of its branches; for if they do, human depravity will surely overcome them and they will lift up their souls unto vanity."[16]

And so we come to the third conversation partner, the Holy Spirit.

3. *Holy Spirit, invited through prayer.* The role of this third conversation partner is so easily misunderstood because of our tendency to use prayer as a last resort. After exhausting all human resources, we pray. I don't want to diminish the value of urgent and even last-minute cries to God. They are thoroughly biblical and entirely appropriate in their place. But emergency prayer is not the same as purifying prayer, a concept that comes much closer to what I have in mind. Let me explain.

The purpose of bringing my crooked heart to God for cleansing or purification is so that my head (heart) might be in a better position to perceive God's will in Scripture. Purifying prayer enables my mind, my reason, to fulfill its proper role in the three-cornered conversation. A purified heart is the only kind that has half a chance of understanding and applying Scripture in accordance with God's will. In emergency prayer, I usually throw up my hands and turn everything over to God, dropping out of the conversation completely. The emergency prayer approach might suggest that I simply open my Bible at random and expect the Spirit to let my finger fall on the right verse.

I suspect that purifying prayer is what Paul had in mind when he admonished the Thessalonian believers to "pray without ceasing."[17] When we are in a constant attitude of prayer we will be in a much better position to represent God's character and will in our decisions. When it comes to our study of Scripture, praying without ceasing means that we will be using our heads more—thinking more, not less. Because we are in an attitude of prayer, God can guide our minds and hearts into proper attitudes and good applications.

In my conversations with other Christians, I am constantly on the lookout for good metaphors to illustrate how prayer works in our lives. One friend suggested that we are like a radio playing God's signal. I complained that a radio was too passive a model. Another friend suggested a control tower at an airport.

That metaphor works better, for it requires the presence of Someone in the tower, but also active decisions on the part of the pilot.

The metaphor I find most useful, however, is the Brita water filter or any kind of chemical filter across a moving stream. The idea of a water filter illustrates the difference between the life that is rooted in prayer and one that is not; for when we are not in communion with God, life goes on. We eat, sleep, talk, work, and play, regardless of whether we are in communion with God. But like the water flowing through a saturated filter that no longer filters, the life untouched by prayer keeps flowing; it simply is not purified by contact with the divine.

There is one other very rational part of this approach to prayer that I discovered when our two girls were young. On those relatively rare occasions when parental direction seemed necessary, I found myself saying, "Ask Jesus to help you." Then I began wondering what I was expecting Jesus to do. Would he come with a giant 20 cc syringe and inject some help?

I concluded that what would be most helpful for them—and for me, too, when I needed special help—was to ask for help and to *remember* asking for help. Somehow it is much more difficult to be nasty when I am actively praying for the other person's good and *remembering* that I have prayed for that person's good.

That same procedure applies when I come to Scripture with my crooked heart. If I can consistently remember that I am doing God's work instead of my own, I will be using my mind, my heart, and my reason all the more, but under the purifying influence of God's Spirit.

Does such an approach guarantee right answers? Not at all. Indeed, when Ellen White was counseling a brother to "educate" himself so that he would have "wisdom to deal with minds," she concludes her counsel on a cautionary note: "Our heavenly Father frequently leaves us in uncertainty in regard to our efforts."[18]

The results

To my grateful amazement, my devotional life as been greatly enriched by my knowledge of the diversity to be found in Scripture and in the church. Instead of an external checklist, I now know that study and prayer are intrinsic to the life of the Christian. Only through study and prayer will I be able to address the needs that I will meet during the day. Every student and every class are a call to prayer, a fresh situation that must be brought before the Lord. Devotions are no longer a chore. I rejoice that I have the privilege of being in touch with God as I seek to be His faithful witness.

It is also a joy to know that I don't have to feel guilty about deciding which part of Scripture is appropriate for any particular person or situation. Nor do I have to "let go and let God" (whatever that might mean). Instead of letting go, I hang on all the tighter, knowing that God expects me to be faithful in my witness for Him.

To sum up, the Bible provides the cases, but never tells me what case I should use in any particular situation. My heart and mind must process the cases in order to make the proper application. But my crooked heart must constantly be brought in touch with God through prayer so that this deceitful chunk of humanity can be purified in God's presence.

After I have done my homework, then I am ready to join my brothers and sisters to ponder the work of the church. If we have each done our personal work, then we will come together as the early Christians did in Acts 15. We will make important decisions when "it has seemed good to the Holy Spirit and to us."[19]

---

1. Matthew 6:5, 6.

2. Matthew 6:7, 8.

3. Mark 1:35.

4. Ellen White, *Testimonies to Ministers and Gospel Workers* (Mountain View, Calif.: Pacific Press® Pub. Assn., 1962), 169.

5. White, *Testimonies to Ministers,* 214.

6. C. S. Lewis to Mrs. Ursula Roberts, Magdalen College, July 31, 1954, in *Letters of C. S. Lewis* (New York: Harcourt Brace Jovanovich, 1975), 256; italics in the original.

7. Matthew 6:5, 6.

8. Luke 18:9–14.

9. Luke 11:1–4.

10. 2 Samuel 12:7. As Nathan did to David after David's sin with Bathsheba and the murder of her husband, Uriah.

11. 2 Samuel 13:12, NASB.

12. Jeremiah 17:9, KJV.

13. Psalm 51:2, 7, 10.

14. W. H. Auden, "As I Walked out One Evening," *The Collected Poetry of W. H. Auden* (New York: Random House, n.d.), as quoted in Roger Robbennolt, *Carnival Tales for Blind Ben See* (Leavenworth, Kans.: Forest of Peace Publishing, 1999), 111, 161.

15. Paul suggests this kind of work by the Spirit in Romans 2:14 when he refers to "Gentiles, who do not posses the law, [yet who] do instinctively what the law requires." That passage seems to lie behind Ellen White's comment in connection with the parable of

the sheep and goats in Matthew 25: "Among the heathen are those who worship God ignorantly, those to whom the light is never brought by human instrumentality, yet they will not perish. Though ignorant of the written law of God, they have heard His voice speaking to them in nature, and have done the things that the law required. Their works are evidence that the Holy Spirit has touched their hearts, and they are recognized as the children of God" (*The Desire of Ages,* 638).

16. White, *Testimonies to Ministers,* 169.

17. 1 Thessalonians 5:17.

18. White, *Testimonies for the Church,* 3:420.

19. Acts 15:28.

Part 3

Liberals and Conservatives: The Labels

The Bible says, "For the whole law is summed up in a single commandment, 'You shall love your neighbor as yourself.' If, however, you bite and devour one another, take care that you are not consumed by one another."[1]

In the three chapters in part 3 we'll try to get a handle on the labels. What do *liberal* and *conservative* actually mean? I suggest that a believing community uses the labels in three ways, having to do with how we think, how we relate to culture, and how we think about God. Those categories are oversimplified, to be sure. But they point in the right direction.

I believe the time has come to take seriously Jesus' second command and explore ways in which liberals and conservatives can work together more effectively. I must admit, however, that not everyone is as optimistic as I am. When I told my "Inspiration" class at Walla Walla University that I was writing this book, a student responded, "I want to know why the church needs both liberals and conservatives. The notion that we can bring together such vastly different people comes either from a man who is way ahead of his time or from one who is crazy. I believe you're the former, but such appreciation of opposites seems rare these days."

He's right in at least one respect: the church isn't an easy place to bring opposites together. But I don't think I'm crazy. And I actually believe that I'm not ahead of the times, but behind, just trying to catch up with the apostle Paul from the first century and Ellen White from the nineteenth. The church should, and could, be a place where liberals and conservatives model to the larger world how believers can work together to bring hope and healing to a torn and bleeding planet, and do so without the slightest compromise of essential convictions.

Furthermore, as scary as the topic may sound, when I have presented it to church groups in various settings, the response has been not just positive, but downright enthusiastic. Key elements have appeared in Adventist publications in 1985, 1989, and 1992. And my sermon on the topic in the Walla Walla College Church in 1989 triggered an avalanche of positive feedback, more than I have ever received for any other sermon or article.[2]

So I believe the time is right. And the conviction has been growing in my soul that our Adventist heritage gives us a significant advantage as we seek to realize the New Testament vision of the church as the body of Christ. Indeed, *Adventist Advantage* was one of the titles I seriously considered for this book.

If we talk about an Adventist advantage, however, I hope we can do so with confidence and conviction but without arrogance. Any claim to be the "remnant" too easily slips toward arrogance even if one believes the claim to be true. But confidence slipping toward arrogance is probably just one of the occupational hazards of being an evangelist. *Humble* and *evangelist* are words that don't easily come together.

In that respect the apostle Paul may be our most vivid example. When he defended his ministry against his detractors at Corinth, he sounded something less than humble: "If they can brag, so can I, but it is a foolish thing to do. . . . Are they servants of Christ? I am a fool to talk this way, but I serve him better than they do. I have worked harder and have been put in jail more times. I have been beaten with whips more and have been in danger of death more often. . . . If I have to brag, I will brag about how weak I am. God, the Father of our Lord Jesus, knows I am not lying."[3]

Humble? Not just yet!

But let's get back to work. I want to make the case that Jesus needs both liberals and conservatives—and so do we.

1. Galatians 5:14, 15.
2. "Adventist Personality Types," *Insight,* August 10, 1985, 6–11; "We Need Your Differences," *Adventist Review,* November 2, 1989, 17–20; "Pictures: The Pie," *North Pacific Union Gleaner,* August 17, 1992; "The Adventist Church at Corinth," (Sabbath sermon, Walla Walla College Church, College Place, Wash., December 9, 1989). A slightly revised version of the sermon with the same title appears in this book as chapter 20. All items are available online at www.aldenthompson.com.
3. 2 Corinthians 11:21–31, CEV.

Chapter 9

It All Started When We Were Kids

The Bible says, "Esau was an outdoorsman; his brother Jacob was a homebody. Esau was Isaac's favorite . . . , Jacob was Rebekah's."[1]

Ellen White says, "God designed that . . . those of varied temperaments should be associated together. . . . Diversities of temperament and character are frequently marked in families; where this is the case there should be a mutual recognition of one another's rights."[2]

Others say, Treating people the same is not equal treatment if the people are not the same.[3]—Deborah Tannen

One doesn't have to listen very long or hard these days to hear vocal comments about "fairness" from American young people, indeed, even from children. When parents from their more mature vantage point, treat their children differently with every intention of being fair, it doesn't take much to set off the howls of protest: "That's not fair!"

We have good evidence from Scripture that parents are quite capable of favoritism. Abraham's preference for Isaac over Ishmael could perhaps be justified because of God's promises concerning Isaac. But what justification is there for the way Isaac and Rebekah treated their two boys? Or for the way Jacob showered favors on Joseph and Benjamin, the sons of his "favorite" wife Rachel? Or for the way David treated his son Absalom?

There are other areas where thoughtful people in our culture would have no difficulty labeling particular actions as unfair. We would universally resent it if a post office clerk sold stamps at half price to the poor, even though we might otherwise be quite sympathetic to the needs of the poor. Likewise, we would not appreciate it if the same clerk, for quite different reasons, gave a discount on stamps to the wealthy. We might agree that major users should get special consideration in some circumstances. But don't try to make any deals at the main desk in the post office while the rest of us are listening in!

In the classroom, lifelong memories are made by teachers who are not fair. I have a vivid memory of a seminary teacher who refused to correct a grading error simply because my calling it to his attention was seen as an inappropriate challenge to the teacher's authority. Similarly, a friend recently shared a forty-year memory of a college teacher who foolishly gave percentage grades on a final test, but then overruled the results because the student who got the 98 percent didn't "try" as hard as the student who got the 90 percent. It was no secret. The teacher bluntly told the 98 percent student his rationale. If a teacher wants to grade subjectively, give an essay test. Don't give percentage scores and then ignore them.

All of these obvious inequities would be universally recognized by thoughtful adults. But that's not the point I want to make here. I'm talking about those legitimate adaptations that wise parents, good teachers, effective pastors, and alert employers make when dealing with those for whom they are responsible. A gentle touch here, a firm touch there; a word of encouragement here, a caution there. "You could have done more," to one; "You are attempting too much," to another.

Even when such adaptations would be recognized as fair and necessary, they feel unfair when the recipients receive their differing treatment in the presence of each other. That's why sensitive adaptations are best done quietly and in private. When we were growing up with our siblings, we were even quicker to spot examples of inequities and label them as unfair. But the mature mind will recognize that such adaptations are quite necessary, and if done well, very fair indeed.

My question is, Why is it that virtually all thoughtful people so easily recognize the need for adaptations to particular needs at home, at school, at work, and even in church life, but resist them when dealing with the teachings of the church or the interpretation of the Bible? Shouldn't the same principles of adaptation apply? How we express our beliefs is linked to our behavior, and how we interpret the Bible is linked to our beliefs. The genes and chromosomes we inherited from our parents and the influence of home and school all play a part too.

That's why the distinctions between liberals and conservatives—along with the labels—as discussed in the following chapters, are important. If we really are different, then we have to work harder to understand each other. Ellen White pointed that out to a brother who was too confident of his own perspective: "You need to educate yourself, that you may have wisdom to deal with minds," she wrote. "You should with some have compassion, making a difference, while others you may save with fear, pulling them out of the fire [Jude 22, 23]."[4] Her next sentence is particularly insightful: "Our heavenly Father frequently leaves us in uncertainty in regard to our efforts." It is that touch of uncertainty that makes it possible for us to learn from each other. And whether we are liberal or conservative, we all have a lot to learn.

---

1. Genesis 25:27, 28, paraphrased.

2. White, "The Mother's Duty—Christ Her Strength," *Signs of the Times* (November 29, 1877). Full quote: "God designed that we should be tolerant of one another, that those of varied temperaments should be associated together, so that by mutual forbearance and consideration of one another's peculiarities, prejudices should be softened, and rough points of character smoothed. Diversities of temperament and character are frequently marked in families; where this is the case there should be a mutual recognition of another's rights. Thus all the members may be in harmony, and the blending of varied temperaments may be a benefit to all. Christian courtesy is the golden clasp which unites the members of the family in bonds of love, becoming closer and stronger every day."

3. Adapted from Deborah Tannen, "Teacher's Classroom Strategies Should Recognize That Men and Women Use Language Differently," *The Chronicle of Higher Education,* June 19, 1991, B3. Exact quote: "Treating people the same is not equal treatment if they are not the same."

4. White, *Testimonies for the Church,* 3:420.

Chapter 10

Liberals and Conservatives: Choosing Up Sides

Some will argue that the words *liberal* and *conservative* have outlived their usefulness. They're too mushy, too elusive, too divisive. It's a valid concern, especially when religion is involved; words are dangerous when used as clubs instead of flashlights.

But I believe careful definitions can be helpful. In this chapter, we'll explore how the words *liberal* and *conservative* are used in our larger, daily world. In our next chapter, we will look more specifically at the different ways they are used in a religious setting.

In general—unless we get into politics and religion—the word *conservative* is less troublesome than the word *liberal*. Its meaning is clear-cut and more neutral than its value-laden counterpart. Without passing any kind of judgment, it simply describes a more cautious approach to life. In finance, for example, a person may adopt a conservative investment plan; in sports, a team may adopt a conservative game plan. In both cases, the term is virtually value free—a conservative plan can be good in some situations, bad in others.

Where caution is deemed inappropriate, however, conservative then shades into the negative and passes judgment. Interestingly enough, every time Ellen White actually used the word, it carried this negative sense. For example, when expressing concern for believers who "discourage any further investigation of the Scriptures," she says that "they become conservative and seek to avoid discussion."[1] Clearly she is passing judgment. In our daily life, the word is frequently used in this judgmental sense even though the essential meaning of the word is neutral.

By contrast and in a curious sort of way, liberal ends up being more troublesome precisely because it starts out on the positive side of the ledger. I suspect, however, that the only context in which a positive meaning for the word is nearly universally recognized is when it refers to someone as a liberal giver in the monetary sense. Even those who know themselves to be stingy will begrudgingly praise the generous by referring to them as "liberal"—as if wishing they could somehow be more liberal themselves. Yet even here criticism lurks close at hand: thrifty people often fear that *generous* really means "reckless." Thus even a "liberal giver" can be viewed with suspicion.

Beyond that narrow monetary application of the word, *liberal* generally implies a more exploratory mode of thinking and acting, often rooted in the abstract and the theoretical. It also suggests a more open, nonjudgmental stance toward people, projects, and ideas. Yet it is precisely those positive impulses that raise a warning flag when the word is used in a political or religious setting. *Exploratory* can be seen as being destructive of traditional values and *nonjudgmental* can be seen as being soft on bad behavior.

But now let's step back and look at some examples of how the liberal-conservative tension plays out in real life. We can start with the university where I have taught since 1970. In our accounting and records offices, for example, we hire conservatives—people who are precise, follow the rules, and pay attention to details. By contrast, in marketing, we hire liberals—creative souls who are eager to adapt to the varied needs and wants of potential university students. Sometimes, maybe even frequently, the conservatives in records and/or accounting rise up in opposition to the liberals in marketing who are so easily tempted to bring in any live body regardless of his or her academic qualifications (records) or financial situation (accounting). The marketing crowd is equally perturbed because their detractors in records or accounting have made their jobs more difficult. Actually, if we wanted to destroy the university, all we would have to do is put the accountants into marketing and the marketing people into accounting! Are both perspectives important? Of course. But both sides must recognize that their strengths can also be their weaknesses. And the creative tension between them often has to be sorted out by administrators who are responsible for keeping the university in balance.

A university setting offers another good example of the liberal-conservative tension: the interplay between faculty who teach in our professional programs (nursing, engineering, business, social work) and the faculty who teach in the liberal arts (English, history, philosophy, chemistry, biology). But the dividing issues are not the same as in the earlier example. Instead of pitting the highly structured and precision-loving accountants against the free-spirited marketers, now the match-up is between the abstract-thinking, theoretically oriented liberal arts teachers and the practical, concrete-thinking faculty in our professional programs.

Given these tensions, faculty meetings are often a real zoo. "Let's get on with it or the patient will die!" exclaim the nurses. "Not so fast," say the humanities people. "We can't make hasty or rash decisions; we must thoroughly explore all the implications." Are both perspectives important? Of course. And blessed be the university president who must moderate the discussion and forge a working environment in which both sides can thrive.

If we shift the scene to politics, the tensions between the two perspectives are vivid and intense. The liberals are strong on compassion and social services. The conservatives are strong on self-reliance and business incentives. Yet typically, at least in America, a slight shift in public sentiment can make a significant difference in who runs the country. Over time, one can plot the swing of the pendulum, from liberals to conservatives, then back to liberals, then back to conservatives. The electorate is healthiest when strong and competent spokespersons are active on both sides.

Not surprisingly, social organisms on either side of the aisle must share some of the characteristics of the other side. A hard-driving business that shows no compassion to workers or customers is not likely to prosper for long. Similarly, a charity that does not follow careful business practices soon loses the confidence of those it seeks to serve.

The same interplay between strengths and weaknesses can be seen to operate within a family. My gentle wife and her hard-driving husband finally were able to admit to each other that each of us had worried about what could happen to our two girls if they were to be left entirely in the care of the other parent. My wife was concerned that if something happened to her, our poor girls could easily be pressed beyond measure by their disciplinarian father. I worried that if something happened to me, our girls would miss the firm guidance their father knew they needed. Somewhat to our surprise, however, we discovered that when I was away, my wife naturally provided a firmer hand; and when my wife was absent, I became gentler. Ideally, with both of us present, the matchup of our differing strengths provided a healthy balance for the family.

One other personal example has shed significant light for me on the life of faith. It comes from a surprisingly secular source—the racquetball court. As I have reflected on the strengths and weaknesses of my various partners over the years, I have come to a startling conclusion, namely, that in any given situation, we have almost no choice over our initial reactions. We don't choose our response—it just happens. And only God knows how much we are able to change. Eventually, I came to the conclusion that I cannot pass any kind of final judgment on those who act in ways I consider inappropriate. I say *final* judgment, for I can still address wrong actions. But what I have to leave open is God's ultimate view of the people involved, for only God knows all the factors that drive our human responses—genetics, upbringing, special circumstances. Only God knows how to factor all that into some kind of *final* judgment.

To describe my position I use the phrase *practical universalism.* That may sound scary, but a practical universalism is a far cry from a pure universalism that claims salvation for everyone regardless of his or her choices and actions. The word *practical* simply reminds me that a *final* judgment is not for me to make. As a result, I am much less judgmental than I once was. My understanding of right and wrong is still very much alive, and I am still quite willing and able to address issues of right and wrong. But I am now more willing to let God be the final judge.

My thinking along these lines was triggered by a comment from one of my racquetball partners years ago. Those of us who regularly played together at that time had quite different strengths. One had the power; another had the reach; I had the speed. One day after a game of singles, my "power" partner opened my eyes with this comment: "Speed on your feet is like perfect pitch in music," he said. "Either you have it or you don't."

Suddenly I realized he was right. All you have to do is watch youngsters at play. Either they can run or they can't. You can command a plodder to run faster, but it won't help. Even with enormous effort, a plodder is still just a plodder. If you have the gift of speed on your feet, fine-tuning can move you up the scale just a bit. But either you have the gift or you don't. You can't choose it.

What surprised me most, however, was how my thinking was transformed as I reflected on my own personal reactions to victory, those exhilarating moments when I turned on the afterburners and left those other guys in the dust. It was always a deliciously wicked feeling, a powerful sense of pride in my own accomplishment. I might note that spectator response suggests that virtually everyone knows the thrill of such a victory. Which Olympic events draw the most attention? The sprints. The one hundred– and two hundred–meter dashes. We are gripped by them.

But when I recognized that my speed was a gift of God, I suddenly realized that my personal pride in my accomplishment was quite misplaced. And I discovered that Paul had words just for me: "What is so special about you?" he wrote to the Corinthians. "What do you have that you were not given? And if it was given to you, how can you brag?"[2]

That principle applies in a host of settings. In school, for example, students with only modest natural abilities can take pride in good grades because of their hard work, not because of their brilliance. "I may not be particularly smart," they will say, "but I worked hard, and it paid off." Fine. But who gave you the ability to work hard? It was a gift of God. It makes no difference where you cut it—we are what we are because of God's gifts. Gratitude, not pride, is the only appropriate response. When we gratefully accept our talents as God-given gifts, using them to bless others, we have fulfilled His purpose in giving us the gifts in the first place.

But I want to make one more crucial application from the racquetball court, one that relates specifically to the life of faith and has contributed significantly to the content of this book. The application began a number of years ago when I reflected on a striking on-court partnership. One man was an energetic, highly motivated, gifted athlete, but whose temper would sometimes flare at the mistakes of lesser mortals. His partner was slower and less gifted, but was steady, dependable, and remarkably patient in the presence of his volatile teammate.

From the standpoint of Christian behavior, both of them displayed admirable traits. In one, quite aside from his raw athletic ability, we could admire the drive, energy, and enthusiasm. In the other, quite aside from his more modest athletic skills, we could admire his unruffled steadiness, his consistency, and his quiet patience under provocation.

Two conclusions, both of which surprised me when they became clear: One was that neither of those men had actually chosen to be who they were. Both the hard-driving, energetic player and the patient laid-back one were born that way. In short, we admired them for traits that were gifts of God.

The second conclusion has been more far-reaching, namely, that in our models of the ideal Christian, we typically have blended the two characters into one impossible ideal: a forceful and energetic person who is also gentle, patient, and unruffled. Impossible. One can be a hard-driving Type A Christian or a patient Type B Christian. One or the other, not both. People just don't come packaged that way. Yet how many Type B Christians feel guilty because they don't have the energy and drive of the Type A? And how many Type A Christians feel guilty because they lack the gentle, even-tempered patience of the Type B? We can learn a great deal from each other and by God's grace knock off some of the sharp edges and fill in some of the valleys. But we are who we are, and we simply must accept that fact rather than suffering guilt for gifts God has not given us. In short, in Christian living as on the racquetball court, the best team is a Type A and a Type B working together, each retaining their strengths, each recognizing their weaknesses.

Finally, I want to illustrate the breadth of human diversity (the differences between liberals and conservatives?) through an insightful quotation about human nature from a British classicist, Richard Livingstone (1880–1960). It has been published twice by *Atlantic Monthly*—first in 1946, and again in 1996—this time in the magazine's "Fifty Years Ago" column. The fact that it is not specifically a Christian quotation can help us understand more clearly how following Jesus enables us to approach the ideal that Livingstone describes. In many ways, the Christian ideal is universally admired. But only those who follow Jesus can claim His way of moving toward that ideal. Here is Livingstone's quote:

> Any attempt to train character is dangerous and must be under-taken with full perception of its danger. Many notes must be harmonized if the full music of the human instrument is to sound: gentleness and courage, boldness and prudence, inquisitiveness and reverence,

tolerance and firmness, confidence and humility, stability and freedom. It is a difficult and risky attempt to make a man, and it is tempting to turn aside from the task. But we have only to look round to see the disastrous results of declining it, as, for the most part, we have hitherto done.[3]

My analysis of the traits Livingstone cites should trigger a lively discussion, especially when I begin to put them under the heading of liberal or conservative. As I go through Livingstone's matched pairs, I see all of them as positive and worth emulating. Yet they come packaged in quite different ways. In my list, three of the pairs divide naturally under liberal or conservative headings. In one case, I put both terms on my conservative list; two other pairs resist the liberal-conservative categorization, with all terms ending up on both sides of the ledger. Here's my list:

1. Clear-cut division between liberal and conservative:

Liberal	Conservative
gentleness	courage
inquisitiveness	reverence
tolerance	firmness

2. Both terms on one side (conservative):

boldness
prudence

3. Both terms on both sides:

confidence/humility
stability/freedom

I put both boldness and prudence on the conservative side of the ledger, even though they are manifested in quite different ways. Whether in politics or religion, conservative spokespersons are much more likely to be known for boldly proclaiming their convictions. Yet, in practical, everyday life, prudence would be seen as a conservative trait.

As for the terms that resist the labels, I have seen both confidence and humility wonderfully displayed by both liberals and conservatives, though rarely in the same person. And both camps will claim stability and freedom for themselves, arguing that their agenda is the only way to true stability. And in their own way, each side will argue for freedom. In western democracies, however, liberals are more interested in social freedom, while conservatives argue the case for political freedom.

To sum up, I hope two truths have become clear: One, that highly valued but opposite traits are almost never manifested in the same person; two, that people with different gifts and different temperaments produce the best results when they learn how to work together so that the strengths of some complement the weaknesses of others.

Christians point to the church—the body of Christ—as the place where a unity is forged out of our differing gifts. Our next chapter will develop the more specifically religious side of the discussion, illustrating why Jesus needs both liberals and conservatives, and so do we.

---

1. White, *Testimonies for the Church,* 5:706, 707.

2. 1 Corinthians 4:7, CEV.

3. Richard Livingstone (British classicist, 1880–1960), *Atlantic Monthly,* July 1946 and July 1996.

Chapter 11

Liberals and Conservatives: Three Flavors

Is it "crazy" to try and bring together in the church "vastly different people"? The student quoted in the introduction to part 3 was inclined to think so. And from a strictly human point of view, it's not just crazy; it's impossible.

But this isn't a human work. It belongs to God. After the scales fell from Saul's eyes and he became the apostle Paul, he could exclaim, "From now on, therefore, we regard no one from a human point of view."[1] We are called to see things from God's perspective. And that means doing our part in shaping the church, the body of Christ, in ways that will enable all God's children to be a part of it.

In this chapter, we will briefly explore three ways in which the liberal-conservative spectrum describes the lives of believers: how we think, how we live, and what we believe about God. These are presented graphically in the pie chart on page 121.

Motivation: Different strokes for different folks

If in business, politics, family, and leisure we can recognize that people respond differently to different emphases, Why not in the church? And the crucial factor is motivation more than mere information. When the teachings of the church are viewed simply as truths in the sense of information, we are in danger of overlooking the fact that certain views of truth will appeal much more strongly to some people than to others. That is especially so when it comes to interpreting the life and death of Jesus.

Given that potential for diverse reactions, I think we should try to view church life in much the same way that we view the children's story at church. The first goal: get their attention and keep it; the second and ultimate goal: motivate them to do better and be better. The second goal is the real one, but you're dead in the water if you don't have their attention. And if you simply feed them information without touching their lives for good, you might as well stay home.

A major challenge to the acceptance of diversity in the church, however, is rooted in the traditional way we have used the word *truth*. Old-timers will remember how Adventists have spoken of people accepting the truth or leaving the truth, as if believers had accepted (or rejected) a clearly defined body of doctrines which all Adventists recognize as truth. There's real truth in that view, especially when applied to the foundational elements in our common ground in chapter 1: the two parts in our name, Sabbath and advent, and the two major points in our original church covenant: "commandments of God and the faith of Jesus."[2] But just how those simple summaries allow for diversity in the church is not so easily addressed.

Interestingly enough, early Adventists did not hesitate to sign a simple twenty-nine-word covenant in 1861.[3] But they staunchly resisted any kind of longer "official" statement, even though in 1872 they published a list of twenty-five "Fundamental Principles" and declared that Adventists held to this longer list "with great unanimity."[4]

Adventists have uniformly declared their opposition to any formal creed other than the Bible itself. In 1898, Ellen White suggested one of the reasons why that might be important: "A jealous regard for what is termed theological truth," she wrote, "often accompanies a hatred of genuine truth as made manifest in life."[5] A fixed creed tempts believers to force their own will on others. Yet, as Ellen White goes on to say, "truth as made manifest in life" should make the believers "sincere, kind, patient, forbearing, heavenly-minded."[6]

But right there is a red flag for many: How can we be gracious when "truth" is involved? Shouldn't we contend for truth, even to the death? Shouldn't we, like Daniel's friends, be willing to stand tall on the plain of Dura? Shouldn't we, like Daniel himself, be willing to be thrown to the lions rather than compromise truth?

Scripture is clear that truth is indeed worth dying for. But the way Jesus faced death, the way Shadrach, Meshach, Abednego, and Daniel faced death, should be instructive for us in our battles for truth. Were any of those great heroes of faith anything less than "sincere, kind, patient, forbearing, heavenly-minded" as they confronted the great forces of evil?

The power of those examples no doubt motivated Ellen White's pointed comments to A. T. Jones, a man inclined to be confrontational in his defense of truth: "The Lord wants his people to follow other methods than that of condemning wrong, even though the condemnation be just."[7]

There are occasions when God's people must address wrong, when we must "cry aloud" and "spare not,"[8] when we must "sigh" and "cry" for the "abominations" in Israel.[9] But it is important to note that the vast majority of the strong statements in Scripture are from credentialed prophetic voices, voices specially commissioned by God to speak strong words.

In that connection, it's worth remembering again Ellen White's caution, cited in chapter 3, to those who might be tempted to follow her sometimes hard-hitting prophetic example: "God has not given my brethren the work that he has given me,"[10] she told an 1881 camp meeting crowd. If others have disregarded God's repeated instructions to be "kind, patient, and forbearing"[11] they alone must answer to God for the results.

The example of Jesus is also crucial here: "tears were in his voice"[12] when He had to speak hard words. That's a tough act for sinful humans to follow, regardless of the intensity of our piety. "We long to see reforms," Ellen White wrote to A. T. Jones, "and because we do not see that which we desire, an evil spirit is too often allowed to cast drops of gall into our cup, and thus others are embittered. By our ill-advised words their spirit is chafed, and they are stirred to rebellion."[13]

So let us be brave, careful, honest, and sincere—and explore how liberals and conservatives could, and should, help each other in the church. Based on my own observations of the religious life, I see three key relationships where the liberal-conservative spectrum can be illuminating. The first focuses on the mind, our intellectual processes, how we think. The second illustrates how we live and act, our lifestyle within our human culture. The third illustrates what we believe about God. In short: mind, culture, God; or, thinking, living, believing. I'm convinced that understanding these three aspects of the body of Christ can make the church healthier and stronger. We'll look briefly at all three here and develop them further in later chapters.

1. The intellectual spectrum (mind): conservatives who love answers, liberals who love questions. When we reflect on the mind and thinking, the spread reaches from highly structured conservatives who deeply value the answers the church has always taught, to exploratory liberals who keep asking questions to help the church stay in touch with changing times. In Adventist jargon, the conservatives celebrate the deeply rooted traditions known as landmarks, while the liberals celebrate present truth, the cutting-edge truths for our day, a meaning that comes clear in Ellen White's use of the statement in 1888: "That which God gives His servants to speak today would not perhaps have been present truth twenty years ago, but it is God's message for this time."[14]

The church urgently needs people who cherish our answers, but it just as urgently needs people who will ask the hard questions. Since it is the very nature of conservative churches to want answers—we'll look at that use of the word *conservative* under category number three (belief) below—the exploratory people eager to ask questions are frequently viewed with suspicion by their fellow church members. Somehow, the church needs to find ways of cherishing both kinds of people—those who ask the crucial questions and those who cherish life-changing answers. Without questions, the answers soon become irrelevant; without answers, the questions can be destructive. If either side of the equation is missing, the church is in trouble. We must find ways to nurture them both.

But both sides need to be sensitive to the deep fears of those on the other side. The liberals are troubled if it appears that they will not be able to ask their questions; the conservatives are concerned that they will not hear the affirmation of truth that is so important to them. Those reactions were vividly illustrated at a camp-meeting book sale when my book *Inspiration* first came off the press in 1991. It was one of those festive Saturday night auditorium book sales in which the book promoters urge the patrons to buy books for all their children, grandchildren, and neighbors. Though I was not there, I heard what happened. For reasons I cannot fully understand, the person promoting my book said right out loud in front of the whole crowd, that some highly placed people in the General Conference did not approve of it. Immediately, some who had raised their hands for the book, put their hands back in their laps! But others shot up! The liberals smelled an exploratory book; the conservatives feared a liberal plot. If the church is going to thrive, it must be sensitive to both impulses.

Another example of how sensitive the issue can be came into sharper focus for me through dialogue with a pastor and a church member who were divided over the question of whether I should come to hold a seminar at their church. The member was more exploratory than the pastor, but the pastor told of conversations with an ordained minister in the church who had dropped out of his doctoral program at a major non-Adventist university just six months from completion. "If I had gone to class one more day," he told his pastor friend, "I would have lost my way spiritually." That's serious stuff.

2. The lifestyle spectrum (culture): conservatives who head to the hills, liberals who run to the city. Looking at how we live is not quite as tidy as looking at how we think, even though living is much more visible than thinking. The muddiness of this category is a main reason some people argue for dumping the labels altogether. At the extremes, however, we find clarity, though to find the real extremes we have to go outside the Adventist church to the conservative monks and nuns who take refuge in cloisters and monasteries, and to the liberal playboys and playmates who head to the bright lights where the action is. Put another way, conservatives try to escape modern culture (and usually attack it); liberals revel in it. To use more technical language, the liberals are the hedonists, lovers of pleasure; the conservatives are the ascetics, those who practice self-denial. If anything looks good, feels good, tastes good, the liberals say, "Give me more!" The conservatives say, "Don't touch!"

Some might be tempted to view introverts and extroverts as characterizing the two extremes, i.e., conservatives are those who try to avoid people and crowds; liberals are those who seek them out at every opportunity. But this is another place where the categories turn muddy, for some introverts are closet hedonists while some extroverts are covert ascetics.

From the standpoint of church life, mainstream churches will always be liberal, because they are culture-inclusive, adapting to human impulses to include as much of the world as possible. Sectarian[15] bodies, those who separate themselves from mainstream communities, will always be conservative, because they are critical of culture in their earnest search to find a closer walk with God. When any body of believers becomes too "worldly," it is ripe for a sectarian uprising, a schism that takes away the more earnest believers to form their own community.

Adventism urgently needs a blend of both impulses. In a sense, the liberals who are drawn to human culture will always be more at risk spiritually, at least in terms of a public commitment to God and church; they are more likely to abandon belief and church completely, in danger of slipping away gradually as the call of this present world becomes louder and louder.

But conservatives are also at risk spiritually, though in quite a different sense. They may be tempted to abandon the church—not for the world, but because the church has become too worldly. They do not turn away from belief in God; in fact, they seek him more earnestly. But in their intensity and passion for God they too easily become angry at those who do not seek God as they do. Thus, at least initially, they are in danger of losing the gentle gifts of the Spirit, in danger of not seeing the beauty in God's created world. They are so preoccupied with escaping sin that the whole world looks grim. Ironically, those who move far to the conservative end of the spectrum, denying all natural bodily appetites, are actually in great danger of abandoning the search for God completely. They can suddenly jump all the way to the other end of the spectrum, immersing themselves in all the delights of the flesh.

For the church, the best evangelistic team would be one made up of an individual from each end of the spectrum, and by "end," I don't mean those clear at the end—they're too scary and volatile. But a moderate liberal knows what's going on in the world, and a moderate conservative knows how to seek God and where. Yes, they are both at risk, but in different ways. If by God's grace they can stay in touch with each other, they will also be more likely to stay in touch with God.

3. The presence of God spectrum (belief): conservatives for whom God is a powerful personal presence, liberals for whom God is a more distant reality. Here the two extremes can really frighten each other. Devout conservatives tend to be certain that their sense of God's overwhelming presence in the world is something that should be shared by all. That's very unsettling for those whose sense of God's presence is less tangible, less focused. Annie Dillard (a liberal) in *Holy the Firm,* neatly captures the contrast between the two perspectives, describing them under the heading of high and low church:

> The higher Christian churches—where, if anywhere, I belong—
> come at God with an unwarranted air of professionalism, with author-
> ity and pomp, as though they knew what they were doing, as though
> people in themselves were an appropriate set of creatures to have deal-
> ings with God. I often think of the set pieces of liturgy as certain words
> that people have successfully addressed to God without their getting
> killed. . . . If God were to blast such a service to bits, the congregation
> would be, I believe, genuinely shocked. But in the low churches you
> expect it any minute.[16]

One senses in Dillard's comments a kind of distant admiration for those who
live in awe of God's immediate presence. But can one expect such a person to
immediately and joyfully turn from high church to low church? From liberal to
conservative? Liberals worry that the conservatives will try to force them to worship a God they do not know and cannot understand. That's frightening.

But the reverse is also true and also scary: the liberal who does not sense a
powerful immediate presence of God can be a real threat to conservative
thought and practice—the other two areas where liberal-conservative tensions
exist. Because the sense of impending judgment is weaker for liberals, it's easier
for them to ask their pointed questions, even in forms that seem blasphemous
to awestruck conservatives.

For the same reason, liberals are much more easily tempted and attracted by the
world, by the enticements of human culture. Their God is not looming near to
pounce on them when they step out of line. Most staunch conservatives are keenly
aware of the pull of human passions and appetites. Without being told, they seem
to sense that if they are surrounded by too many liberals, even in the church, they
could be swept away, falling into dangerous and destructive temptations.

Often the fear of sex and violence is especially keen in the minds and hearts
of conservatives. The record of physical abuse found in conservative churches
and a divorce rate virtually equivalent to that found in the liberal churches are
sobering realities that hint of the real fears lurking in the conservative soul.
They know full well the destructive power of worldly temptations. Liberals

could save themselves a great deal of heartache and pain if only they would listen more carefully to the concerns of their conservative brothers and sisters.

Tragically, the relationship between the two extremes has too often been characterized by horror and scorn: horror from the conservatives at the easygoing and exploratory liberals; scorn from the liberals at the highly structured and more cautious conservatives. Conservatives know they are at risk, indeed they all too often crash and burn when the call of this present world becomes too loud. Liberals are equally at risk; they just don't feel it as keenly. Without realizing it, surprised liberals may find themselves side-by-side with remorseful conservatives, both having been blindsided by sin in ways they never thought possible.

Somehow, in the church, believers on both ends of the spectrum must find ways to communicate with each other without horror from the conservatives and scorn from the liberals. What conservatives often do not realize is that the Bible illustrates with remarkable clarity the experience of devout believers for whom God's presence is not so immediate and so powerful. If conservatives could glimpse the genuineness of that kind of experience, seeing it illustrated in the Bible, they wouldn't have to be so troubled at every kind of "liberal" impulse. They could see that not all liberals are necessarily liberals across the board. There are liberals in thinking, for whom God is more distant, but who can still be very careful in matters of lifestyle. And some for whom God seems more distant may not even feel the need to ask hard questions. In other words, they are liberal only in the one sense of experiencing God as being distant, rather than near.

And that leads me to an observation that I hope could be grasped by all sides in the discussion. I have discovered in my years of teaching and ministry that liberals in the larger (secular) world are quite willing to be wicked, and cheerfully so. Note this conversation described by David Ansen, a movie critic:

> A few years ago, at a wedding reception in Waco, Texas, a young man of deep religious convictions, hearing that I was a movie critic, struck up a conversation. I asked him if he saw many movies. "Oh, no," he said, his politeness barely concealing his horror. "They pollute me." This was a real conversation stopper. Feeling like a toxic-waste dump (and feeling good about it, mind you), I turned away.[17]

That "toxic-waste dump" reaction is not a believer's response, but it is an attitude shared by many in the "world." They enjoy the pleasures of sin, reveling in them and taking a perverse pleasure in the expressions of horror that come their way from devout conservatives.

But if some liberals in the world actually revel in the horror dumped on them by conservatives, no one at the conservative end of the spectrum enjoys the scorn dumped on them by liberals. Indeed, no one—not anyone, anywhere, liberal or conservative—wants to be told that they are stupid. Yet that is precisely the message often communicated by liberals, even in the church: conservatives are blind, closed-minded, and stupid. So there!

No so fast, please. And here let me be extraordinarily candid: I know what it means to be treated with condescension by liberals in the church. That's why I rarely get angry at conservatives, even though many of them are horrified at my "honesty" with the Bible. I know what it feels like to be treated condescendingly, and I don't like it. By God's grace, I don't ever want to treat anyone condescendingly. When Jesus said that treating others the way we want to be treated is the law and the prophets,[18] He gave us *the* touchstone for our lives. I have no right, ever, to treat any of my brothers and sisters with condescension, a principle that applies to our treatment of every human being on earth. And if Jesus' words aren't clear enough, Ellen White presses the point home.

In 1879, she wrote to a family of brothers who were not living exemplary lives. They held influence in the church, yet were "worldly and scheming, [watching for] their opportunity to make a close bargain. . . . They [were] envious, jealous, puffed up." Ellen White told these men that "effectual service to Christ" meant that they should "always manifest kindness, respect, noble love and generosity, toward even wicked men."[19]

To A. T. Jones, one of the great spokespersons for righteousness by faith at the famous 1888 General Conference, but who was also known for his harsh treatment of opponents, Ellen White penned these words: "In the advocacy of the truth the bitterest opponents should be treated with respect and deference. . . . Treat every [person] as honest. Speak no word, do no deed that will confirm any in unbelief."[20]

In my own experience, I believe the condescending attitude toward me was intended to be kind and considerate. My liberal friends were convinced, I think, that if I knew what they knew, I couldn't believe what I believe. That attitude is rooted, in part, in the popularity of developmental models for understanding human experience such as Lawrence Kohlberg's six stages of moral development or James Fowler's six stages of faith. But I have never seen anyone appeal to a developmental model without triggering significant anger in those deemed to be "below" them on the scale. On the surface, it sounds so gracious to say that the Lord needs all kinds of people in the church: I have my work to do; you have yours; and God wants us all to work together to make the church strong. But when such a statement comes from a self-proclaimed stage-six person speaking to a stage-four person, the result is anger, not joy.

Another widespread prejudice in our culture is the idea that abstract-thinking people are simply more intelligent than practical, concrete-thinking people. Abstract thinking is always pegged at the upper levels of the developmental scale. Though there is undoubtedly some truth in that perspective, it is very misleading simply to equate the ability to think abstractly with higher intelligence. And that's not just a subtle undercurrent in our culture. It's there, printed in black and white. The well-known 16PF[21] personality test, for example, an instrument that has been in use for more than forty years, has consistently stated right on its printed form that abstract thinking marks one as "more intelligent"; concrete thinking marks one as "less intelligent." I much prefer a temperament test like Myers-Briggs that uses nonjudgmental language. That makes it much easier for each of us to recognize that our strengths are also our potential weaknesses.

In my own case, I sensed that the condescension of some of the liberals was directed at my conservative view of a personal God who revealed Himself in Jesus Christ, who is still active in our lives, who answers prayers, performs miracles, and is coming again as He promised. Because of powerful influences at work in our culture, many liberals, both in and out of the church, are easily tempted to view such concrete belief in a personal, miracle-working God as childish. Indeed, *childish is* the very word used by Rabbi Harold Kushner (famous for his book *When Bad Things Happen to Good People*[22]) in his discussion of a new Torah and commentary he coedited for the Jewish community. As quoted in a review of the book, Kushner noted that many Jews are now "very sophisticated and well read about psychology, literature and history, but they are locked in a childish version of the Bible."[23]

The "grown-up" view? According to the review, Kushner's book argues that Abraham probably never existed, nor Moses, and that the Exodus from Egypt probably never happened. And all this is said to be "proven" by archaeology. While such sentiments are rarely expressed openly within the Adventist community, their presence in the larger culture means that they do have an effect.

Admittedly, it is a more liberal view that allows for some parts of the Bible to be symbolic, rather than historical. Yet even very conservative Adventists would admit, for example, that the story of Lazarus in Abraham's bosom[24] is figurative, not literal; symbolic, not historical. But if some of the Bible is figurative, it is not a necessary conclusion that all of it is and that biblical history is simply not reliable. For reasons that seem highly illogical to me, the differences between the parallel accounts in the four Gospels lead some critics to reject their historical value completely. G. A Wells, for example, a radical critic of the Gospels, in his book *Who Was Jesus?* suggests in his "Introduction" that Jesus was nothing more than a "legendary figure." And the last two words in his book refer to the Scriptures as "ancient fantasies."[25]

Gotthold Ephraim Lessing (1729–1781), the great German dramatist and philosopher, already questioned the logic of the critics in his day. Referring to a list of highly respected ancient historians, he said: "If we are likely to treat Livy and Dionysius and Polybius and Tacitus so respectfully and nobly that we do not put them on the rack for a single syllable, why not also Matthew, Mark, Luke and John?"[26]

But if liberal critics overstep their logic in taking the Bible apart, why must its conservative defenders overstep their logic and refuse to see what is obvious in Scripture? Conservatives have been so afraid of the liberal slippery slope that they have made impossible claims for the Bible. And many of them are frightened and angry because deep in their souls they sense that their position is vulnerable.

Let's put our heads and hearts together and avoid the two extremes. Most of us are not triple liberals or triple conservatives—those who are will need more help! For the most part, we are a mixed bag, with one liberal leg or two and one conservative leg or two. We can help each other. Let's listen to all of Scripture, to all of God's family, and to the Spirit of God at work in our midst. We will need to muffle our feelings of horror and scorn long enough to hear all of us express our needs, our fears, and our deep desire to be faithful to God. I believe this is a great day of opportunity for the church. If by God's grace and through His power we can come together, we would be the most unique church on the face of the earth.

But in that very connection, a word of caution—just in case our longed-for unity begins to emerge: let's be careful how we trumpet our uniqueness to the world. A light doesn't have to announce its presence. It simply does its God-given work. And people rejoice because the light has made it possible for them to see.

1. 2 Corinthians 5:16.

2. "Commandments of God" and "faith of Jesus" are the closing words in the three angels' messages in Revelation 14:6–12.

3. Quoted at the beginning of chapter 1: "We, the undersigned, hereby associate ourselves together, as a church, taking the name, Seventh-day Adventists, covenanting to keep the commandments of God, and the faith of Jesus Christ." Original church covenant used to organize Adventist churches when organization first began to happen 1861. Published in "Doings of the Battle Creek Conference, Oct. 5 & 6, 1861," *Review and Herald*, October 8, 1861. See *Seventh-day Adventist Encyclopedia*, 2nd rev. ed., s.v. "Covenant, Church."

4. The 1872 statement, along with the 1931 and 1980 statements, are published in appendix 1 of Gary Land, ed., *Adventism in America* (Grand Rapids, Mich.: Wm. B. Eerdmans, 1996), 231–250. All three statements are laid out in synoptic format in Rolf Pöhler, *Continuity and Change in Adventist Teaching* (New York: Peter Lang, 2000).

5. White, *The Desire of Ages*, 309.

6. Ibid., 310.

7. White, *Testimonies for the Church*, 6: 121.

8. Isaiah 58:1, KJV.

9. Ezekiel 9:4, KJV.

10. White, *Testimonies for the Church*, 5:20.

11. Ibid.

12. White, *Steps to Christ*, 12.

13. White, *Testimonies for the Church*, 6:122.

14. White, Manuscript 8a, 1888, *The Ellen G. White 1888 Materials*, 1:133.

15. The word *sectarian* is used here in the value-free sociological sense, referring to a body which is counter-cultural rather than culture-inclusive. Typically, sectarian bodies form because believers crave a more intense experience of holiness (sanctification) than the culture-inclusive "mainstream" church is able to provide.

16. Annie Dillard, *Holy the Firm*, quoted in Annie Dillard, *The Annie Dillard Reader* (New York: HarperCollins, 1994), 447.

17. David Ansen, "A Century at the Movies," *Newsweek*, June 29, 1998, 15.

18. See Matthew 7:12.

19. White, *Testimonies for the Church*, 4:331.

20. White, *Testimonies for the Church,* 6:122.

21. 16 Personality Factors, developed by Raymond B. Catell.

22. Harold Kushner, *When Bad Things Happen to Good People* (New York: Shocken Books, 1981).

23. Michael Massing, "New Torah for Modern Minds," *New York Times,* March 9, 2002, review of *Etz Hayim* ("Tree of Life"), a Torah and commentary published by the United Synagogue of Conservative Judaism.

24. Luke 16:19–31.

25. G. A. Wells, *Who Was Jesus? A Critique of the New Testament Record* (La Salle, Ill.: Open Court, 1989), 4, 194.

26. Gotthold Ephraim Lessing, cited by H. M. Kuitert, in *I Have My Doubts: How to Become a Christian Without Being a Fundamentalist* (Valley Forge, Pa.: SCM/Trinity, 1993), 279.

Part 4

The Pie: Introduction to Myers-Briggs

The Bible says, "What then is Apollos? What is Paul? Servants through whom you came to believe, as the Lord assigned to each. I planted, Apollos watered, but God gave the growth."[1]

The Bible says, "For just as the body is one and has many members, and all the members of the body, though many, are one body, so it is with Christ."[2]

For a number of years now I have used the pie to illustrate the diverse strands in the Bible, in the church, and in the world. Articles describing the pie have appeared in *Insight* magazine and in the *Adventist Review.*[3]

The pie is organized around the three different ways we use the terms *liberal* and *conservative* in the church—referring to how we think, how we relate to culture, and what we believe about God. These categories were introduced in chapter 11 with the following descriptions:

1. The intellectual spectrum (mind): conservatives who love answers, liberals who love questions.
2. The lifestyle spectrum (culture): conservatives who head to the hills, liberals who run to the city.

3. The presence of God spectrum (belief): conservatives for whom God is a powerful personal presence, liberals for whom God is a more distant reality.

The pie is laid out so that liberals are on the left and conservatives on the right, following the traditional use of the words in the political world. As the "presence of God" spectrum is depicted on this chart, it flows from a strong sense of His personal presence on the right to a decreasing sense of His presence on the left. As one moves towards the right, the sense of His presence feels ever more threatening. Conversely, as one moves towards the left, the sense of His presence diminishes until it finally disappears entirely.

After I had been using the pie for some time, I discovered a rather tidy correlation with Myers-Briggs temperament types. When some faculty colleagues introduced me to David Keirsey's elaboration of the Myers-Briggs schema in *Please Understand Me II*,[4] I added some elements from Keirsey's perspective as well.

Colleagues tell me that other temperament analyses are more accurate and more carefully nuanced than Myers-Briggs is. Some schemes are certainly more rigorous. In fact, one could be more blunt and simply say "nastier," in keeping with the spirit of the more rigorous tests. Taylor-Johnson, for example, a temperament test that many in our School of Theology find useful for premarital counseling, is rigorously normed and uses strong language: nervous, inhibited, indifferent, dominant, submissive, hostile, and impulsive. Strong words can be useful for diagnostic purposes, especially in premarital counseling, but they can also be devastating.

Myers-Briggs is much more affirming in its language. In every case, the labels are positive or at least neutral, making it easier to recognize that our strength is frequently—maybe always—our weakness. Keirsey's book, in particular, makes a point of affirming different kinds of intelligence. He notes four major types: tactical, logistical, diplomatic, and strategic.[5] That kind of positive assessment I find much more helpful than the 16PF test, which, astonishingly, describes concrete thinkers as "less intelligent," abstract thinkers as "more intelligent"![6]

A brief introduction to the Myers-Briggs categories helps explain how the pie works.

Myers-Briggs and the pie

Myers-Briggs uses these four matched pairs to describe key temperament features:

1. I/E: Introvert/Extrovert. This category is straightforward. Extroverts are energized by people; introverts are exhausted by people. My favorite quick check is simply to ask what happens when the telephone rings: Do you hurry to answer or do you hope someone else will?

2. S/N: Sensing/iNtuition. Sensory refers to hands-on concrete thinking; intuitive describes the abstract thinker. This category is a key factor in the discussions of liberals and conservatives. Conservatives tend to be sensory; liberals, intuitive.

3. T/F: Thinking/Feeling. The divide in this category is straightforward: Does one make decisions and respond to life situations based on logic or on feeling?

4. J/P: Judging/Perceiving. Here the divide is between planning and spontaneity. The judging person has life planned out; action is prompt and decisive. By contrast, the perceiving person likes to respond to creative alternatives along the way. Put bluntly, the judging person is on time; the perceiving person arrives late.

One selection from each of the four categories is used to make up one's temperament type. My basic type is ENTJ, described in some handbooks under the heading of "commandant." If you have a problem, fix it! Interestingly enough, the need to adjust to my wife's health limitations has resulted in an ENFJ result for me—i.e., the catalyst; one who seeks to bring people together. This book reflects that heightened F factor in my own experience. My problem is that I have worked with Myers-Briggs so much that I can tweak the test to make it come out any way I want. When I asked my colleague and good friend Larry Veverka, our local expert on Myers-Briggs, how he assessed me on the scale, his comment was, "Thompson, when you are on a roll, you are a pure ENTJ."

My book *Inspiration* reflects the ENTJ impulse: Why wouldn't we want to be honest with all the evidence in Scripture? Let's get it out on the table so that we can look at it. For me, it was a real shock to learn that not everyone was as eager as I am to deal with the evidence.

Four basic types: Guardian (SJ), Idealist (NF), Rationalist (NT), Artisan (SP)

In Keirsey's scheme, four couplets are the dominant types. The SJ Guardian and the NF Idealist are conservative because of what he calls their "cooperative use of tools," a more cautious spirit driven by a desire that the whole community move together cooperatively. By contrast, the SP Artisan and the NT Rationalist are liberal because of their "pragmatic use of tools," a more daring spirit marked by a willingness to bend the rules under the influence of the perceived needs of the moment. The key elements in these four types can be summarized as follows:

1. Intellectual Conservative. The SJ Guardians are the ones who preserve the traditions of the community. "We haven't done it that way before" is a likely response to innovative ideas. These are high-structure people who like answers better than they like questions. They perform well when expectations are clear. This is the army crowd that doesn't really mind when a dictator is in charge.

2. Lifestyle Conservative. The NF Idealists are the ones who seek to escape the distractions of contemporary culture in search of the ideal. The beauties of nature in desert and mountain are much more attractive to them than the fast life in the city. In a religious community, these Idealists can easily turn into monastics who seek passionately after God.

3. Intellectual Liberal. The NT Rationalists are intrigued by the allure of new ideas. They chafe in a world that craves answers but does not encourage the inquiring mind. These are the skeptics who are very much at home in the university.

4. Lifestyle Liberal. The SP Artisans are the ones who thrive among people and on stage. Energized by a crowd, these party people are drawn to the richness of city life where the joys and temptations of modern culture beckon on every hand.

The pie chart on page 121 illustrates these elements along with many of the related aspects discussed in chapters 11 to 13. The chart at the top of page 122 focuses more specifically on Keirsey's four basic types.

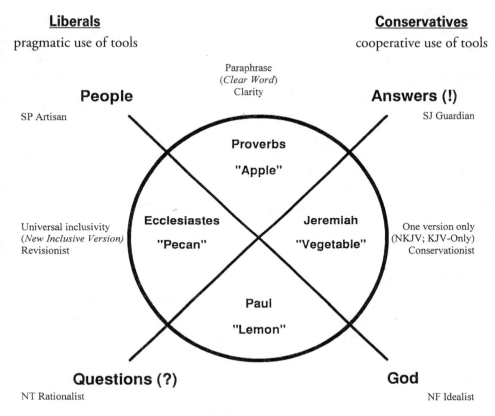

Liberals
pragmatic use of tools

Conservatives
cooperative use of tools

People
SP Artisan

Answers (!)
SJ Guardian

Paraphrase
(*Clear Word*)
Clarity

Proverbs
"Apple"

Universal inclusivity
(*New Inclusive Version*)
Revisionist

Ecclesiastes
"Pecan"

Jeremiah
"Vegetable"

One version only
(NKJV; KJV-Only)
Conservationist

Paul
"Lemon"

Questions (?)
NT Rationalist

God
NF Idealist

Parallel translations
(CEV [dynamic]/NASB [formal])
Clarity and Reliability

Liberals and Conservatives: The Three Flavors

1. Intellectual spectrum (mind): conservatives who love answers, liberals who love questions.

2. Lifestyle spectrum (culture): conservatives who head to the hills to be with God, liberals who run to the city to be with the people.

3. Presence of God spectrum (belief): conservatives for whom God is a powerful personal presence, liberals for whom God is a more distant reality.

See David Keirsey, *Please Understand Me II: Temperament, Character, Intelligence* (Del Mar, Calif.: Prometheus Nemesis, 1998).

In chart form, Keirsey's four types can be visualized as follows:

Type	Passion	People	Place	Myers-Briggs
The Conservatives: Cooperative use of tools:				
Intellectual Conservative:	Answers	Dictators	Army	SJ Guardian
Lifestyle Conservative:	God	Monastics	Desert	NF Idealist
The Liberals: Pragmatic use of tools:				
Intellectual Liberal:	Questions	Skeptics	University	NT Rationalist
Lifestyle Liberal:	People	Party people	City	SP Artisan

The four kinds of pie

The merging of two types in each of the four quadrants yields the four kinds of pie, representing four kinds of church members and four biblical perspectives:

1. Proverbs: Apple Pie. These are the people who love answers and revel in the company of other people. By far the most dominant personality in church circles, Apple Pie Christians thrive in a world of potlucks and Proverbs. The kind of practical wisdom found in Proverbs makes such good sense, and church pot lucks are so much fun! One pastor told me of a woman who was so eager to join the church that she was ready to skip the Bible studies. "Just tell me what to believe, and I'll believe it!" she exclaimed. "I want to belong." Practical, buoyant, and helpful, these sociable people are the backbone of the church.

2. Jeremiah: Vegetable Pie. These double conservatives are very serious about their religious beliefs and practices. The pure type would be best represented by Job's early experience when he could still exclaim, "The LORD gave, and the LORD has taken away; blessed be the name of the LORD."[7] But, as Job discovered, that stiff upper lip is not easily maintained. After seven days of silence in the presence of his friends, "Job opened his mouth and cursed the day of his birth."[8] Many of those in this quadrant have been converted from a life of unrestrained pleasure. Their search for God has moved them so far in the opposite direction that anything that looks good, tastes good, or feels good is a cause for concern. Vegetable pie, a pie without sugar, indeed, a pie that isn't even dessert, symbolizes the ascetic impulse that so easily surfaces in this quadrant. Jeremiah fits better than Job here because Jeremiah knew what it was to live an unhappy, austere life and wasn't afraid to say so.

3. Paul: Lemon Pie. Fully aware of the pain and complexity of our troubled world, the Lemon Pie people are still keenly aware of God's inescapable presence in their lives and in the world. For them, the presence of God is the sugar that turns lemons into lemon pie. They are exploratory and eager to ask their questions. But, like Paul, they sense when it is time to shut up and let God be God.

4. Ecclesiastes: Pecan Pie. These double liberals are most at risk in the church. They may be as fully aware of the church's shortcomings as the double conservatives. But they don't have a stomach for the fight and simply slip away after dark. They are drawn to the rich nuances of human culture in music, literature, art, and drama. But because the world often makes no sense, they resonate with the puzzled wisdom of Ecclesiastes. They will be faithful to God, but from a distance. Pecan pie is the dessert of choice here, perhaps the richest of desserts, a dessert where a little goes a long way.

In the two chapters that follow, the pie provides a pictorial backdrop for addressing liberal and conservative issues in the church. The first chapter in this section focuses on church life in general, the second one zeroes in on the question of Bible translations, a very practical issue for which the pie is a convenient springboard to discussion.

---

1. 1 Corinthians 3:5, 6.

2. 1 Corinthians 12:12.

3. See page 91, endnote 2.

4. David Keirsey, *Please Understand Me II: Temperament, Character, Intelligence* (Del Mar, Calif.: Prometheus Nemesis, 1998). Kraig and Julie Scott introduced me to Keirsey. Kraig is an SJ Guardian whose field is music. Julie is an NT Rationalist whose field is business.

5. Keirsey, 286–330.

6. 16 Personality Factors. The "less intelligent" and "more intelligent" labels appear on the standard summary sheet. Interestingly enough, another analysis based on a 1994 technical manual, heads in the opposite direction. After using the "less intelligent" and "more intelligent" labels under the "reasoning" heading, the "abstraction" category uses the words *absentminded* and *impractical* to describe the supposedly "more intelligent" abstract thinker, but *practical* and *solution-oriented* for the "less intelligent" concrete thinker. See S. R. Conn and M. L. Rieke, eds, *The 16PF Fifth Edition Technical Manual* (Champaign, Ill.: Institute for Personality and Ability Testing, 1994).

7. Job 1:21.

8. Job 3:1.

Chapter 12

The Pie: We Need Your Differences

As the 1980s were drawing to a close, the church was continuing to struggle with theological challenges. A crucial question loomed large: what are the limits of diversity? What follows is a slightly revised version of an article that addresses that issue. It was published in 1989 in the *Adventist Review*.[1] Since it is based on the pie, you will hear echoes from the introduction to the pie at the beginning of part 4.

As I began this article, I was unnerved and somewhat startled by the intensity of my emotions. You won't understand unless you, too, love the church, and people, and God— and want to spend an eternity as one happy family.

A sobering public lecture triggered this piece. Never before has the nation been so fragmented between liberals and conservatives, observed the speaker. New alliances are being forged across traditional boundaries. Jews, Catholics, and Protestants are breaking ranks to choose up sides as liberals or conservatives and then making common cause together.

I pondered the tensions in my church between liberals and conservatives and all the pain linked with those tensions. If only we could press together, work together, sing and pray together. But the heart has to be in it, and the conscience must come along unscathed.

So let's talk about it.

First, the annoying labels. We use them in two ways.[2] As lifestyle markers, they distinguish those who like to pray from those who like to play; those who flee to the desert to be with God from those who rush to the city to be with people.

As markers of intellectual patterns, they distinguish those who lay claim to clear answers from those who love to ask questions; those who prefer the disciplined obedience of the army from those who prefer the probing creativity of the university.

As illustrated in the pie diagram, overlaying the two ways of using liberal and conservative yields a quadrant of four basic types: a double conservative, a double liberal, and two types that are half and half. The church urgently needs all four perspectives—and can make excellent use of all the variations in between, including those who are a lively blend of all four extremes. That means there is room in the church for both thee and me, even if we do have to curb some of our excesses.

Interestingly enough, the differences in the church today are mirrored in Scripture. We can roughly match biblical books or authors with each of the basic types.

In my church, for example, I think of *Brother and Sister Proverbs,* hardworking, practical, optimistic. They are convinced both of God's goodness and of the value of human effort. They thrive on church socials and picnics. They love people, and they love the Lord. They like what they see in church papers: *Review, Insight, Signs.* For secular literature, they are likely to pick up the *Reader's Digest.*

Then we meet *Brother and Sister Jeremiah,* faithful, intense, devout. They are deeply concerned about the loss of spiritual fervor in the church and the subtle inroads being made by the world. You can count on them to be at prayer meeting, Sabbath School, and church services. They are inclined to read *Our Firm Foundation,* being rather troubled by what they consider a worldly tendency in our church papers. They read very little in secular literature, preferring to spend their time with the Bible and the writings of Sister White.

Brother and Sister Ecclesiastes are probably the most difficult for the church to understand. They don't have much time for church work since they are so busy with the symphony, the art gallery, and the museum. Yet they have made some remarkable contacts for the church in the community, and on occasion, have been known to be quite generous in supporting worthy projects. Probing, curious, questioning—if someone mentions a good article in a church paper they might ask for a copy, but they're not likely to subscribe. Even *Adventist Today* and *Spectrum* are journals they read only occasionally. *Harper's Magazine, The Atlantic,* and *The New Yorker* are the magazines you'll likely find around the house.

Brother and Sister Paul are also a perplexity for the church. They seem so devout—indeed, they are devout—but they keep asking questions about matters that the church decided long ago. Their Sabbath School class seems radical, almost heretical. But they attend church faithfully and are loyal supporters. They will tell you that they would like more substance in church papers. They subscribe to *Adventist Review* as well as *Spectrum* and *Adventist Today.* They also read broadly in secular literature, but not with a consuming passion.

What is very puzzling for my church right now is the fact that Johnny Jeremiah, the son of Brother and Sister Jeremiah, has struck up a real friendship with Brother and Sister Ecclesiastes, intrigued by their broad range of interests. The Jeremiahs just don't understand. But to make the picture more complex, Susie Ecclesiastes, the daughter of Brother and Sister Ecclesiastes, has found the fervent piety of the Jeremiahs to be very appealing. Her parents don't understand either.

Can we handle such diversity in Adventism?

When describing ideal Bible teaching, Ellen White addressed that very issue: Students should not have the same teacher "year after year" even if it means using instructors who may not "have so full an understanding of Scriptures." Why do we have four Gospels instead of just one? she asks. "Because the minds of men differ." There is no ideal teacher; the ideal is reached only through a community of teachers. "The whole truth is presented more clearly by several than by one. . . . Often through unusual experiences, under special circumstances, He gives to some Bible students views of truth that others do not grasp. It is possible for the most learned teacher to fall far short of teaching all that should be taught."[3]

We need each other if we want the church to be strong.

A word to the conservatives

Now, a word directly to you who are drawn by the commands and promises of a changeless God, not by the ever-changing fashions of a restless world; to you who yearn for purity, not relevance; to you for whom obedience to a Holy God is infinitely more important than exploring the mysteries of the universe.

If you are alarmed at the loss of fervor in the church, the lowering of standards, the inroads of alien theology—if you long for the straight testimony but feel driven to independent publications or private camp meetings to hear it, then this part is for you. Read on. These are your strengths, weaknesses, challenges, and besetting sins.

1. Piety, commitment, conviction. If you're hungry for spiritual food and lonely in the church because it seems listless and lukewarm, don't give up. The church needs you more than ever right now. You sense its weakness; you know where it needs to go for strength. In a time of prosperity, the "naturally devotional" (to borrow Ellen White's phrase) dare not abandon the church to those attracted by material and worldly interests.

Sensing the weakness of the church, you may be tempted to pull away with the rest of the "pure" saints and establish your own "pure" community. But when has the church ever kept its act together for more than a few minutes at a time? Read Scripture. Read the *Testimonies*. When were the good old days, and how long did they last? God is patient. We must be also.

2. Anger. The anger and hostility I find in much of your literature concerns me. To A. T. Jones, Ellen White once wrote, "Every sermon you preach, every article you write, may be all true; but one drop of gall in it will be poison to the hearer or the reader." Under the influence of the holy oil of the Spirit flowing into the heart, His words should "reform, but not exasperate."[4]

Give your anger to the Lord. Immerse yourself in 1 Corinthians 13 and plead with Him to make it happen.

3. Change. That's an uncomfortable word for you. You would rather be guardians than explorers. And the church needs the stability you bring. But you will have to make peace with change as well. That goes for standards and for doctrines. Early Adventists were critical of any woman without a bonnet and any man without a beard. Even mustaches were off-limits. Modesty is something perceived by culture, and culture changes.

As for doctrine, Ellen White signaled the need for change at the 1888 General Conference Session: "That which God gives His servants to speak today would not perhaps have been present truth twenty years ago, but it is God's message for this time."[5]

How can we know what change is legitimate? By studying Scripture and the writings of Ellen White. Both can help us establish the breadth of God's activity as well as the limits.

4. *Diversity.* This word is almost as dangerous as *change.* Read the parallel passages in Scripture and learn to appreciate why the different writers told the same story in different ways. Diversity gives us a net big enough to do the job.

5. *Authority.* You are impressed by divine authority. Appeals to authority are powerful, but can be short lived and dangerous if not supported by sanctified reason.

In her very first counsel on education, Ellen White warned against holding the minds and wills of the students by "absolute authority."[6] The attempt to ensure stability by the hand of authority can be the very means of destruction.

The church needs you, conservatives. And you need the church. Your great strength is also your great weakness. Share your strength with the church, and let the church help you with your weakness. Send your children to the church's schools; they are your schools, our schools. There will be moments of discomfort for all of us. But we must learn to live together. After all, we'll be neighbors in the kingdom.

A word to the liberals

Now, a word to you who find the world a very intriguing place. As far as the church is concerned, you tend to be less bombastic than the conservatives. You don't go away angry; you just go away. Later, the church wakes up and suddenly remembers, "Whatever happened to . . . ?" But it's too late. The pew has been empty too long.

Actually, to pin the label of liberal on an Adventist isn't quite fair. In the broader religious world, any Adventist willing to carry the name is hopelessly conservative. After all, we believe in a God who hears and answers prayers. That makes us conservative regardless of the labels we use among ourselves.[7]

Still, under that conservative Adventist umbrella, some differences are worth noting. A liberal, for example, finds the creation at least as interesting as the Creator, much prefers a probing question to a revealed answer, and is tempted to spend more time with human beings than with God.

So if you are a liberal Adventist—not wild, just liberal—concerned about the shallowness of the church's preaching and writing, alienated because you have ventured thoughtful questions when the saints wanted clear-cut answers, and feeling condemned because your love of beauty stands in a certain tension over against the church's call for simplicity, sacrifice, and practicality, then this part is for you. Read on. These are your strengths, weaknesses, challenges, and besetting sins:

1. Intellect, curiosity, a love of beauty and excellence. If you're hungry for a thought-provoking sermon, and the church seems austere, without aesthetic qualities, don't give up. The church needs you more than ever right now. You recognize its weakness. You have the sensitivity to help bring it to maturity.

The world is populated by mostly average folks. So is the church. That spells a lonely life for exceptional people. They are seeking answers to questions most have never asked, and conversation partners are rare.

If you are one of the lonely bright ones, you need to know that there are others like you in the church. You need to find each other. Then, together, you can help us shape a believing community for all the people.

And then there is your love of beauty and excellence. Adventism's Puritan heritage makes us intensely practical. Aesthetics are easily ignored. We build no museums or art galleries. You can show us the beautiful in a chaotic world.

2. Patience. This is a hard one. When your outstretched gift finds no receptive hand, and your cry for help no listening ear, you could be excused for looking elsewhere. Because we have so far to go, the church will often appear barren and austere. But it needs your talents.

Pray that you might find in the church the receptive hand and the listening ear. And pray that the Lord of Creation will grant you patience to endure both the average and the mediocre while the church struggles to appreciate your gifts.

You will also need patience to understand those who are so overwhelmed by the divine presence that they obey without questioning. You may feel that you can challenge God, like Abraham or Moses did. Don't neglect that precious right—just remember that others simply melt in His presence.

3. Gifts. Conservatives are gripped by their convictions and give accordingly. The church would be more vibrant if liberals would do the same. Our schools, in particular, could do exciting things if they really enjoyed the wholehearted support of the church. Think about it. Pray about it. Then do something about it.

4. Worship. Liberals tend to be better at probing and exploring than they are at worshiping. And by worship, I don't mean just sitting in church. I'm thinking of an attitude toward God, an attitude of submission and acceptance.

Now I don't mean to diminish your ability to confront God with your questions and perplexities. Not at all. Some of you have struggled long and hard to win through to that openness. But there comes a time when questions fall silent—we admit that God is God and that we are merely His creatures. That is true worship. As Job said, "Behold, I am of small account; what shall I answer thee? / I lay my hand on my mouth."[8]

A more recent pilgrim, C. S. Lewis, a conservative liberal (or was he a liberal conservative?), described his own surrender after a long and arduous search:

> You must picture me alone in that room in Magdalen, night after night, feeling, whenever my mind lifted even for a second from my work, the steady unrelenting approach of Him whom I so earnestly desired not to meet. That which I greatly feared had at last come upon me. In the Trinity Term of 1929 I gave in, and admitted that God was God, and knelt and prayed: perhaps, that night, the most dejected and reluctant convert in all England.[9]

As you search after God, you can know that He is searching after you too. So don't give up too easily. Lay claim to your blessing and don't let Him go. Stay with it—until, like Jacob, you have the blessing in hand.

I want our church to be a channel for at least part of that blessing. That will be difficult, I know, for conservatives have a hard time understanding liberals. Some even think you are out to destroy the church. I'm not telling you anything new. That's part of the loneliness you've learned to live with.

But maybe we are all lonelier than we care to admit. That's why the blessed hope is so precious. Let's share that hope and keep it alive. That's what the body of Christ is all about.

Postscript: The differences summarized

1. Ecclesiastes. The double liberal is full of questions, not very sure of clear answers, intrigued by men and affairs, and does not say very much about God.

2. Jeremiah. The double conservative is dominated by an intense passion for God, pained by the presence of those with a superficial commitment, and often suffers alone.

3. Proverbs. The lifestyle liberal, intellectual conservative believes obedience and hard work bring tangible rewards, a disciplined life makes good sense, and the creation is good—let's enjoy it.

4. Paul. The lifestyle conservative, intellectual liberal believes Christ has brought a creative ferment to the world; the old has passed, in Christ all things are new; God's hand is on the helm, but expects us to be all things to all people.

---

1. Cf. Alden Thompson, "We Need Your Differences," *Adventist Review,* November 2, 1989, 17–20.

2. In this book I have added a third way of using the liberal and conservative labels— the Presence of God spectrum. It is a pattern that overlays the pie as a whole, with the right side representing those who sense God as very near, and the left side representing those for whom God seems more distant.

3. White, *Counsels to Parents,* 432, 433.

4. White, *Testimonies for the Church,* 6:123.

5. White, *The Ellen G. White 1888 Materials,* 1:133.

6. White, *Testimonies for the Church,* 3:134.

7. That is, conservative in the "Presence of God" spectrum, the third way the words *liberal* and *conservative* are used in the church.

8. Job 40:4, RSV.

9. C. S. Lewis, *Surprised by Joy: The Early Shape of My Life* (New York: Houghton Mifflin Harcourt, 1966), 228, 229.

Chapter 13

The Pie and Bible Translations

One of the troubling perplexities of church life these days is that we don't know what to do about Bible translations. Believers are using such a wide variety of different translations that we can't even read Scripture together, much less repeat it out loud together. And which translation should we use for memorization?

This chapter uses the pie as a basis for understanding the rich diversity of Bible translations available today. But to understand the diversity in preferences we need to know the difference between the two basic translation styles, the two poles between which all translations can be placed. The goal of a formal equivalent style of translation is to reflect as closely as possible the language and structure of the original document. By contrast, the goal of a dynamic equivalent style is to make a translation that is as clear and as understandable as possible to the modern reader. Understanding these two translation styles is important for grasping the wide diversity of modern translations.

Formal equivalent translation

A formal equivalent translation is one that seeks to come as close as possible to the language of the original document that is being translated. It is sometimes called a literal or even a word-for-word translation. Such a translation will never be as exciting or as smooth as those translations that try to help modern ears "hear" in their own language and idiom what the original author said. But for those who produce formal equivalent translations, words such as *faithful* and *accurate* are the important ones.

Examples of formal equivalent translations

KJV. The King James Version of 1611, also known as the Authorized Version (AV), was the capstone English translation of the Reformation Era. It drew on a number of earlier English translations, especially Tyndale's New Testament (1525), the Geneva Bible (1560), and the Bishops' Bible (1568, 1602).

In the Reformation Era, the explosion of translations that led up to the KJV came as a result of two powerful movements: one scholarly, one popular. On the scholarly front, the original languages had become very important. Instead of relying on the Latin, scholars wanted to go back to the Hebrew for the Old Testament and to the Greek for the New Testament.

At the popular level, the public clamor to have the Scriptures available in the language of the people reached a fever pitch. The KJV brought together both the scholarly and the popular impulses. On the one hand, it was a Bible in English that was faithful to the original languages; on the other, it was also understandable by ordinary people. The KJV was destined to become a classic.

RV. The first major revision of the KJV was completed in Britain in 1885 and marked the beginning of a new surge of interest in English translations. This time, two quite different impulses were at work: first, the English language had changed significantly since 1611; second, recent discoveries had brought to light a host of old manuscripts. The mandate to the Revised Version translators was a conservative one: stay as close as possible to the KJV, but where the language needed to be updated and where manuscript discoveries pointed to a superior text, changes should be incorporated.

ASV. The American Standard Version of 1901 was based on the British RV, but it incorporated American vocabulary and spelling. The ASV was the foundation for the New American Standard Bible.

RSV. The Revised Standard Version (1946, 1952) took a significant step toward modernizing the language of the Bible. In particular, *thee* and *thou* were replaced by *you* in all cases except where Deity was addressed. The RSV also continued the ASV practice of presenting poetry as poetry and using paragraphs for prose.

NRSV. The New Revised Standard Version of 1989 continued the modernizing process evident in the RSV. In the NRSV, *thee* and *thou* disappeared completely in favor of *you*. In addition, gender accurate or gender inclusive language was used wherever it was clear that both genders were intended in the biblical text. Interestingly enough, the KJV had already used some gender inclusive language. In the Old Testament, for example, the descendants of Jacob/Israel were frequently called "children of Israel," not just "sons." And in the New Testament, the peacemakers in Jesus' sermon on the mount were called "children of God," not just "sons."[1] Toward the latter part of the twentieth century, the gender issue became a volatile one and spawned translations on both sides of the fence.

NASB. *The New American Standard Bible* appeared in 1960–1971 and in an updated version in 1995. Produced by Evangelicals,[2] it is considered by many to be the best study Bible currently in print, especially for those who do not know the biblical languages. A formal equivalent translation that faithfully and consistently reflects the original language, it does not use inclusive language.

NKJV. The New King James Version appeared in 1982 as a more conservative alternative to the dynamic equivalent New International Version. But in one important respect, the NKJV is absolutely unique in its conservatism—it is the only modern translation that does not incorporate new manuscript evidence that has come to light since 1611. From the practical standpoint of worship habits, the implications of such an approach are significant, for in the NKJV, nothing ever goes missing; everything in the text of the KJV is preserved. Only the language is updated.

Two notable examples illustrate how the NKJV parts company with other modern translations. On the basis of manuscript evidence that suggests late additions to the biblical text, most modern translations omit the doxology from the Lord's Prayer in Matthew 6:9–13 and the Trinity proof text from 1 John 5:7. The absence of such passages from the Bible, however, can be unsettling for some believers. For that reason, the NKJV elected to base its translation on the same Greek text that the KJV translators used. For practical purposes, that means that the NKJV is simply the KJV in modern language. Put another way, the KJV translators evaluated manuscripts and made choices. The translators of the NKJV chose not to continue with that process.

Produced by Evangelicals, the NKJV handles the gender issue in the same way as the NASB and NIV, the other major Evangelical translations. That is particularly striking in the case of the NKJV, for its model, the KJV, used inclusive language in the Beatitudes—the peacemakers are "children of God." In the NKJV, they are " 'sons of God.' "[3]

ESV. The English Standard Version of 2001 also stands in the KJV tradition. Its starting point is the RSV of 1971. Some concessions are made on the gender question, but " 'sons' " is typically not expanded to "children"[4] and *sisters* is not added to "brothers" as is consistently done in the NRSV.[5]

All the above translations are formal equivalent in style, seeking to stay as close as possible to the "form" of the original language. The other translation choice is to focus on the receptor language, a style that is called dynamic equivalent.

Dynamic equivalent translation

A translation that focuses on the receptor language, the language of the modern audience that will be using the new translation, is called a dynamic equivalent translation. The word *paraphrase* is sometimes used to describe these versions. In its more radical form, such translations actually change imagery and vocabulary in an effort to communicate to the modern reader a dynamic equivalent of the ideas and language heard by the original audience. In the Sermon on the Mount, for example, when Jesus tells His audience to look normal instead of "dismal" (NRSV) or "gloomy" (CEV),[6] the NRSV gives a formal equivalent translation: "Put oil on your head and wash your face." But the dynamic equivalent CEV has "comb your hair and wash your face."[7] The point in both cases is the same: look normal! But the CEV uses an idiom that is more understandable in our modern world.

Examples of dynamic equivalent translations

Phillips. J. B. Phillips's *New Testament in Modern English* was published in 1958.[8] Phillips was a young pastor who discovered that the language of the KJV simply was not touching the young people with whom he was working. So he produced his own translation. The language flows easily, is somewhat expansive, but seeks to remain faithful to the original even where it has been adapted to a modern audience.

GNB. Though the first edition of the New Testament of the *Good News Bible* was published by the American Bible Society in 1966, the first complete GNB was published in 1976, combining the newly completed Old Testament with the fourth edition of the New Testament. Also known as *Today's English Version* (TEV), the GNB was largely the work of Bible Society translator Robert Bratcher, even though his name generally is not published in connection with the translation itself. Though the language is not intentionally inclusive, in most versions it does use "children" for "sons" when the intent is inclusive.[9] One of its great strengths is the simplicity of its language and vocabulary.

NIV. The complete New International Version was first published in 1978. It is probably the most popular dynamic equivalent translation in use today. Produced by Evangelicals, it does not use inclusive language, a feature that would be incorporated, however, in the TNIV.

TNIV. Today's New International Version was published in 2005. It is an inclusive language version of the NIV. When the word went out that Zondervan was planning to publish an inclusive language version of the NIV, a number of conservative Christian spokespersons objected.[10] The furor led the publisher to put the project temporarily on hold. Ultimately, however, Zondervan moved ahead with the TNIV while promising that the traditional NIV would remain in print.

CEV. The Contemporary English Version was published by the American Bible Society in 1995. Its most noteworthy feature is that it is the first translation designed to be heard by the ear rather than read by the eye. The Bible Society wanted this kind of translation because it concluded that given the changes in modern culture, more people will be "hearing" the Bible than "reading" it. It is an inclusive-language translation and makes generous use of dynamic equivalents.

NLT. The New Living Translation was published in 1996. Based on Kenneth Taylor's enormously popular *The Living Bible,* it is an inclusive-language Bible published by Evangelicals. Originally appearing in sections, *The Living Bible* was published as a complete Bible in 1971. The New Living Translation is the work of a full translation committee that has thoroughly reworked *The Living Bible* into a viable and well-researched translation.

The Message. *The Message* is Eugene H. Peterson's lively rendition of the

Bible in contemporary language. Appearing in sections beginning in 1993, it was published as a complete Bible in 2002. Its fresh and exciting language does not shrink from using modern idioms, even ones that more traditional ears might find jarring. In the last lines of the temptation account of Matthew 4, for example, the NRSV has Jesus saying, "Away with you, Satan!" *The Message* has "Beat it, Satan!"

A touch of history

Throughout history, the clamor for new Bible translations would probably be seen as a liberal phenomenon, even when it is driven by the desire of devout believers to have the Bible in their own language. Deeply rooted in the human soul is the desire to preserve the Bible as the *unchanging* Word of God. "I am the LORD, I change not," declares Malachi 3:6 in the ringing words of the KJV. If God does not change, why should His Word?

Those who chafe at the widespread "KJV-only" attitude that persists in our day, would do well to remember how tenacious that same attitude toward Bible translation has been at a number of points in history; three, in particular, are worth special attention.

From Hebrew to Greek. The Jewish historian Josephus (ca. A.D. 37–100) expressed the traditional view of an unchanging Hebrew Bible: "Although such long ages have now passed," he wrote, "no one has ventured either to add, or to remove, or to alter a syllable."[11] The spread of Greek culture, however, gave birth to a Greek translation of the Bible. Even then, the idea of an unchanging text persisted. When "The Letter of Aristeas" tells the story of the origin of that Greek translation (the Septuagint), it reports that after the translators had finished their work, the leaders of the Jewish community pronounced a curse on "anyone who should alter the version by any addition or change." The words of the new translation were to be "preserved completely and permanently in perpetuity."[12]

From Greek to Latin. Just as Greek had displaced Hebrew, so Latin gradually displaced Greek in the world of Western Christianity. In the process, Latin Bibles came to be widely used. However, after the transition from Greek to Latin was virtually complete, the great biblical scholar Jerome (ca. A.D. 325–420) decided that a new Latin translation was urgently needed. He had discovered that the

Latin translations in use in his day had been carelessly done and were based on the Greek translation of the Old Testament instead of on the Hebrew original and on inferior Greek manuscripts for the New Testament. His decision to base his translation on the Hebrew original and on better New Testament manuscripts, however, meant that some familiar passages would not be quite the same—and that meant trouble.

Jerome knew what he would be up against. "With my eyes wide open," he wrote, "I thrust my hand into the flame."[13] When his critics complained, as he knew they would, he did not flinch. "Two-legged asses," he called them, and "filthy swine who grunt as they trample on pearls."[14] In time, Jerome's Latin Vulgate weathered the storm and became fully accepted as the new standard. But the initial resistance is worth noting.

From Latin to English. Even though the Renaissance had awakened interest in the original biblical languages (Hebrew and Greek), Latin was not easily displaced. The editors of one of the early parallel Bibles, the *Complutensian Polyglot* (1514–1517), explained that the Latin translation had been printed between the Hebrew and the Greek just as Jesus had been crucified between two thieves![15]

At the time of the Reformation, resistance to the Bible in English was powerful and deadly. Of all the early English translators, only one, Miles Coverdale, died in bed.[16] That conservative impulse left other scars as well. In July 1546, a royal decree from Henry VIII declared that "no man or woman, of what estate, condition, or degree, was after the last day of August, to receive, have, take, or keep, Tyndale's or Coverdale's New Testament."[17] A pathetic human response to the ban is reflected in a handwritten note on the flyleaf of a copy of Polydore Vergil's *History of Inventions:*

> When I kepe Mr. Letymers shepe I bout thys boke when the Testament was oberragated, that shepeherdys myght not rede hit. I pray God amende that blindness. Wryt by Robert Wyllyams, keppyng shepe upon Seynbury hill. 1546.[18]

Four perspectives in the translation debate: The pie to the rescue

By applying the pie to the question of Bible translations, we can begin to understand that no single approach to Bible translation is likely to be seen as the right one. Different temperaments will naturally gravitate to different translations. Whatever our personal preferences may be, we will need to learn to live with diversity. Furthermore, by looking carefully at the pie, we could conclude that both conservative and liberal stereotypes take a bit of a beating. If a conservative is anyone who has at least one conservative leg, then three of the four quadrants can be seen as conservative. Similarly, if a liberal is anyone with at least one liberal leg, then three of the quadrants can also be seen as liberal. That could mean that only the double liberals and the double conservatives would be at deep odds with each other.

Looking more closely at each of the four quadrants can help us understand the characteristics that shape a particular preference for a particular translation.

1. Intellectual liberal and lifestyle conservative

Lemon Pie and Paul: A parallel Bible using the NASB and CEV. I start with the Lemon Pie quadrant because it is my "home." This is the piece of the pie that brings together the liberal exploratory impulse with the deep-rooted conservative impulse that seeks God's presence. For someone like me, God's Word is especially precious. But it serves a dual function in my life, inspiring a deep sense of reverence on the one hand, but triggering a great deal of inquisitiveness on the other. That tension between reverence and inquisitiveness is one of the matched pairs cited by Richard Livingstone in chapter 10.[19]

That's why I could never really be satisfied with just one translation, whether a formal equivalent or a dynamic equivalent. I want a parallel Bible that puts the two side by side. For the formal equivalent, I would probably choose the NASB; for the dynamic equivalent, I would probably choose the CEV or the GNB. In real life, I use the NRSV. But if I could pull it off, I would like a parallel Bible that would give me the best of both worlds.

2. Intellectual conservative and lifestyle liberal

Apple Pie and Proverbs: GNB, TNIV, The Message, and The Clear Word. Most church members are in the Apple Pie quadrant. As lifestyle liberals, they love people; as intellectual conservatives, they find it easy to accept what the church teaches. As for Bible translations, they simply want a Bible that makes sense and preserves what they believe is important. Intuitively, one might suspect that this crowd would simply grab the KJV and run with it. And many do. But the Apple Pie crowd also loves exciting Bibles that bring a breath of fresh air to the reading and hearing of God's Word. That's why you will find an eager interest in the dynamic equivalent translations. GNB, CEV, NLT, NIV, and TNIV all find a welcome home here. *The Message* is also very popular. These are devout believers who love people, love the church, and love the Lord. Anything that makes the Word of God come alive works well for them. In short, when it comes to Bible translations, the Apple Pie people are light-years removed from the King James–only view of the Vegetable Pie people.

Left to my own devices, I never would have dreamed the extent to which this is true of Apple Pie people. But the response of Adventists to *The Clear Word,* an expanded paraphrase by Jack J. Blanco,[20] has made a believer of me. At the high risk of being misunderstood, I will comment further on the *Clear Word* phenomenon. It is a powerful demonstration of our preference for positive thinking. The response of Adventists to *The Clear Word* confirms that at a very deep level, we really do want to think good thoughts about God and about people. We have affirmed Ellen White's counsel: "The Lord wants His people to follow other methods than that of condemning wrong, even though the condemnation be just."[21]

Before I go further, however, I should share my own view; namely, that *The Clear Word* is a commentary—not a Bible translation. My conclusion is based on the fact that *The Clear Word* handles the biblical text with a freedom that sets it apart from even the most vivid dynamic equivalent translations. But because so many people are using it as if it were a translation, it needs to be addressed here.

Popular views of the Bible are such, however, that any attempt to evaluate *The Clear Word* will be seen by some as an attack on God's Word. When *The Clear Word* first appeared, I wrote an evaluative piece for the *North Pacific Union Gleaner.*[22] I attempted to be evenhanded, expressing my positions under the three headings: "Admiration," "Puzzlement," and "Alarm." But at least one reader objected. "Let's quit criticizing the different Bibles," said the letter to the editor. "When we criticize the Word, we are criticizing God."

If we were to take such sentiments seriously, it would be impossible to evaluate any translation for its strengths and weaknesses; we would be obligated to praise every translation however strong or weak it might actually be. I do believe God can use any Bible, any translation, to His glory. The King James Version translators affirmed the same, declaring in the KJV preface: "We affirm and insist that the very worst translation of the Bible in English . . . contains the word of God, or rather, is the word of God." They even lauded the usefulness of translations produced by "vile heretics"![23] But affirming the value of a Bible or translation should not prevent a careful evaluation of its strengths and weaknesses.

Blanco is fully aware of what he has done. Responding to articles and letters that appeared in the *Adventist Review,* he wrote, "Thank you for your caution regarding the use of *The Clear Word.* . . . Its purpose is devotional and not for serious study, as the preface clearly states. Also, it is an expanded paraphrase and not a translation, as you correctly stated."[24]

At the level of intentions, I want to commend Blanco for the remarkable labor of love represented by *The Clear Word.* It is obvious that he desires to draw people to the Bible by making it more attractive and readable and by speaking well of God. And he has done just that. For the first time, many Adventists are hearing biblical content in language they can actually understand.

Where I take issue with him, however, is the methodology by which he has accomplished his goal; namely, dramatically altering the content of Scripture through omissions and additions, and by modifications that actually reverse the original reading. Many of the changes are in passages where the plain reading of the text seems to portray God as harsh or violent. Thus, in *The Clear Word,* Moses commands the death of adult males instead of male children[25]; in Samuel's command to Saul to destroy the Amalekites, the babies are simply dropped from the list.[26] Eli's sons must die because they don't repent—instead of not repenting because God already intended to kill them.[27] And the reluctant midnight friend in Jesus' story responds *because* he is a friend, even though the original text explicitly says that the man did *not* respond because of friendship; it was persistence that brought results.[28] In short, *The Clear Word* is not just a paraphrase, clarifying obscure language or interpreting ambiguous passages; it changes passages that are painfully clear, making them more palatable to sensitive readers. There are times and places when that is the right thing to do. But

I am concerned when we are reluctant to confront the extent to which the Bible reveals God's condescension to radical human evil.

Every parent and every teacher knows the challenge of opening the hard words of Scripture to sensitive minds. The Apple Pie people find it difficult to read the tough stuff. And I am very sympathetic to that gentle impulse. We should never read all the Bible to all people all the time. God expects us to be selective. But if we remodel the Bible after our own inclinations and do not expose ourselves to what the Bible *really* says, we may be missing out on important truths.

The response to *The Clear Word* has emphatically demonstrated that the church wants to think good thoughts about God. Never have I seen an Adventist publication that has swept through the church as *The Clear Word* has done. When I ask in my classes how many of my students have at least heard of it, virtually every hand is raised. I know of no other Adventist book that could get that kind of reaction.

3. Intellectual conservative and lifestyle conservative

Vegetable Pie and Jeremiah: KJV only. The Vegetable Pie people in Adventism are the double conservatives. They are conservative on the intellectual level, preferring solid structure and clear answers rather than creativity and exploratory questions. They are also conservative in lifestyle, preferring to move away from the allurements of modern culture into safer and quieter enclaves, even out in the wilderness, if possible.

Maybe it shouldn't be surprising that the Vegetable Pie people would want a traditional Bible that cannot be moved, not even a syllable of it. But surprising or not, a strong contingent of KJV-only defenders call Adventism their home. And I will admit that in the 1990s I was indeed surprised to discover the strength of the KJV-only movement in Adventism. Shocked, might be a better word.

My eyes were opened on the day I received a telephone call from a former head elder in the church where I had been the pastor. With alarm in his voice, he told me of a large Adventist church in which some sixty members had signed a petition to remove the NIV pew Bibles and replace them with the KJV. I thought we had solved the Bible translation issue years before. Not only had

Ellen White begun to use the Revised Version almost as soon as it appeared, but Adventist scholars have made a significant contribution to the literature on the subject.

In 1975, for example, Zondervan Publishing House brought out a fine little handbook on Bible translations, authored by two Adventist scholars, Sakae Kubo and Walter Specht. Titled *So Many Versions?* the book carefully analyzed the remarkable variety of English translations that had appeared in print up to that time. The book was revised and reissued in 1983.

Surprise! The battle had not been won and probably never will be. If Kubo and Specht have represented the Lemon Pie people in print, Wilkinson and Standish are the well-known names and published authors among the Vegetable Pie people.[29]

And once my eyes were opened, I discovered a significant number of non-Adventist voices who also have eagerly gone into print in defense of the KJV, and not just in defense of the KJV, but in defense of the KJV as the *only* legitimate Bible translation.

One of the more flamboyant names in the battle is G. A. Riplinger. The cover of her 690-page book *New Age Bible Versions* announces, "An exhaustive documentation exposing the message, men, and manuscripts moving mankind to the antichrist's one world religion." For emphasis, a further line at the bottom of the front cover announces, "The new case against the NIV, NASB, NKJV, NRSV, NAB, REB, RSV, CEV, TEV, GNB, Living, Phillips, New Jerusalem, & New Century."[30]

If you are thinking that there aren't many Bible translations left, you're right. The last line on the cover of her book reads, "The latest research supporting the authorized King James Version."

I do not intend to critique or defend the KJV-only position here. But I do want to express my astonishment that a church that can give birth to *The Clear Word* can also nurture a vibrant KJV-only community. Both perspectives are conservative with reference to God. That is, they both would affirm God's presence and activity in our world. But they are worlds apart when it comes to their views of the Bible. The Apple Pie people will accept almost unlimited change in their sacred text; the Vegetable Pie people don't want to move even so much as a syllable.

Perhaps the best that can be said of such a situation is that both groups may exercise a kind of restraining influence on the potential extremes of which the other side is capable. Admittedly, the Lemon Pie people look with amazement at both the freewheeling Apple Pie crowd and the highly structured Vegetable Pie people. Yet all of us still affirm the commandments of God and the faith of Jesus. And all of us, like Abraham, look "for a city which hath foundations, whose builder and maker is God."[31]

4. Intellectual liberals and lifestyle liberals

Pecan Pie and Ecclesiastes: An inclusive version.[32] The fourth quadrant is home for the Pecan Pie people. These are the double liberals. Drawn to everything that is human in the world, they see the pain and the beauty, and they are full of questions. Because they are without at least one conservative leg, they are at risk in the church. In fact, it would be difficult to find a spokesperson for this group within Adventism. But they are scattered here and there throughout the church, living a quiet, but often painful life.

So let me speak briefly on their behalf, and I will do so by sharing an experience that opened my eyes.

I was holding a weekend seminar for young adults in which we were exploring some difficult biblical passages. At one point, we broke into small groups to discuss the story of the dismembered concubine in Judges 19–21. It's not a happy story. Indeed, for several reasons, I consider it to be the worst story in the Old Testament.[33]

Now something would be wrong with us if we didn't experience some discomfort with the story. But in one group, I noticed one young woman who was experiencing something considerably beyond mere discomfort. She was in deep emotional distress. The girl's mother sensed my concern and took me aside, quietly explaining that because of some abusive family relationships, her daughter was likely to be deeply traumatized by any biblical story in which women were mistreated.

The New Testament and Psalms: An Inclusive Version is designed to help just such a person. God is no longer referred to as male, and anything offensive to women has been rendered in neutral terms. Most ordinary people would likely be puzzled or even annoyed at such efforts to render the Bible safe. But my glimpse of one child of God who had been deeply wounded by people who should have known better, helped me appreciate the value of the *Inclusive Version*. It will never meet the needs of very many in the church. But for those few who desperately need help, it can be a source of life.

Summary

The diversity represented by the pie continues to amaze me. And nowhere does one see that diversity more vividly than in our preferences for particular Bible translations. The fact that the inhabitants of the four quadrants can live together at all is truly a miracle. I hope we can keep praying for that kind of ongoing miracle. By God's grace, there will be a place for Apple Pie, Vegetable Pie, Lemon Pie, and even Pecan Pie in the church. After all, if there is that kind of diversity in the Bible, shouldn't we nurture it in the church too?

---

1. Matthew 5:9.

2. The term *Evangelical* carries a more-or-less technical meaning in North America, referring to Christians who affirm the teachings of the Bible and God's active involvement on earth today. Developing in the 1940s and 1950s as a more moderate form of fundamentalism, Evangelicals stand in a certain tension with so-called mainstream Protestantism, typically a more liberal form of Christianity that tends to be less enthusiastic about the miraculous elements in Scripture and is less likely to stress God's personal presence and activity on earth today. While there is often a fair bit of overlap between the two groups, the differences can be marked. Two different journals serve the two constituencies: *The Christian Century* caters to mainstream Protestantism; *Christianity Today* is distinctly Evangelical.

3. Matthew 5:9.

4. E.g., Matthew 5:9 in the Beatitudes.

5. Galatians 5:13, NRSV: "For you were called to freedom, brothers and sisters." The ESV does not add *sisters*. The NRSV consistently indicates in the footnotes whenever it adds *sisters* to make a text gender inclusive.

6. Contemporary English Version.

7. Matthew 6:16, 17, NRSV and CEV.

8. It was published in sections beginning in 1947. A revised edition was published in 1972.

9. E.g., Matthew 5:9 in the Beatitudes.

10. The attack was led by James Dobson of Focus on the Family, *World* magazine, which is a conservative Evangelical news magazine, and by the conservative elements in the Southern Baptist Convention.

11. Josephus, *Contra Apion*, 1:42 , Loeb edition, H. St. J. Thackeray, trans. (Cambridge, Mass.: Harvard University Press, 1956), 179, 180.

12. R. J. H. Shutt, "Letter of Aristeas," in *The Old Testament Pseudepigrapha*, vol. II, ed. James. H. Charlesworth (New York: Doubleday, 1985), 33, line 311.

13. From Jerome's preface to Isaiah, quoted in J. N. D. Kelly, *Jerome: His Life, Writings, and Controversies* (Westminster, Md.: Christian Classics, 1980), 159.

14. Kelly, *Jerome,* 89, 157.

15. Quoted in Ira M. Price, *The Ancestry of Our English Bible,* 3rd ed. (New York: Harper & Row, 1956), 35.

16. An observation by J. Isaacs in H. Wheeler Robinson, ed., *The Bible in Its Ancient and English Versions* (London: Oxford University Press, 1940), 182.

17. Ibid., 180.

18. Ibid.

19. Livingstone, *Atlantic Monthly,* July 1996.

20. Jack J. Blanco, *The Clear Word Bible* (1994). It is printed and distributed, but not published, by the Review and Herald® Publishing Association in Hagerstown, Maryland. Later editions dropped the word *Bible* from the title. A revised edition appeared in 2000 in which all references to the Review and Herald® have been removed.

21. White, *Testimonies for the Church,* 6:121.

22. Alden Thompson, "Adventist Bible, Adventist Message," *North Pacific Union Gleaner,* December 12, 1994, 11.

23. The most readily accessible form of the preface is in the edition edited by Erroll F. Rhodes and Liana Lupas, *The Translators to the Reader: The Original Preface of the King James Version of 1611 Revisited* (New York: American Bible Society, 1997). This edition prints a photocopy of the original, a literal transcription in modern type font, and a modern form with updated language. The phrase "worst translation" (78) is the modern form of "meanest translation"; "vile heretics" (79) is the same in the original.

24. Letters, *Adventist Review,* NAD ed., June 1995, 2.

25. See Numbers 31:17.

26. See 1 Samuel 15:3. *The Clear Word* revision of 2000 adds the babies back to the list of those who are to be destroyed.

27. See 1 Samuel 2:25.

28. See Luke 11:8.

29. Benjamin G. Wilkinson, *Our Authorized Bible Vindicated* (Washington, D.C.: privately printed, 1930), and Russell and Colin Standish, *Modern Bible Translations Unmasked* (Rapidan, Va.: Hartland Publications, 1993).

30. G. A. Riplinger, *New Age Bible Versions* (Munroe Falls, Ohio: A. V. Publications, 1993).

31. Hebrews 11:10, KJV.

32. Victor R. Gold et al., eds., *The New Testament and Psalms: An Inclusive Version* (New York: Oxford University Press, 1995).

33. I discuss the story more fully in chapter 6 of *Who's Afraid of the Old Testament God?* "The Worst Story in the Old Testament: Judges 19-21," in *Who's Afraid of the Old Testament God?* (Paternoster, Zondervan, Pacesetters, 1988, 1989, 2000, 2003).

Part 5

Fears and Hopes

Liberals and conservatives don't fear the same things, at least not at a focused, specific level. They may not even have the same hopes. But if we can somehow get past our more specific fears and hopes, as different as they may be, we can begin to realize that our ultimate hopes are amazingly similar. By keeping those ultimate hopes clearly in view, we can begin to see how the more specific fears—the ones that may look frightening to the "other side"—can actually help us reach and celebrate our ultimate goals.

As a practical example, let's imagine that we're heading to Grandpa and Grandma's house for a family reunion. All of us have agreed (perhaps reluctantly) that we do want to go, but for different reasons. The party people want nonstop chattering, good food, and exciting games. What fun! The more private people are willing to put up with some of that, but what they really want is to head out into the woods and hills for some quiet time in nature. What joy! But neither of those goals can be reached if we don't actually arrive at Grandpa's and Grandma's. So there is a common goal even while there are differing expectations.

Enter another factor: time. If the early birds win, our part of the family could arrive before the grandparents are ready. A big family event means getting house and garden tidied up and the food all ready. That takes time. In some families, many hands make light work, and an early arrival simply means that everyone pitches in to help. But in other families, too many cooks spoil the broth, and everything needs to be in order before the tribe arrives. For that kind of family, an early arrival is a real pain.

And if the tardy or late risers win? The leisurely trip en route may be renewing and relaxing, but they miss out on half the party (for those families who start on time, anyway), or they make everyone wait for the big dinner (for those families who have to wait until everyone is there), which can be another real pain. Even the later risers may admit to some regret at the chaos they have caused.

In short, if the early birds and late risers can put their heads together, our part of the tribe won't arrive too late or too early. Then, both the party people and the nature lovers can find their joy, and the trip will be a success. But if we can't work together, the trip may be cancelled and everyone will just stay home to "enjoy" more bickering.

Does that kind of thinking work for church? I think so. The five chapters in part 5 explore the possibilities further.

Chapter 14

Important Words Heard During the Day: *Liberty, Authority,* and *God*

The Bible says, "Nobody will tell anybody what to do. Everyone will do what's right simply because they know Me."[1]

The Bible says, "Out in the world, strong-armed rulers keep everyone in line. That's not My way. In My kingdom, everyone helps everyone else."[2]

Ellen White says, "When we depend on God instead of people, we actually end up trusting people more. Our faith in God is altogether too feeble and our confidence in one another altogether too meager."[3]

Others say, "I have come to suspect that when people complain about 'organized' religion what they are really saying is that they can't stand other people."[4]—Kathleen Norris

This chapter tries to sort out three tantalizing words that are important in the liberal-conservative debate: *liberty, authority,* and *God.* For most of us non-experts, it's a zoo. The crucial question is, What does *good* mean for us and our world? To what extent can we have liberty and freedom? Who has the right to tell us what to do or what not to do? How does the freedom of one relate to the freedom of others?

Actually, one other word can help us sort out the issues: *libertarian*. It's a scary word because it sounds like anarchy. And for some wild-eyed people, that's exactly what it means. But looking at the different ways the word is used can help us sort out the issues, even though the different senses often overlap with each other.

Liberty and the libertarians

In its raw, basic meaning, *libertarian* emphasizes the freedom of the individual. Five more specific uses can help us grasp the different aspects of the word, especially as they might apply to the liberal-conservative spectrum.

1. Political libertarians. The word is actually used by people at both ends of the liberal-conservative spectrum. On the left (liberal) side of the spectrum are the pure anarchists who don't want restrictions on anyone. It's a free-for-all. Interestingly enough, the term can also refer to those who would make everyone free by leveling the playing field completely and keeping it that way by doing away with private property. No one would own anything; everything would belong to everyone. Of course, to make that happen it would require a great deal of coercion, all in the name of liberty! Communism tried this. The result? A horrific example of how enforced goodness is one of the worst forms of evil.

On the right (conservative) side of the spectrum, political libertarians, especially in America, stress the individual's right to own property and carry weapons for the purpose of defending one's property. In this sense, political libertarianism often links up with capitalism and economic libertarianism, making the distribution of wealth very uneven. Usually, the rich get richer, and the poor get poorer.

2. Social libertarians. In a sense, the social libertarians represent a reaction to the political libertarians. Social libertarians represent a striking blend of moral liberalism combined with social intervention. In most Western countries, the social libertarians are drawn to the needs of the vulnerable members of society, those who are most often hurt by the excesses of capitalism—the victims of the greed of others. At the same time, gay rights, abortion rights, and family planning are areas that social libertarians strongly support. Thus, at the personal level, they tend to be moral liberals. But when it comes to issues of justice and equality for the socially vulnerable, they take the moral high road.

3. Economic libertarians. Particularly in America, economic libertarianism is often linked with the political libertarianism of the right. Capitalism finds its strongest defenders here. Government should get out of the way so that business can do what it needs and wants to do. In such a society, the gulf between the rich and poor is often enormous.

4. Educational libertarians. Here the contemporary impulse is almost entirely secular. Authority, divine or human, has no right to restrict the free exchange of ideas—unless, of course, they happen to be religious ideas, which may not be allowed into the discussion at all. In short, the practice of the educational libertarians can be highly intolerant and highly controlling.

5. Religious libertarians. Here the words are nearly contradictory. It would be more accurate to speak of a "libertarian with reference to religion," for religion itself virtually disappears. Freethinkers put themselves in this category. Affirmation of any kind of Divine Authority would be seen as a restriction of human freedom.

So how should Christians respond to all these cries for liberty and freedom? Perhaps an example from sports can help make the point that true freedom exists only within a framework of discipline. Those who attempt to play tennis without mastering the strokes find that they are never really "free" to play the game effectively. Discipline is the route to freedom. Within the framework of Christianity, Elton Trueblood notes the "paradox of freedom," namely, that "we are most free when we are bound."[5] James's "law of liberty"[6] points in the same direction.

In that same connection, Frederick Buechner talks about the nature of law, more specifically the "law of love," in a way that takes us directly to our next key word: *authority.* Buechner says that it is a "tragic misunderstanding" to think that the word *obey* necessarily means doing something for someone else's sake. "When Jesus asks people to obey above everything the Law of Love," he notes, "it is above everything for their own sakes that he is asking them to do it."[7]

If it is indeed true that we are most free when we obey, how does authority relate to personal freedom?

Authority

From a Christian perspective, authority is not an issue in a perfect world—neither before sin nor after it has been dealt with. God's will and the human will blend in perfect harmony. The law of love is a natural law, like the law of gravity. Rebel sinners stand in selfish opposition to the law of love; saved sinners are in the process of learning it, a process that could be compared to learning certain natural skills, such as walking, riding a bicycle, or swimming. Suddenly, it begins to happen, and it simply becomes part of you, naturally.

In a world where sin abounds, however, the issue is complex. Most of us don't want to be told what to do. "Because I said so" is the last-ditch effort of human authority figures to assert their authority and bring rebels into line. When all other arguments seem to have failed, parents, teachers, and others in authority are tempted to appeal to their authority as a reason for subordinates to obey.

In our daily lives, we accept certain rules and laws as essential for our common lives. In some cases, such as with stop signs and traffic lights, the laws clearly are intended to make life easier for everyone, and we quite readily support such laws. Speed limits have a similar purpose, though the need for a particular limit is not always as self-evident as the need for stop signs and traffic lights. But the intervention of the authorities can reach even more deeply into our lives, becoming more bothersome and intrusive, like mandatory seat belt laws, for example.

Given the fact that wearing a seat belt is now required, with real money as a penalty, you might ask yourself, What made me buckle up for the first time? Or maybe you are one of the remaining renegades who insist on a life of unfettered freedom. I don't remember when or why I started wearing a seat belt. Typically, I'm fairly obedient in practical matters; I rebel only when someone tells me I *have* to do something.

Initially, I buckled up more faithfully when I was driving than when I was a passenger. But since the winter of 1963, I wear a seat belt all the time. That was when I was a passenger without one and popped my head through the windshield. I can still rub the scar on my forehead and feel it in the middle of my scalp. It's a convincing argument in favor of seat belts.

But if seat belts are such a benefit, why doesn't everyone wear them? Of course, they restrict our freedom, and yes, they're uncomfortable; one can even cite examples of accidents in which it was more dangerous to wear a seat belt than to be without. Still, the evidence in favor of seat belts is overwhelming.

So our good-hearted officials have decided to help us wear our seat belts. The first efforts were gentle and kind, buckles in the shape of hearts with a loving message: "Buckle up—we love you!"

It didn't work. They tried a harder line: "Buckle up! It's the law." Stronger words, but still not much muscle. Sometimes the hard rhetoric was softened just a bit: "Buckle up! It's our law."

But only when the penalty turned expensive—"Click it or ticket"—did the habit begin to catch on. In Washington State, where I live, the fine is $101 for riding without a seat belt. Next door in Oregon, it costs only $94. But in both states, the authorities issue tickets with no qualms of conscience. Still, I am amazed at how often the report of a fatal accident includes the line: "The driver was not wearing a seat belt."

God as Authority

Now let's bring God into the picture. Should God be concerned about such things as seat belts? Why not, if God, like John, wants us to "prosper and be in health"?[8]

So God sets about the task of helping us protect ourselves and others. In short, to *make* us be good. Well, *make* is a bit strong. *Encourage? Entice? Coax?*

You see the problem. Paul lays it out—his dilemma, ours, and God's: "What would you prefer? Am I to come to you with a stick, or with love in a spirit of gentleness?"[9]

God's goal—ours, too, unless we are still in rebellion—is to point us to a life of natural obedience, for our sake and for the sake of everyone around us. But until God recreates us and restores us to a new world, we won't necessarily do what is right of our own free will. Sinners are rebellious libertarians by nature. Believers know that God is interested in us as individuals. If we are spiritually mature, however, we will recognize that God is even more keenly interested in how we relate to others. Indeed, the parable of the sheep and the goats in Matthew 25 makes our relationship to others *the* crucial issue in the judgment. God's decision in judgment turns on just "one point," notes Ellen White: what we "have done or have neglected to do for Him in the person of the poor and suffering."[10]

That responsibility to others explains why the church also becomes involved with issues of authority. Thus each of us must decide how to relate to leaders, both elected and charismatic, and to group decisions, as well as to official documents adopted by the group. Exploring the role of those kinds of authorities goes beyond the limits of this chapter. But one such authority is crucial for us here, namely, the authority of the written Word of God, words that have gained the respect of the community by a Spirit-guided process now hidden from our view. Within the pages of the Bible, God's hand may be presented as heavy or light; God can be portrayed as reassuring, challenging, or threatening, depending upon the needs of particular people. But that very diversity within Scripture explains why we need *all* of Scripture to meet the needs of liberals and conservatives today. And that diversity also explains why we need the continued guidance of the Spirit and the wise counsel of our brothers and sisters if we are going to be faithful to God's calling.

In our age, what has proven so deadly for belief in God is the satanic deception that God is always and only heavy-handed and arbitrary, allowing no questioning of His authority. Some of the staunchest defenders of the Bible have contributed unwittingly, but directly, to the rage of atheists, many of whom had inquiring minds early in their youth but whose questions were squelched by heavy-handed Christians. Thus, the atheists angrily denounce both the Bible and the "God" they think the Bible describes. Ellen White candidly identified that demonic process when she said that "arbitrary words and actions stir up the worst passions of the human heart."[11]

The appeal to hell as the primary weapon in God's arsenal is part of the same picture. Noting that the doctrine of hell has driven many to skepticism, Ellen White comments that for some "it is impossible . . . to accept doctrines which outrage [their] sense of justice, mercy, and benevolence" and because "these are represented as the teaching of the Bible, [they] refuse to receive it as the word of God."[12]

But when the story of Jesus is our guiding star, then the Bible actually reveals a God who can be heavy-handed when necessary, but always and only as a last resort. God as revealed in Jesus pointed to the glorious ideal of a universe where the law of love has made everyone free, more interested in helping and serving others rather than in simply pursuing their own selfish ends.

Those who follow Jesus look forward, of course, to God's future kingdom where even the animals are vegetarians and where no one will "hurt or destroy" on all God's holy mountain because the "earth will be full of the knowledge of the LORD / as the waters cover the sea."[13] But the really important part is that Jesus' followers find it just as important, indeed, more important, to do all in their power to help make this world as much like the next one as possible. In short, to recognize that treating others the way we would want to be treated if we were in their place[14] is not only the law of the future kingdom, it is the law of God's kingdom now.

That means caring deeply for the needs of the liberals. That means caring deeply for the needs of the conservatives. That means recognizing that where the one side is weak, the other side is strong. And that it works both ways.

In the end, therefore, the astonishing truth that emerges is that God is the greatest libertarian of all. And He made it happen by giving up His liberty, His freedom, dying on the cross so that the law of love could once again become the law of the universe. If God can die for us, then surely we should be willing to live for Him by living for all His children.

---

1. Jeremiah 31:34, author's paraphrase.

2. Matthew 20:25–27, author's paraphrase.

3. White, *Testimonies to Ministers,* 214, author's paraphrase. Actual quote reads, "When men cease to depend upon men, when they make God their efficiency, then there will be more confidence manifested in one another. Our faith in God is altogether too feeble and our confidence in one another altogether too meager."

4. Norris, *Amazing Grace,* 258.

5. Elton Trueblood, "Freed by Our Bonds," in *The New Man for Our Time* (New York: Harper & Row, 1970), quoted in *Leadership* vol. 10, no. 3 (Summer 1989), 60.

6. James 2:12.

7. Frederick Buechner, *Whistling in the Dark* (San Francisco: Harper, 1993), 98.

8. 3 John 2, KJV.

9. 1 Corinthians 4:21.

10. White, *The Desire of Ages,* 637.

11. White, *Testimonies for the Church,* 6:134.

12. Ellen White, *The Great Controversy,* 525. Full quote states, "The errors of popular theology have driven many a soul to skepticism who might otherwise have been a believer in the Scriptures. It is impossible for him to accept doctrines which outrage his sense of justice, mercy, and benevolence; and since these are represented as the teaching of the Bible, he refuses to receive it as the word of God."

13. Isaiah 11:9.

14. Matthew 7:12; 22:35–40.

Chapter 15

Scary Words Heard After Dark: *Pluralism, Relativism, Contradictions*

The Bible says, "I planted, Apollos watered, but God gave the growth."[1]

The Bible says, "When arguing with fools, don't answer their foolish arguments. . . . When arguing with fools, *be sure to answer their foolish arguments.*"[2]

Ellen White says, "We differ so widely in disposition, habits, education, that our ways of looking at things vary. We judge differently."[3]

Others say, "There are just too many molecules involved in a 'fact' for a declarative sentence to cover them all. When you speak, you simplify. And when you simplify, you lie."[4]—Bart Kosko, *Fuzzy Thinking*

This chapter deals directly with the words that scare conservatives: *pluralism, relativism,* and *contradictions.* I want conservatives to read it. But liberals need to read it, too, if they are going to understand enough about conservatives to be able to work together with them.

And right here, I will say more about my own liberal/conservative pedigree, because I know that I am a curious half-breed, a puzzle for both liberals and conservatives. A student once told me that he first thought I was the most liberal teacher he'd ever had, but the more he listened and watched, the more he was convinced that I was the most conservative! A noted liberal in the church—for whom I am a curious specimen, I suspect—once exclaimed to me, "Thompson, do you have any kindred spirits at all in the church?"

A major reason for this puzzlement stems from the assumption on both sides of the aisle that someone who is liberal or conservative in one area must surely be a liberal or conservative in all areas. Most easily tempted in this respect are the triple conservatives and triple liberals, those whose conservatism or liberalism is rooted in all three areas: (1) thinking/the mind, (2) living/lifestyle/culture, and (3) believing/God. And there are enough spectacular examples of dramatic switches from one end of the spectrum to the other to make an all-or-nothing conclusion almost believable.

Thus, if triple conservatives hear me asking exploratory questions about the Bible, they conclude that after dark I must surely be leading a wild and undisciplined life, that my confession of faith is fake, and that I am, in fact, an atheist. Indeed, at a church seminar recently, a woman came up to me and said that she had heard with her own ears an Adventist professor exclaiming about "that atheist at Walla Walla who wrote that book *Inspiration!*" That would also explain why an e-mail critique of the book described it "as one of the most dangerous books ever published by our denomination."

Interestingly enough, the woman who told me about the atheist exclamation, said that she had marched right down to the Adventist Book Center®, bought a copy, read it, and found it very helpful.

But if you are tempted to think that simply reading my books is the solution to all the world's problems, think again. Several years ago, a woman came up to me at a seminar I was holding and told me how helpful she had found that same book *Inspiration.* But she added that her husband—"who is a lot brighter than I am," she said—had found the book very troubling. She and her husband were both physicians, Loma Linda University graduates.

That's a modern confirmation of Ellen White's comment: "Our understanding of truth, our ideas in regard to the conduct of life, are not in all respects the same. . . . The trials of one are not the trials of another. The duties that one finds light are to another most difficult and perplexing."[5] But attempting to illustrate those differences raises a real dilemma for me, because even mentioning the strong conservative reaction against my writings could actually make matters worse, tempting liberals to give up the battle in amazed discouragement because the gulf seems so wide and deep.

A case in point: some months ago as I was presenting to a group of "liberals" some of the challenges and dilemmas facing the church, one disenchanted listener exclaimed in the middle of it all, "Why bother?" I was startled because he and his family have benefited enormously as a result of the Adventist message and the Adventist educational system. I tried to stay calm (and practice what I preach) because I realized that he doesn't have my body chemistry, and I don't have his. Still, what I really want is increased understanding, not increased hostility. And I really do believe there is good reason to hope that the disparate segments in the church can actually work together toward our common goals. In other words, I have a host of good reasons for bothering!

Both sides must realize that generalizations usually lead to overreactions, and it happens on both sides. If some conservatives assume that all liberals are dangerous and undisciplined, living wild lives, asking destructive questions, and denying the existence of God, it's also true that some liberals assume the same in reverse, namely, that those who are conservative in one area must surely be conservative in all three areas—usually *very* conservative, they assume. I have been startled, for example, to note how many people who are already aware of, in general, my conservative lifestyle, are surprised to learn that I eat dessert, even ice cream. They assume that conservative means vegan, no sugar, no oil— a position, I might add, that is nowhere supported in the writings of Ellen White, at least not that I know of. And they have a hard time understanding a deeply rooted conviction of mine that the Lord created raspberries for the specific purpose of being eaten with ice cream!

From the liberal side, the most deadly assumption, and the one where I personally feel most misunderstood, is that anyone who affirms a miracle-working, prayer-answering, personal God must surely be close-minded and fearful of hard questions. The fact that most Evangelicals believe in the inerrancy of Scripture no doubt contributes to that liberal assessment of conservative Christians. My own firmly held conviction is that it is possible to believe in a miracle-working, prayer-answering, personal God without also believing in the inerrancy of the Bible, but that continues to be very much a minority position. In a sense, the battle is raging as we speak.

In any event, in the larger culture, the assumption that conservatives in the realm of belief are reluctant to ask the hard questions is deeply rooted—not without some justification. I believe Adventists could help to change that image, but it will be a significant challenge.

As a first step in addressing the generalizations of my own positions, let me give a brief and candid assessment of my own standing on the three liberal-conservative scales. At the same time, however, I will cite counter examples of devout Adventists whose reactions are quite different from mine. In doing so, I hope to make clear that my personal reactions and decisions may be reassuring and helpful to some, but should not be seen as applying across the board to the entire church family.

To make the point simply, I see myself as conservative in two of the three areas: lifestyle and belief about God, though with some significant crossover into liberal terrain in both of these areas. The one area where I am clearly a liberal is in the life of the mind: I will ask my questions, and virtually any question is fair game. But even there, my questioning mind is securely anchored in conservatism by some immovable answers from Scripture, namely, those things in Scripture that never change: Jesus' two great commands (love to God and love to each other), and the Ten Commandments. That stable law pyramid is, indeed, my anchor, my umbilical cord, so to speak, securing me to the spaceship when I head out "into space" to explore both Scripture and the world.

But let me expound further on my statement: "Virtually any question is fair game." Why *virtually*? Why not *all*? Because I sense my vulnerability in key areas directly linked to another liberal-conservative spectrum, the one involving culture and lifestyle. And here my responses are distinctly conservative, especially as they relate to three aspects I know I must carefully monitor: sports, sex, and violence. At best, all three areas represent distractions; at worst, they could prove destructive. Lifestyle issues are significant and deserve more extensive treatment. Here I will only comment significantly on one of the three areas, sports, using it as an illustration of how lifestyle questions can have a real bearing on how we live and act.

An illustration of lifestyle complications: Sports

I should say at the outset that part of the challenge in dealing with lifestyle issues in the church today stems from the fact that most mainstream Adventists have little feel for the stark conservatism that marked much of Adventism in its early years. That is particularly true with reference to sports and recreation. Can you imagine the president of a modern Adventist college or university giving the order to convert an athletic field into a farm? Yet that is exactly what happened at Battle Creek College in 1897. President E. A. Sutherland "got out a plow, Dean Magan drove the team, and a 225-pound J. G. Lamson sat on the beam as they plowed the recreation grounds of the college and planted them to potatoes!"[6]

That kind of conservatism may help explain why Christians, in general, and Adventists, in particular, have done such a poor job of addressing lifestyle issues, especially as they relate to inspired counsel. A popular saying perhaps characteristic of the attitude of people in conservative religious circles clearly works against any effort to encourage thoughtful evaluation of biblical counsel: "The Bible says it. I believe it. That settles it." Adventists have our own version— "Sister White says . . ." That appeal to raw inspired authority has often led to one of two unhappy results representing opposite ends of the spectrum: (1) preparation of random and highly selective lists of approved and forbidden acts, or (2) ignoring inspired sources completely.

In Adventism, for example, boarding schools have banned chess, checkers, and cards (because Sister White says so), but have allowed Rook and Monopoly to take their places, games that are potentially just as deadly. From my own study of Ellen White's comments about recreation and games, I have concluded that one of her key concerns is the danger of addiction, qualified in a number of instances by the phrase "in the minds of some" or something similar. That is an important qualification. I know of an Adventist professor who could learn his Hebrew vocabulary while watching football on television. That's impossible for me because I am glued to the screen. Another professor does the family ironing while watching football on TV, which is another impossibility for me. If I am going to watch, I must watch. Radio is different. I can multitask and do something useful like clean the basement while listening to a game.

But even if radio allows me to multitask, radio sports still represents a deadly distraction from the things I want to do and the person I want to be. Others, such as my two TV-watching colleagues noted above, have quite different experiences. But I have to be honest and admit that my tendency to be fully absorbed by any kind of competitive event can seriously detract from my ability to treat others as I want to treat them, as Jesus would treat them, and as Jesus would want me to treat them. If I am engrossed in any kind of competitive event, I ignore other people, give them the cold shoulder, and speak abruptly. To be perfectly blunt, Jesus' second great command simply disappears from my horizon. That's why during peak sporting seasons I sometimes handle the temptation by turning it into a reverse game, vying with myself to see how many major sporting events I can actually avoid!

Recently, however, I had a revealing conversation with a devout and serious-minded colleague who told me that in his experience, sports were his best points of contact with other people and a real source of enrichment and personal satisfaction. In his early years, since he wasn't gifted musically, sports provided focus, fellowship, and a sense of accomplishment. In his view, given the myriad temptations facing modern youth (sex, drugs, computer and video games, and online pornography), sports provide an important and healthy alternative for our young people. In general, I'm inclined to agree.

I should also note one disastrous result of the Adventist avoidance of organized sports: adult Adventists are often very poor sports. When I was a youth pastor, our church used to schedule a weekly father-son softball game every Sunday. We had to quit because the fathers were so ill-tempered. Graduates of public high schools have told me how appalled they are at Adventist behavior during sporting events. "Anyone acting like that in public school," they tell me, "would be benched immediately." Learning how to win and lose graciously is an important life skill. When we avoid sports completely, we lose an important opportunity for essential character development.

Having said all that, however, I still must say that I understand all too well Ellen White's cautions about games. Nevertheless, it would be unwise for a highly competitive person like me to attempt to dictate to the whole community. My conservative stance, driven by personal issues, must be balanced with some good sense from moderate liberals.

One final concern before we turn to the three big words that trouble conservatives, and that is to note the importance of stepping back to take a more global look. Adventists represent a strand of Christian thinking that is particularly concerned about holy living, *sanctification,* to use the classic Reformation word. The description of my own experience reveals a heavy emphasis on the inner life. That kind of soul searching can yield positive results. But introspection can also make us forget our calling to reach out to a world in desperate need. That's where I believe the liberal impulse with its interest in the larger non-Adventist culture can be a helpful corrective to the more introspective tradition that has dominated our Adventist history. I don't believe God simply wants holy people as if that were an end in itself. He wants holy people who are so moved by God's holiness that they have no choice but to move out resolutely into the world, determined to make a difference in God's world for God's sake.

Now, if you have stayed on board thus far, you may have begun to sense the importance of that phrase that has become a favorite of mine: "the problems are the solution." It's time to look at the three scary words themselves: *pluralism, relativism,* and *contradictions.*

Biblical pluralism: 1 Corinthians

"Each of you says, 'I belong to Paul,' or 'I belong to Apollos,' or 'I belong to Cephas.' "[7]

With so many fragmenting forces threatening the church, devout believers are sometimes fearful of looking at the diversity in Scripture. It just feels scary. And I must admit that the phrase "unity in diversity" is often used to bring things into the church I don't think really belong there. Yet I strongly support the concept in principle. It is thoroughly biblical. And there is no better place to find it taught and illustrated than in Paul's first letter to the Corinthians.

Paul was deeply troubled that the church he had founded was being torn apart by factions, each group claiming their favorite preacher. His letter provides a wonderful illustration of how Paul worked with the church to shape a truly biblical pluralism. Five points are worth noting:

1. If you destroy the church, God will destroy you. One of the most sobering church passages in the New Testament is found in 1 Corinthians 3:16, 17. It's easy to overlook the primary thrust of the passage because the phrase "You are God's temple" sounds like health reform. But for health reform, the right temple passage is 1 Corinthians 6:19, 20, "Your body is a temple of the Holy

Spirit." There the primary focus is on sexual purity, but the application to healthful living in general is only a small step away.

The temple passage in 1 Corinthians 3, however, is about church, not health. The clue is in the original language (Greek) where *you* is plural. Our English word *you* fails us here because it includes both singular and plural. The only way to make the text clear is to say "all of you" or "y'all" (with an accent from the American South). Either way brings the message home: "All of you," says Paul, "are God's temple and His Spirit dwells in you. If anyone destroys God's temple, God will destroy that person. For God's temple is holy, and all of you are that temple." In short, we are called to do everything we can to preserve God's temple, the church.

2. The building: different materials. The forceful temple passage in chapter 3 is part of a larger picture that Paul is developing (see verses 9–17), namely, the picture of God's building that different people help construct. What is so intriguing here is that this building is constructed of materials that differ widely in quality: gold and silver at the top all the way down to wood, hay, and straw at the bottom. In other words, God's building is for rich and poor, skilled and unskilled, indeed, for anyone who wants to build on Jesus, the True Foundation. That's a message worldwide Adventism needs to hear again and again.

3. Baby food: nourishment for needy Christians. At the beginning of the chapter (verses 1 and 2) Paul introduces another model for diversity: food. It's milk for the kids and solid food for adults. He's not talking about children chronologically, but children spiritually. He would love to give solid food to all of them, but they're not ready. So they get milk. What a marvelous picture of a patient God who stocks the fridge with food for every need and ability! As an important aside, here, it's worth noting that *milk* is used both negatively and positively in the New Testament. In Hebrews 5:12, 13, it is used in the same slightly negative sense as Paul does here—i.e., grow up so that you can eat solid food! But in 1 Peter 2:2, Peter uses the term positively, urging the believers to "long for the pure, spiritual milk."

4. Field and farm: different roles for different preachers. The various models that Paul develops in chapter 3 all focus on different aspects of church life. The building model focuses on materials that differ widely in quality, yet are all acceptable to God; the baby-food model reveals a God who condescends to give milk when the believers really should be on solid food; one more model follows hard on the baby-food illustration, namely, that of the field and the farm (see verses 6–9), emphasizing that different preachers play different roles in the church and may even present different doctrinal emphases.

In chapter 1, Paul gives us some background information that helps us understand the passion that drives this farming model. He, of course, was the founding father of the Corinthian church. But while he was away, the believers began choosing up sides behind their favorite preachers and were tearing each other apart. Instead of working together for the good of all, some claimed to be followers of Peter, some of Paul, some of Apollos. One group (arrogantly?) attempted to stand above the fray, claiming to follow only Christ. Paul was horrified, deeply troubled, and angry. Unmistakable traces of all those emotions are sprinkled throughout his letter.

In his letter to the Galatians, Paul confronts Peter by name. Here he does not. He blames the congregation, not the preachers. But with the farming model, he points to a possible solution to the tensions in the church, one that could be crucial for Adventism today: different believers have different needs that will be addressed differently by different preachers. The key line is in chapter 3, verse 6: "I planted, Apollos watered, but God gave the growth." If we take Paul's metaphor quite literally, he probably means that he saw himself as an evangelist and Apollos as a pastor. But both of them, like all God's workers, are simply God's servants, all doing their part to help the plants grow. The spiritual needs of new Christians are not the same as the needs of those who have followed Jesus for some time. All the workers have a common purpose, says Paul. But God is the one who makes things grow.

In short, we need a variety of workers in the church, and not all of them will give the same emphasis, the same message. We hear a clear echo of this idea from Ellen White when she says: "It is possible for the most learned teacher to fall far short of teaching all that should be taught."[8]

5. *The body: the parts belong together.* One other model for unity in diversity comes later in Paul's letter. Unlike the food, farm, and building models, this one has no sharp edges. With his picture of the body, Paul is neither attacking nor defending; he is simply describing how God wants the church to work together. Every body part is different, but all the parts depend on each other. In the body,

there is a variety of gifts, services, and activities. But there is only one Spirit, one Lord, one God, "the same God who activates all of them in everyone."[9]

If Paul could make such a powerful case for unity and diversity, should we not be able to find a way to make it happen more readily in God's church? We address that question in several different ways throughout this book, often with reference to the three different ways in which the liberal-conservative spectrum is used in connection with religion. In summary, we can cautiously speak of a biblical pluralism, a pluralism that is absolutely committed to faithful obedience and reflects the diversity that is found in Scripture itself. This is not an anything-goes pluralism, but one that is rooted in God's Word, a pluralism that we neglect at our peril.

Biblical relativism

For my thoughts are not your thoughts,
　　nor are your ways my ways, says the LORD.
For as the heavens are higher than the earth,
　　so are my ways higher than your ways
　　and my thoughts than your thoughts.[10]

An anything-goes relativism in Scripture? Not at all. A biblical relativism? Yes, if you want to call it that. In the Bible, we find God's radical adaptations to human needs. The great principles of His law never change; His character never changes. And for those very reasons, He is willing to be "all things to all people,"[11] to borrow the words of the apostle Paul.

Was Paul a bit on the exuberant side, overstating his case? Probably.

But now the crucial point: If Paul could be all things to all people, as he tells us he was, shouldn't we also be willing to allow the same privilege to Paul's Lord, the Master of the universe? Shouldn't God be all things to all people? After all, Christians believe that Paul was inspired by God.

Of course, of course, of course. But it is easier said than done, because it feels so chaotic, so erratic—yes, and so relativistic. And for most devout conservatives the word *relativism* feels almost like a swearword.

But now for an illustration from the classroom. Recently, a student in my Old

Testament History class described the God of the Old Testament as a "moral relativist." How could God command from Sinai, "Thou shalt not kill," but also command Israel to destroy the surrounding nations, including their children and babies (see 1 Samuel 15:3)? If God is indeed a moral relativist, this student continued, then 99 percent of the Old Testament is irrelevant for us today.

The student comes from a stable Adventist family, has attended Adventist schools all the way through, and is currently active in church life. He is not an evil-minded critic. He is simply being honest.

I explained my approach to the Old Testament God, the short version being that the violence of the Old Testament tells us first about the violence of the people God is trying to reach as He patiently uses the only language violent people could understand. Five steps spell out the essential elements in that approach:

1. Jesus is the clearest revelation of God. For the all-important truth that Jesus is the revelation of the Father, two passages from John's Gospel lay the foundation: John 1:14, "The Word became flesh," and John 14:9, "Whoever has seen me has seen the Father."

But a not-so-subtle bombshell lurks in this claim that Jesus is the clearest revelation of God. It means that God has given other revelations of Himself that are not as clear! Of course, and why not? In the first grade, we teach first-graders what they need to know in a way that they can understand. The teaching in high school, college, and university will be better and clearer, at least in one sense. But in the first grade, it is exactly what is needed. The same principle applies to God's dealing with the human race. After sin had taken its dreadful toll on the human mind and soul, God gave the people what they needed in a way that they could understand, first-grade stuff, so to speak. The revelation of God in Jesus Christ can be better than anything else God has ever done without denying the value of the earlier revelations. Indeed, those lesser revelations were just what the people needed. That's what happens in a good first grade.

Can such an approach be confirmed in Scripture? Yes. Matthew 5, the first chapter of the Sermon on the Mount, tells us exactly that. With six clear comparisons, Jesus contrasts the Old Testament understanding with His own teaching, "You have heard. . . . But I say . . ." To cite just one example, the Old Testament forbids murder, but Jesus forbids the murderous anger that precedes murder.[12] And Jesus calls His way better.

2. The Old Testament was Jesus' Bible. In spite of—or maybe we could even boldly say, because of—the six contrasts between old and new in Matthew 5, Jesus fully supported the authority of the Old Testament, insisting, "I have not come to abolish the law and the prophets, but to fulfill."[13] The Old Testament was Jesus' only Bible. The six examples clearly show that Jesus was not doing away with the Old Testament but filling it full of richer meaning. Thus, Jesus Himself teaches us that it is entirely legitimate to claim that Jesus gives us a better and clearer revelation of God, while fully affirming the binding authority of the old revelation.

3. The Old Testament dramatically illustrates the catastrophic impact of sin on the human family. Telling the story of a succession of disasters, Genesis 3–11 documents an avalanchlike falling away from God: sin in the Garden, Cain's murder of his brother, the Flood, and the Tower of Babel. At the bottom of that avalanche, comes one of the most startling statements in all Scripture: Joshua 24:2 declares that Abraham's own family worshiped other gods. From that point on, the Old Testament illustrates how God slowly, but patiently, led a chosen people to the point that they were finally ready to hear the story of Jesus, a stunning, nonviolent revelation of God, the clearest revelation of God the universe had ever seen.

Why the long, slow road? Because of the great cosmic conflict between good and evil, between love and selfishness. Love must be seen to be love, and sin, most vividly illustrated in the form of selfishness, must be seen to be sin. God allowed sin in the first place only so that His way, the way of love, could be seen to be good. Satan and selfishness would have their day in the sun to show what selfishness could do—thus the long slide in Genesis 3–11. God intends to win His people back, but love can only win; it cannot coerce. Thus, God embarks on a daring, but dangerous, rescue effort, even using the language and method of violence to reach a people enmeshed in a violent culture.

4. Fearful people and authorities turned violent are the most dramatic results of sin. Genesis 3 begins to reveal the deadly results of sin. A gentle God comes looking for a frightened Adam. Through the generations that follow, Adam's fear develops into a full-fledged horror of any authority—human or divine—authority that manifests its power on earth through violent punishments, and from heaven with the demand for painful sacrifices, ultimately the sacrifice of one's firstborn son.

In subtle ways, the story of God's command to Abraham to sacrifice Isaac (see Genesis 22) confirms that humanity had accepted that terrible satanic "truth" that the gods are violent. Abraham offers not one word of complaint at God's command. In Genesis 18, he had confronted God over the possibility that innocent people could be destroyed in Sodom. But he offered no challenge whatsoever when God commanded him to sacrifice his firstborn son. Thus, God dramatically began the transformation of Satan's most horrid lie—that sin demands a human sacrifice—teaching Abraham that humans cannot pay for their own sin; God Himself will provide the Sacrifice. Abraham was pointed to the ram in the thicket; we are pointed to the death of Jesus on the cross.

The most pointed confirmation of this dramatic human acceptance of the satanic lie is found in Micah 6:6–8. Here the prophet begins with the question, "With what shall I come before the LORD?" Each answer then ups the bid: "Burnt offerings, with calves a year old?" "Thousands of rams, with ten thousands of rivers of oil?" And finally: "Shall I give my firstborn for my transgression, / the fruit of my body for the sin of my soul?"

Without any reference to sacrifice at all, the famous verse 8 declares that the Lord requires His people "to do justice, and to love kindness, / and to walk humbly with your God."

That's not the last word, however, for even though Micah himself says nothing about God's ultimate solution, the story of Jesus testifies that Micah's powerful affirmation of sinful human thinking is finally put to rest by God's ultimate sacrifice on the cross.

5. In a world where even the gods demand violent sacrifices, God condescends to speak a language that violent people understand. Thus, the Old Testament can be seen as a powerful testimony to a patient God, the same God who revealed Himself in Jesus, a God who reaches people where they are.

When I talked with the student who had called God a moral relativist, it was clear that in two respects his own thinking about the Bible was different from mine. First, he held the position that the Bible is, or should be, an absolute reflection of God's goodness. Second, he assumed that the Bible characters would have thought about God the same as we think today.

Was he convinced? The jury is still out. If he continues to hold his present position, he is in danger, as he himself said, of making the Old Testament 99 percent irrelevant. I believe that all the examples in Scripture give us insights as to how God dealt with particular people in particular times and places. Paul teaches as much 1 Corinthians 10:11, "These things happened to them to serve as an example, and they were written down to instruct us, on whom the ends of the ages have come."

If we want to speak of relativism, then we are speaking of a biblical relativism, which is exactly what the Bible teaches in Isaiah 55:8, 9. God's ways and God's thoughts are not ours.

> For as the heavens are higher than the earth,
> so are my ways higher than your ways
> and my thoughts than your thoughts.

If that's not clear enough, Ellen White put it this way: "God and heaven alone are infallible."[14] I think Ellen White was right. So was Isaiah.

Biblical contradictions?

"What would you prefer? Am I to come to you with a stick, or with love in a spirit of gentleness?"[15]

If the Bible is going to be the kind of book that God's people need to guide them to the kingdom, it will have to be throbbing with apparent contradictions. But the word *apparent* is crucial here. When seen in the larger context of the great struggle between good and evil, what appear to be raw contradictions are actually marvelous adaptations to particular needs. The differences in circumstances and the differences in people require a Sourcebook that is alive with a host of examples. "Rightly understood," wrote Ellen White, the apparent contradictions "are in perfect harmony."[16] "The illuminated soul sees a spiritual unity," she wrote, but discovering that unity "requires patience, thought, and prayer."[17]

In my more playful moments, I have threatened to write a book with the title *There Are No Problems in the Bible.* What does that mean? It means that if we could see any particular situation from the perspective of the people who are involved—and from God's perspective in seeking to help them—it would make perfectly good sense. But even a small gap in time and place often leads us to considerable puzzlement. If, however, we are willing to allow God to adapt to particular needs in different ways, then the pieces of the puzzle fall neatly into place.

Why are we so frightened of contradictions? Because we worry too much about the critics—those who doubt the inspiration of the Bible. I have a collection of letters from thoughtful and conscientious Christians who are uncertain about what to do with my more open approach to Scripture simply because they are afraid of the critics. They worry that by pointing out the differences in the Bible I am playing directly into the hands of crowing critics and we will be left speechless.

My response to the critics would be forthright and direct. First, I would say that the Bible is our Book, not theirs. It doesn't belong to the critics. And given what God needs to do in the world, what the critics call contradictions are essential to the very nature of Scripture. How could Scripture be clearer than by putting two proverbs side by side, one counseling us to not answer fools according to their folly, the next one counseling us to answer fools according to their folly? The same principle lies behind that question Paul posed to the quarreling Corinthians; Shall I "come to you with a stick, or with love in a spirit of gentleness?"

Most of Ellen White's uses of the word *contradictions* are in a "Yes, but . . ." setting in which she is addressing those who object to the Bible or to her own writings because of the contradictions they have found. Some fifteen times she uses the word in this way. In such cases, she almost always points to the larger "spiritual unity" or the "underlying harmony." But in one remarkable instance in *The Desire of Ages,* she actually uses *contradictions* as a positive description of the life of Christ: "Great contradictions presented themselves in Jesus," she wrote. "He was the divine Son of God, and yet a helpless child. The Creator of the worlds, the earth was His possession, and yet poverty marked His life experience at every step."[18]

Here we can sense precisely why there must be contradictions. How could there be an Incarnation, God in human flesh, unless it also presented us with this enormous mystery of the Creator of the universe coming to earth as a helpless child? The story cannot be told without those glorious contradictions.

Based on my own observations, the critics who sneer at the contradictions in the Bible (or at the contradictions in the writings of Ellen White) are almost always those who have run up against one or more examples that cannot be solved by the appeal to raw authority: "The Bible says it. I believe it. That settles it." An inquiring mind is simply angered by that kind of arbitrary answer. Indeed, in her counsels on education, Ellen White quite candidly states, "Arbitrary words and actions stir up the worst passions of the human heart."[19] Nowhere is that illustrated more clearly than in the response of the critics to the arbitrary defense of the Bible. The critics are angry because they have been told not to see what they have already seen or that what they think they have seen isn't there at all. Adventists have a marvelous opportunity to show a better way if we can honestly say, without anger, "Yes, you have seen what you have seen. Isn't that what we should expect in a Book that is adapted to the practical needs of a great variety of people living in a difficult world?"

In short, I believe we can be honest with the contradictions. We need them. We can leave the critics speechless if we simply admit that the contradictions are there, and, in fact, are essential if God's Word is to be effective in reaching all kinds of people.

---

1. 1 Corinthians 3:6.

2. Proverbs 26:4, 5, NLT; emphasis supplied.

3. White, *The Ministry of Healing,* 483. (1905).

4. Bart Kosko, *Fuzzy Thinking: The New Science of Fuzzy Logic* (New York: Hyperion, 1993), 86.

5. White, *The Ministry of Healing,* 483.

6. Merlin L. Neff, *For God and C.M.E.* (Mountain View, Calif.: Pacific Press®, 1964), 63.

7. 1 Corinthians 1:12.

8. White, *Counsels to Parents,* 433.

9. See 1 Corinthians 12:4–6; 1 Corinthians 12:6.

10. Isaiah 55:8, 9.

11. 1 Corinthians 9:22.

12. See Matthew 5:21, 22.

13. See Matthew 5:17.

14. White, *Selected Messages,* 1:37.

15. 1 Corinthians 4:21.

16. White, *Patriarchs and Prophets,* 114.

17. Ellen White, *Selected Messages,* 1:20.

18. White, *The Desire of Ages,* 87, 88.

19. White, *Testimonies for the Church,* 6:134.

Chapter 16

The Greatest Fear: Change, Diversity, and Rebellion Against God

The Bible says, "After Jehudi had read several columns from Jeremiah's scroll, the king would cut them off with his penknife and toss them into the fire. Even after the entire scroll had gone up in smoke, neither the king nor any of his people were afraid. No one."[1]

Ellen White says, "As real spiritual life declines, the search for truth stops. People are content with what they know and discourage serious Bible study. They become conservative and seek to avoid discussion."[2]

Others say, "Those who attempt anything for the public, especially if they try to make the word of God understandable, set themselves up to be frowned upon by every evil eye, and cast themselves headlong on a row of pikes, to be stabbed by every sharp tongue. . . . Even if people don't like what they have, they still don't want it changed."[3]—Translators of the King James Version of the Bible

Others say, "When everybody knows that something is so, it means that nobody knows nothin'."[4]—Andrew Grove, founder of Intel

The purpose of this chapter is to bring together several closely related concerns that flow into one great fear, namely, that if we use our own human reason to recognize change and the diversity of application in Scripture, we have rebelled against God. Devout conservatives will know what I mean. I pray that the liberals will listen in carefully, for they live in quite a different world.

The first three statements at the head of this chapter illustrate the painful truth that change involving religion is just hard work. Nowhere is that illustrated more vividly than by those who no longer believe. Atheists gleefully, or angrily, sound off against a monolithic view of religion and God, assuming that whatever was once held to be true—though they have now rejected it—will always be held as true. Many such atheists give clear evidence that they simply ignore the progressive and creative scholarly work of Evangelical believers simply because they assume that anyone who believes must surely be a rigid fundamentalist.

One of my students shared with me some poignant quotations from two well-known and competent Evangelical scholars who have been immersed in the study of the historical Jesus, a topic that has stirred wide interest in recent years. Ben Witherington, for example, observed with some frustration, that "a large number of mainline scholars . . . continue to simply ignore the work of critical evangelicals, as if it were not scholarly work." In some cases, he observed, "they appear ignorant of its existence."[5]

In a similar vein, N. T. Wright, the gifted and prolific bishop of Durham, comments candidly in one of his books: "I live in a world where Christian devotion and evangelical piety have been highly suspicious of and sometimes implacably opposed to serious historical work on the New Testament, and vice versa." Calling this situation "deeply destructive of the gospel," Wright continues, "I have done my best to preach and to pray as a serious historian and to do my historical work as a serious preacher and pray-er. This has resulted in some fellow-historians calling me a fundamentalist and some fellow-believers calling me a compromised pseudo-liberal. The irony does not make it any less painful."[6]

Just how difficult it is for nonbelievers and/or nonpracticing believers to accept change is reflected in the remarkable response to the liberalizing Roman Catholic Vatican Council II (1962–1965). The most hostile reactions often came from lapsed Catholics, ex-Catholics, and non-Catholics. The American Catholic author Garry Wills offers this generic quote as an illustration of the widespread reaction against changes adopted at the council: "I don't go to Mass myself, any more, but if ever I do, . . . I want to find the Latin Mass still there!"[7]

In that same connection, I would mention the comments of a former student of mine who was a Catholic when Vatican II rolled out its changes. He was about twelve years old and not particularly devout when the church announced that Catholics could now eat meat on Friday. "It blew my mind and shattered my faith," he said. "I'd always been taught that you go to hell for eating meat on Friday. Now what are we going to tell all those guys in hell?" He simply turned away from any kind of faith and stayed away for several years.

The fourth quote at the beginning of this chapter, affirming that when everybody knows something, then nobody knows anything, comes from Andrew Grove, cofounder of Intel. He's talking about the business world. What he describes is now being called the "curse of knowledge," a phrase that refers to the closed thinking of those who are too comfortable in their established roles to be able to think creatively. Exploratory thinking simply stops when you, and everyone around you, are convinced that everything you know and do is true and right.

The same article that quotes Grove refers to a striking 1990 experiment that demonstrated how far removed from reality common perceptions can actually be. The experiment focused on popular songs, attempting to find out how many people could actually recognize a tune simply from the rhythm thumped on a tabletop.

Psychologist Elizabeth Newton set up two groups of people, the "tappers" and the "listeners." But before the experiment, she asked each of the tappers to estimate how many of the tunes they thought the listeners would get right. On average, the tappers thought the listeners would get about half of them right. In actual fact, the listeners guessed only 3 of 120 songs, or about 2.5 percent. The tappers were astounded. Said the *New York Times* reporter, "The song was so clear in their minds; how could the listeners not 'hear' it in their taps?"

Casebook: A story

Against that backdrop of general resistance to change, here's a story, a series of events, that shows how difficult it is for believers to accept a new perspective, even though it clearly describes what they do in actual practice. How is it possible to do one thing in practice, but resist hearing that practice described? If you are already practicing what the preacher is preaching, why not let him preach it? Maybe it's a little like a wedding or funeral in which everyone knows things that no one would dare say in public! Every spring I begin to act that way about my garden. I fear that during the winter the gophers have gone to work and rooted around where I didn't really want them to be. But as long as I don't actually go out and look, I can almost convince myself that there really aren't any gophers there.

I have discovered a similar impulse with reference to the Bible. At a deep, subconscious level, we want to believe that the Bible applies to all people everywhere. But we don't have to look far before it becomes clear that not all commands, not all advice in the Bible can apply across the board. The clearest examples come from the book of Proverbs:

> Do not answer fools according to their folly, or you will be a fool yourself (Proverbs 26:4).

> Answer fools according to their folly, or they will be wise in their own eyes (Proverbs 26:5).

Such contradictions abound whenever we use proverbs: "Too many cooks spoil the broth," but "many hands make light work." Jane Merchant (1919–1972) put this paradox into verse:

> "He who hesitates is lost"
> or "Look before you leap."
> The sages proffer good advice
> To spur us on to victory
> In sayings pithy and concise
> And flatly contradictory.[8]

Now is it possible to describe these contradictions accurately and place them in a framework where they all make sense? When I wrote my book *Inspiration*,[9] I thought most everyone had seen what I had seen in the Bible and would like to put the pieces together in a logical framework. To borrow terms from the experiment mentioned above, I was one of the "tappers" who thought that most of the people would get it. This is a story that begins to explain why many "listeners" did not.

I don't remember the student's name, the date, or the class. But I do remember the moment, the student's gender, the classroom, and the seat—for "old" Walla Walla University people, it was Fine Arts Center, room 120, middle of the second row. And I vividly remember the quote: "What you're talking about," he exclaimed, "is a casebook approach!"

All of a sudden, the lights came on. That was it! A perfect description of how we relate to Scripture and the writings of Ellen White. Since then I have used the phrase all the time and am almost as excited about the clarity it brings as I was at first. But I must admit that I have been startled—though also greatly intrigued—by the widely diverse reactions to the idea. Indeed, the casebook/codebook distinction has probably stirred up more of a ruckus than anything else in my book.

But first, a clarification for those who are mystified by the word but feel too sheepish to ask. *Casebook* is a legal term, but it is also used in such disciplines as psychology and sociology. It refers to a collection of cases, or excerpts from cases, that a student is supposed to analyze. The cases illustrate various options rather than dictate a particular course of action. Since a casebook contains only descriptions, it demands analysis and decision.

The contrasting word is *codebook*, another legal term, one that is widely used to refer to fixed laws. To put the contrast bluntly, a *codebook* simply requires obedience; a *casebook* requires thought and application.

As applied to the Bible and the writings of Ellen White, a casebook flies directly in the face of the popular motto: "The Bible says it. I believe it. That settles it." With a casebook approach, that motto gets rewritten into something like this: "The Bible says it. I believe it. That doesn't settle it at all." No one is capable of doing all that the Bible says because many of the commands speak to opposite conditions. And nothing in the Bible or in the writings of Ellen

White can tell me what I should put in this chapter or how I should say it. What I do have, however, in the Bible and in the writings of Ellen White are many examples from which I must choose in order to know how to live and act.

Immediately, however, instead of hearing "choose," some will hear the more negative phrase, "pick and choose," often a description of what happens when someone wants to go his or her own way instead of following God. But whether we *choose* or *pick and choose,* the words still describe what we have to do all the time, every day.

Putting that all solidly within a religious context would mean that if a casebook doesn't settle it—and I am convinced that it doesn't—it certainly is a call to prayer. For the believer, it helps explain why Paul could invite us to live in an atmosphere of prayer, to "pray without ceasing."[10] As I described in chapter 8, in my own experience, a casebook approach transformed my devotional life. And that is a crucial part of this whole story.

Idaho

In what follows, I describe the events in a rough chronological order, although in some cases, I did not find out about them until much later. That is certainly the case with the Idaho Conference workers' meeting at Camp Ida-Haven in January 1986. Years later, one of the pastors in attendance told me that at the time of that workers' meeting, he had quietly been asking some questions of his faith and was frightened by what was happening. He actually wondered if he was losing his mind. "Your presentations that year," he said, "were the first clue I had that I wasn't going out of my mind. What a relief!"

He also told me that during the breaks between presentations, he discovered that many of the pastors in attendance did not want to come back in to hear more. When he tried to find out why, asking them how they would deal with the issues I was discussing, their answers were evasive; they just knew that they had heard enough. Because they were conference employees, they did come back in but probably did not receive a great blessing. At the time, I was blissfully unaware of all that turmoil. But I continue to ponder why what I call "solutions" are so often viewed by others as "problems."

Scotland

The next significant event came as I was putting the finishing touches on my book *Inspiration*[10] and meeting every week with a couple of pastors in Scotland to work through some of the issues. One day, I was hammering away at the idea of the law pyramid—the *one*, the *two*, the *Ten* Commandments, and the many[11]—arguing that in our sinful earth, the *one-two-Ten* law pyramid never changes; it represents the enduring, unchanging core of Scripture. But the principles embedded in the *one*, the *two*, and the *Ten* Commandments are applied more specifically by the many. All the rest of Scripture is encompassed in the many—the applications of the *one*, the *two*, and the *Ten* Commandments in time and place. Suddenly and quite spontaneously, one of the pastors exclaimed, "That sounds like only the one, the two, and the ten are really inspired, and everything else is merely human!"

I was caught by surprise. Where did such a feeling come from when my intention was to emphasize, and I mean emphasize, that *all* of Scripture is inspired, even the most specific applications? During our sessions, I had sensed some uneasiness, but it wasn't until ten years later that the pastor revealed his true feelings. We had maintained occasional contact over the years, so it wasn't just a bolt out of the blue. Still, I was once again startled by his exclamation: "Thompson," he said, "you made me so angry. Every week after our meetings I would go home in turmoil. But then, as I thought about it over the next few days, I had to admit to myself, 'But he's right!'"

During the intervening ten years, he had made peace with the ideas we had worked on. In fact, he was instrumental in inviting me to speak to a group of British pastors. Still, hearing of his anger was a sobering moment for me.

And now, nearly another ten years later and just days before I sat down to write this chapter, another scene in the drama opened up in conversations with this same pastor. As I was describing what I hoped to do in this book, he commented, "I hope you will address the issue of disappointment with God."

"What do you mean?" I asked.

"When I began to see those things in Scripture that changed my view of things," he said, "I was nearly swept away by a keen sense of disappointment with God. Why had He let me down?"

That's an important question to which we must return. But let's finish this story first.

Switzerland

My Scottish friend's delayed and reluctant admission of anger at the implications of the law pyramid (*one-two-Ten*) was so striking because it came hard on the heels of a similar exclamation from a retired pastor in Switzerland. When *Inspiration* appeared in German translation,[12] I was invited to speak on the topic to Adventist audiences in Germany and Switzerland—weekend seminars in Darmstadt and Friedensau and an evening seminar in Basel. My wife and I also spent three days with the Swiss Adventist pastors in St. Stephan, the only occasion during our two-week itinerary when those with serious reservations about my book joined in the dialogue.

Two reactions from that meeting with the Swiss pastors loom large in my thinking. One, reported to me secondhand, was the comment from a number of the pastors: "We're glad we heard Brother Thompson, because now we know he's not out to destroy the church."

The second reaction was the exclamation that foreshadowed what I would hear in Scotland. Toward the end of our meetings, one of the pastors, who obviously had read my book, took me aside and spoke earnestly with an obvious desire to help me: "Brother Thompson," he said, "you need to say that it's not *just* the one principle of love, Jesus' two great commands, and the Ten Commandments that are inspired. The entire Bible is inspired. You haven't said that in your book, and you need to."

What sobered me about his comment was the realization that he was just beginning to hear one of the most important messages I wanted to communicate in my book, namely, that the whole Bible is inspired, not just the parts we use or like. It was the oral presentation that opened the door just enough so that he could begin to hear what he had not heard in my book, in spite of all my efforts to make the point clear in print.

Now, when someone tells me that it sounds like only the *one*, the *two*, and the *Ten* Commandments are inspired, I usually respond somewhat as follows: "I never said that, did I? But that's what it feels like, right?"

"Yes," is the typical response. "You didn't say it, but it certainly felt like you said it."

Student reactions

The final chapter to this story isn't finished yet, but this is part of it. I continue to be amazed at how hard it is to get my point across. While I was actually in the process of writing this chapter, I received an e-mail from a former student, now an Adventist pastor. He was asking for materials to help one of his devout and active church members, who was beginning to grapple with inspiration issues, especially in connection with the experience of Ellen White.

I sent him some material, and in my response, I related to him an experience involving one of his college classmates, a close friend of his. The friend, also an Adventist pastor, had called me on a Friday night many years ago to thank me for one of my classes—but also to tell me how he had come to a place where he could be thankful for a class that had made him very angry while he was actually taking it. "When I was in your class on Ellen White, my freshman year," he said, "you made me so angry; I was your worst detractor." Then he went on to explain what had just happened that precipitated his call.

A woman preparing for baptism in his church had been given an anti–Ellen White book. She told the pastor that she couldn't be baptized unless someone could go through the book with her and help answer her questions. So they sat down together and went through the book—all of it. "Because of your class," he said, "I was able to address all the major issues. There were a few minor things that were new. But in general, you had covered all the bases."

He told the woman that if she had found answers to her questions, the church would be delighted if she could be baptized with the others on Sabbath. She came, and she was indeed baptized. My former student had called me to thank me, in effect, for making him so angry!

In what follows, I will share additional insights that I have learned from my students. But first, an important word on how I grade their work. In short, I consider it fair game to expect correct information when my students write an examination. But some issues are not clear-cut and generate a variety of positions and responses. For such questions, a factual answer does not exist. When I address such issues, I want my students to understand the issues and the options, and I usually want them to know what my position is. But I have a mortal fear of pressuring them into accepting my position just to get a grade. Typically, I will introduce such controversial questions with the phrase, "According to your instructor . . ." My intention is to liberate the students to recognize my position without obligating them to accept it just to get a grade. I am delighted, of course, if they find my answers helpful. But I want them to be free to make their own decisions.

Ironically, this method sometimes has exactly the opposite effect of what I intend, leading some to think that I am imposing my convictions on them. How do I know this? Because at several points during the term I require them to give me their own personal reactions and reflections. They get full credit if they give any evidence at all that they are alive and well. And at the final exam in my senior-level Inspiration and Revelation class, I require a one-page reflection on the quarter's work. I ask the students to be candid and tell me what worked and what didn't. They get full credit for whatever they write. It's interesting stuff, and it tells me a great deal about both students and teacher.

But the examinations have been a puzzle, for when I ask the students simply to identify my position, a certain number of them object. To them it feels coercive, even though my intention is to liberate them! My most memorable failure came when I was teaching in Germany and a student did very poorly on the first examination. When I talked with him, he admitted that during class he had taken notes only on the things he agreed with. With such a perspective and the highly selective set of notes that such an approach would produce, he had no idea what the perspective of the teacher might be.

But I have been equally unsuccessful with some of my American students. In a recent class, after one student grumbled about the need to recognize the instructor's perspective, he admitted that he didn't really want to learn what any particular person thought. In his final comments on the class, he said that he simply was bored with the pie chart that I use to illustrate how different people think.[13] "It wasn't very useful or even terribly interesting," he wrote. "I don't really care how we differ."

Try again, Thompson. One of my major teaching objectives is to help students see how different people view the same passage of Scripture in very different ways. We even do some small-group work in class where the students discover in face-to-face conversations with each other how much they differ in their reactions to the same passage of Scripture. But if, from the outset, a student doesn't care how we differ, the challenge is significant.

In any event, I began to realize that some students were still having a hard time accepting—or even hearing—my position that *all* the Bible is inspired. It would appear that my preferred cure for all-or-nothing thinking, namely the law pyramid (*one-two-ten*), is in some ways still problematic, even though my students tell me with remarkable consistency that the law pyramid is one of the most helpful concepts they get from my classes. And to be fair, I point them to Ellen White's *Patriarchs and Prophets* as the source of my inspiration.[14]

The first time I saw the bright red flag was in the summer of 2002 when I was teaching History of Adventism to a group of highly motivated upper-division students and some teachers returning to work on certification requirements. It was a great class. The students were eager, devout, and bright. That's why I was stunned when, on the first test, eleven out of the fifteen got the wrong answer to my loaded question. Here it is as it appeared on the examination:

> Question: Select the one answer most likely to represent your instructor's position on the applicability of Ellen White's messages:
>
> A. Ellen White's general counsels were inspired and universally applicable; by contrast, her specific counsels to individuals were simply practical counsel given by a godly woman and should not be considered inspired.
>
> B. Because of the principle of "once true, always true," all of Ellen White's writings are universally applicable, rising above the normal limits of time and place.
>
> C. Even Ellen White's most specific counsels are inspired and illustrate larger principles which others find useful.

I wanted students to mark C: specific counsels illustrate larger principles. To my amazement and horror, eleven of the fifteen marked A: only the general counsels are inspired; the specifics are not.

Since then I have continued to experiment in virtually every class, trying to find a more effective way of making my position clear. In my Old Testament classes, the issue is the same, but applied to biblical material instead of to Ellen White. In short, I want my students to recognize the *one-two-ten* as a rock-solid nucleus, an anchor that never moves, but also to see the more specific counsel and laws as inspired applications of the enduring principles.

I began reading the test question orally in review sessions before the examination, identifying my position with great emphasis and telling the students that the same question would be on the test—the options would be scrambled, but exactly the same wording would be used. Up to a third of the students have still been getting it wrong!

Finally, in the winter of 2008, I tried a new wrinkle. I actually printed out the question on the official review sheet. But before the students got the review sheet, I passed out slips of paper, gave them the question, and asked for unsigned responses. Here are the results:

A.	Only the general principles are inspired	10 students
B.	Universal applicability	1 student
C.	The specifics illustrate larger principles	8 students

Then I gave them the review sheet, pounded my desk, and shouted a little louder. The exam? Four of twenty-seven still missed it! Finally, in the spring of 2008, after recounting the updated saga, I "bullied" the entire class into marking the correct answer. Finally. Finally!

What further intrigues me is that although almost no one actually marks the option for "universal applicability," still the process of interpreting in time and place seems to result in the feeling, at a deep subconscious level, that the more narrowly focused specifics really aren't inspired by God, precisely, because they are not universally applicable.

As I have grappled with this issue, I have decided that sin has deeply imprinted in the human psyche the suspicion, maybe even the conviction, that God doesn't really want us to think and decide for ourselves. If a message is really from God, surely it must be absolute and eternal. We are not called to think and choose, but simply to obey.

Is that kind of thinking linked in some mysterious way to Isaac's reaction to the blessing that he had just pronounced on Jacob, the son who had so cruelly duped his aged father in order to steal the blessing, with his mother's less-than-subtle approval, no less? In our secularized day, any son who would deceive his parent to steal a blessing would most likely be stripped of any and all blessings. Yet when Isaac learned that he had been cruelly deceived, he blurted out to Esau, the defrauded brother, that he had already blessed Jacob. "Yes," exclaimed his father, "and blessed he shall be!"[15]

Does the story of Daniel in the lions' den reveal the same kind of universalizing logic? "The laws of the Medes and Persians . . . cannot be revoked," declared the king.[16] The logic held even when King Darius discovered that he had been deceived. If human laws and the decrees of the king "cannot be revoked," surely the word of the "gods" must be even more enduring.

I don't know if my classroom illustration solves the problem, but I ask my students to imagine with me a plan to motivate a specific sleepy student to get to class on time. Suppose I were to suggest the following: "Shall I come to your room at seven forty-five in the morning and wake you up with a glass of cold water in the face?" That personalized threat to one student would come from the teacher just as much as would the course outline, but only the course outline would apply to the whole class.

In the same way, all of Scripture comes from God and is inspired of God. But not all of it is universally applicable, however uncomfortable that may feel in the depths of human experience. No one on earth is capable of doing all that God says should be done—not because they are rebellious, but because God has adapted His specific counsel to meet opposite needs. One person is always too early, another too late; some students write too much, some not enough. Each gets the right message—but not the same message. To the extent that the Bible can help us in our daily living, it must be full of many contradictory examples.

Thus, by God's grace, liberals and conservatives need to work together and tussle together, in our efforts to understand and apply God's Word in our lives. We will frequently be astonished at each other's reactions. But in the end, we will all be stronger, wiser, more patient, and more like God. That will mean great joy in heaven—and maybe even more joy on earth. The more nonchalant attitude of the liberal can help to overcome the cautious fears of the conservative, and the carefully nurtured structure of the conservative may keep the liberal from slipping into deep trouble.

But now it is time to bring part 5 to a close on a positive note, namely, a glimpse of our greatest hope, one that early Adventists loved to call "the blessed hope." That's the story of the next two chapters.

---

1. Jeremiah 36:23, 24, author's paraphrase.

2. Ellen White, *Testimonies for the Church,* 5:706, 707, author's paraphrase.

3. Paraphrased from Erroll F. Rhodes and Liana Lupas, eds., "The Translators to the Reader," in *The Translators to the Reader: The Original Preface of the King James Version of 1611 Revisited* (New York: American Bible Society, 1997), 69.

4. Andrew S. Grove, cofounder of Intel, quoted in Janet Rae-Dupree, "Innovative Minds Don't Think Alike," *New York Times,* December 30, 2007.

5. Ben Witherington, *The Jesus Quest: The Third Search for the Jew of Nazareth* (Downers Grove, Ill.: InterVarsity, 1997), 256, 257.

6. N. T. Wright, *The Challenge of Jesus: Rediscovering Who Jesus Was and Is* (Downers Grove, Ill.: InterVarsity, 1999), 191, 192.

7. Garry Wills, *Bare Ruined Choirs: Doubt, Prophecy, and Radical Religion* (Garden City, N.Y.: Doubleday, 1971), 3.

8. Jane Merchant, "Look Before You Leap, or He Who Hesitates Is Lost," *Halfway Up the Sky* (Nashville: Abingdon, 1965), 42.

9. Alden Thompson, *Inspiration: Hard Questions, Honest Answers* (Hagerstown, Md.: Review and Herald®, 1991).

10. 1 Thessalonians 5:17.

11. In this book, the idea of the law pyramid is addressed most specifically in chapter 2. It refers to the progressive adaptation of God's law of love to human need: the *one* great principle of love, its application and adaptation in Jesus' *two* great commands, and its further adaptation in the *Ten* Commandments. The most complete development of the casebook/codebook distinction and its application in the law pyramid is found in chapters 7 and 8 of *Inspiration,* 98–136. Chapter 7, "God's Word: Casebook or Codebook?" was reprinted in *Ministry,* July 1991, 6–10. In my own experience, the original source of the idea came from two chapters in Ellen White's *Patriarchs and Prophets,* "The Law Given to Israel" (chapter 27) and "The Law and the Covenants" (chapter 32). The most telling quotes in *Patriarchs and Prophets* are found on pages 305, 310, 311, 363, 364, 372.

12. Alden Thompson, *Inspiration: knifflige Fragen—ehrliche Antworten* (Möckern-Friedensau, Germany: Theologische Hochschule Friedensau, 1998).

13. See part 4, "The Pie: Introduction to Myers-Briggs," and chapters 12 and 13.

14. See esp. *Patriarchs and Prophets,* 303–314 (chapter 27), 363–373 (chapter 32).

15. Genesis 27, especially verses 30–40; Genesis 27:33.

16. Daniel 6:12.

Chapter 17

Greatest Hope, Blessed Hope: Dinner and Dessert

The Bible says, "The wolf shall live with the lamb,
the leopard shall lie down with the kid,
the calf and the lion and the fatling together,
and a little child shall lead them.
The cow and the bear shall graze,
their young shall lie down together;
and the lion shall eat straw like the ox.
The nursing child shall play over the hole of the asp,
And the weaned child shall put its hand on the adder's den.
They will not hurt or destroy on all my holy mountain;
for the earth will be full of the knowledge of the LORD
as the waters cover the sea."[1]

The Bible says, "For in hope we were saved. Now hope that is seen is not hope. For who hopes for what is seen? But if we hope for what we do not see, we wait for it with patience."[2]

Ellen White says, "The great controversy is ended. Sin and sinners are no more. The entire universe is clean. One pulse of harmony and gladness beats through the vast creation. From Him who created all, flow life and light and gladness, throughout the realms of illimitable space. From the minutest atom to the greatest world, all things, animate and inanimate, in their unshadowed beauty and perfect joy, declare that God is love."[3]

Others say, "Then the new earth and sky, the same yet not the same as these, will rise in us as we have risen in Christ. And once again, after who knows what aeons of the silence and the dark, the birds will sing and the waters flow, and light and shadows move across the hills, and the faces of our friends laugh upon us with amazed recognition.

"Guesses, of course, only guesses. If they are not true, something better will be. For 'we know that we shall be made like Him, for we shall see Him as He is' [1 John 3:2]."[4]—C. S. Lewis

Others say, "We must never speak to simple, excitable people about 'the Day' without emphasizing again and again the utter impossibility of prediction. We must try to show them that the impossibility is an essential part of the doctrine. If you do not believe our Lord's words, why do you believe in his return at all? And if you do believe them must you not put away from you, utterly and forever, any hope of dating that return? His teaching on the subject quite clearly consisted of three propositions. (1) That he will certainly return. (2) That we cannot possibly find out when. (3) And that therefore we must always be ready for him."[5]—C. S. Lewis

Others say, "When you expect the world to end at any moment, you know there is no need to hurry. You take your time, you do your work well."[6]—Thomas Merton

The blessed hope, the hope of restoration, is part of the glue that bonds Adventists together. We are convinced that God can do better than this. And we live in that hope.

Some twenty years ago, I wrote an article about the new earth that was published in *Signs of the Times®* (1985). I still like it. Here it is.

I'll add comment and analysis in the next chapter. But dinner and dessert come first. Afterward, we'll slip back to the kitchen, so to speak, to find out what went into the meal; we might even go out into the garden. But first, dinner and dessert:

Safe streets and doors without locks[7]

No barking dogs. Neighbors who are friendly and helpful. Happy children. Lush green lawns and brilliant flowers. Perfectly safe streets and doors that need no locks. Sound almost like heaven?

It probably would be heaven, or at least a new earth. And that would be part of my list if I could speak my piece to the planning commission. And I'd go further: why not on-time buses that also wait for the tardy? TV programming that is exciting, but without violence or perversity? I'd like a world without fear, where promises are kept and the innocent are free—a world alive with the answer to the little girl's prayer: "Please make all the bad people good and all the good people nice."

I think it would be fun to compare my list with yours. Maybe you have a special love for onions, melons, or mangoes and would like nothing better than to grow them trouble free in your garden.

Dreaming about the perfect world is a good idea once in a while. But can the dream come true? Christians say Yes.

We'll take a closer look at that Christian hope. But first, a word to those of you who stand outside the house of faith wistfully looking in—who long to believe, yet wonder if you ever can.

You've explored the possibilities for patching up this world. A less than cheery picture, isn't it? What are our chances of making all the bad people good and all the good people nice? And supposing for the moment that by some radical turn of events, everyone *did* become kind and sweet, could we convince nature to behave? Would she cheerfully, or even grudgingly, relinquish her famines, earthquakes, and floods?

Patchwork. Miserable patchwork is the best we could ever do. And the patches would be forever tearing loose.

Let's face it: we need a fresh start. And that's really the essence of the Christian's hope: an ideal world, a new heaven and a new earth.[8]

It is a precious hope—but only for those who believe. This is not the place to mount a full-fledged argument for believing in God and His Word. Christians have often appealed to various natural and logical proofs, to archaeology and to fulfilled prophecy. Many have found faith and strengthened faith through those means. For those who want to believe, however, and are finding it hard, let me suggest that the most helpful argument in behalf of the God of Scripture is not so much an argument as it is a witness, namely, the words and lives of those who have believed.

The authors of Scripture believed, and they tell of other godly men and women who believed. Are you longing to believe? Let believers help you. Are you attracted by their experience? Let them tell you what God has done. What you once thought strange can become precious—and a powerful force in your life.

We need to remember, however, that forceful witnesses can lead us astray. They can make us believe almost anything—hundreds of people died in Jonestown because they believed the words of a powerful witness. So use your head; test your experience; pray. The great God of the universe is eager to send His Spirit to help you find the truth and believe.

But now let's talk more directly about the Christian's hope of a new earth. Is it really that important? Some Christians say it isn't, arguing that the Christian life in the here and now is its own reward. I can think of at least one famous Christian who would heartily disagree: the apostle Paul.

In 1 Corinthians 15, Paul challenges those who deny the resurrection and the hope of a future life: "If for this life only we have hoped in Christ, we are of all men most to be pitied."[9]

Now I wouldn't want to discount the value of the Christian way for our present life, not for a minute. I am deeply grateful to my parents for nourishing the Christian principles that have brought stability and meaning to my life. It is a heritage I intend to pass on. But I'm with Paul when it comes to the value of the future life. The hope of a new earth is the sugar in the lemonade—take it away and all you have left is lemon juice.

Other Christians hesitate to stress the material joys of the new earth, believing that mature Christians should focus their thoughts on God and God alone.

Reunion with God is indeed central to the future hope. John tells us that one day God will dwell with humanity: "God himself will be with them," he says, and there won't even be a temple there because "its temple is the Lord God the Almighty and the Lamb."[10]

As important as reunion with God is, however, I cannot imagine Him in isolation from His gifts. When we visit friends or loved ones, hospitality and gifts are just part of the package. As a student, I eagerly anticipated visits home. I went to visit Mother and Dad, of course—and to munch away on home-baked bread, cinnamon rolls, potato salad, and mushroom patties. I couldn't conceive of Mother locking the kitchen to see if I was coming home for the "right" reasons.

Similarly, I'd really feel cheated if someone were to strip away the houses, gardens, and fruits—the "home-cooking"—from the new earth. People make the home, but tucking the home into the right house makes it cozy. And homes were meant to be cozy.

That raises the tantalizing question which we can't avoid: what will the new earth really be like? I may have startled you with my earlier suggestion of buses and TV for the new earth. Actually, I was being cautious—snow skiing and windsurfing could have made the list just as easily! But don't take my list too seriously; I simply was trying to make the point that the new earth is a real place for real people. Of that we can be sure. But beyond that, we're in for some real surprises.

We can let our imaginations run wild until our mouths water at the prospects. But be prepared. The real thing will boggle the mind and dazzle the eye. How do I know? From reading Scripture. Let me explain.

First, we need to note that the Christian hope of an ideal world is bound up with two important Christian doctrines: Creation and resurrection. Sometimes Christians have followed the lead of the ancient Greeks and have looked forward to a strictly "spiritual" (nonmaterial) future life. The ancients typically considered the material side of man as inherently evil and the source of human depravity. Admittedly, we have difficulty conceiving of a perfect material world. If I stub my toe and crack my head against a tree, it hurts. Soil is composed of dead and decaying organisms. Plants and creatures regularly dispose of waste.

How will such problems be resolved in a perfect world?

I don't know. But I do know the verdict pronounced on a world created by God: "And God saw everything that he had made, and behold, it was very good."[11] That world was a very earthy place, and God called it good. If He can make a perfect world once, He can do it again. And He has promised to let us share in that new world—with bodies somewhat remodeled to remove the ravages of sin, to be sure—but with bodies nevertheless.[12]

Oscar Cullmann, a well-known New Testament scholar, caused quite a stir in Christian circles with his Ingersoll Lecture in 1955.[13] In the lecture, he compared the Christian and Greek views of life and death, contrasting Jesus' tears and agony in the face of death with the philosopher Socrates' calm acceptance of the hemlock poison. For Jesus, death was an enemy; for Socrates, it was a friend, liberating his soul from its fleshly prison. Cullmann argued that the biblical view of creation demands the resurrection of the body. The concept of an immortal soul that receives its reward apart from the body arose from a nonbiblical perspective.

Given the deep respect for Creation and the promises of resurrection in Scripture, we can expect the Bible to describe the future ideal world as a real place for real people. But a word of caution is in order, for the Bible contains several different "pictures" of the new earth. That's partly why I can let my imagination run riot—while recognizing that the real thing could easily be quite different. An exciting prospect for some could be meaningless or even distasteful to others. No point in advertising a new earth that the customers won't buy!

Understandably, Christians tend to take their picture of the new earth from the New Testament, especially from Revelation 21 and 22. A comparison with an Old Testament passage, Isaiah 65, reveals some interesting differences. The New Testament proclaims that death, sinners, and everything "accursed" are gone.[14] Isaiah simply promises the elimination of premature death and the effective control over sinners: "No more shall there be in it an infant that lives but a few days, or an old man who does not fill out his days, for the child shall die a hundred years old, and the sinner a hundred years old shall be accursed."[15]

Why the difference? God was simply describing the kind of world which His people at that time could appreciate. As strange as it may seem to us, resurrection and eternal life just weren't important to them; they lived on through their children.[16] The conclusion to Job's experience is a typical happy ending for the Old Testament, for he "saw his sons, and his sons' sons, four generations. And Job died, an old man, and full of days."[17]

An art teacher from a boarding high school once told me that her students tended to draw pictures of mountains like those nearest home: students from the heart of Idaho drew the jagged Sawtooth Mountains, those from eastern Montana sketched rolling hills. Pictures of the new earth are like that, too, as God shows us what we can know and love. In Isaiah's day, the people longed for a settled homeland; they wanted to build and plant, to live and harvest in peace. That's what God promised.[18] He promised to transform the animals too. Wolves won't eat lambs anymore, and the lions will live on straw, just like the ox. No one will "hurt or destroy" on all God's holy mountain.[19]

In the visions the Lord gave John, we discover an ideal city of the first century, with walls and gates. Had John lived in an African village or an American town, God might have changed the scenery. Now I won't be at all disappointed if the eternal city turns out to be exactly as John described it. But as I study Scripture, I have the suspicion that we might be in for a surprise—not a disappointing one, a surprise more delightful than anything we can imagine.

Finally, we must come back to earth and ask what we should do while we wait for that ideal world. To be perfectly blunt, Jesus doesn't want His followers just to sit around and wait. However hopeless this world might appear, He expects us to make it as much like a new earth as possible. Quoting Isaiah 61, Jesus outlined His program to His fellow citizens at Nazareth. It was His agenda, of course. But that just means that it's ours until He returns: " 'He has anointed me to preach good news to the poor. He has sent me to proclaim release to the captives and recovering of sight to the blind, to set at liberty those who are oppressed, to proclaim the acceptable year of the Lord.' "[20]

Was all this new earth restoration waiting to be fulfilled at the end of time? Hardly. Jesus Himself said, "Today this scripture has been fulfilled in your hearing."[21]

So let us be up and doing while we wait. Let's keep our dogs quiet; be friendly and helpful; make our neighborhoods lush with grass and bright flowers. And let's follow Jesus' example: helping the poor, the blind, and the oppressed. After all, the Christian's hope is not just for those who believe, but for those who act.

Comments and analysis? That comes in the next chapter. This has been dinner and dessert. Now we head into the kitchen, maybe even into the garden, to find out what went into the meal.

---

1. Isaiah 11:6–9.

2. Romans 8:24, 25.

3. White, *The Great Controversy*, 678.

4. Lewis, *Letters to Malcolm*, 124.

5. C. S. Lewis, *The World's Last Night: And Other Essays* (San Diego: Harcourt Brace, 1987), 107.

6. Thomas Merton, quoted in Rodney Clapp, "Overdosing on the Apocalypse," *Christianity Today*, October 28, 1991, 29, on the Shaker ability to produce such fine furniture while believing in the imminent end of the world.

7. Cf. Alden Thompson, "Safe Streets and Doors Without Locks," *Signs of the Times®*, October 1985, 20–22. The version published here differs only slightly from the one published in 1985.

8. Revelation 21:1; cf. Isaiah 65:17; 66:22.

9. 1 Corinthians 15:19, RSV. Unless otherwise noted, all Scripture quotations in this chapter are from the RSV.

10. Revelation 21:3, 22.

11. Genesis 1:31.

12. See 1 Corinthians 15:35–54.

13. Oscar Cullmann, "Immortality of the Soul, or Resurrection of the Dead?" Ingersoll Lecture for 1955, in Krister Stendahl, ed., *Immortality and Resurrection* (New York: Macmillan, 1964), 9–33. Also published in book form in 1958 by Epworth Press, London.

14. Revelation 21:4, 8; 22:3.

15. Isaiah 65:20.

16. Interestingly enough, C. S. Lewis, a strong believer in an eternal hell and in the immortal soul, doesn't see either as being at all prominent in the Old Testament. His most candid discussion is in chapter 4, "Death in the Psalms," in his *Reflections on the Psalms* (London: Fontana Books, 1958), 34–41. In chapter 4, paragraph 6 is this pointed statement: "It seems quite clear that in most parts of the Old Testament there is little or no belief in a future life; certainly no belief that is of any religious importance."

17. Job 42:16, 17.

18. Isaiah 65:21–23.

19. Isaiah 11:6–9; 65:25.

20. Luke 4:18, 19.

21. Luke 4:21.

Chapter 18

Greatest Hope, Blessed Hope: Into the Kitchen, Even the Garden

Crucial Question: When God predicts the future, does He always get it just right?

Answer: Always. But God's response is always linked to the response of the people.

Illustration: Jonah. When the people repent, God repents.

The Bible says, "And God saw their works, that they turned from their evil way; and God repented of the evil, that he had said that he would do unto them; and he did it not" (Jonah 3:10, KJV).

Illustration: King Saul. If the people do not repent or if they repent after it is too late, God repents.

The Bible says, "The LORD repented that he had made Saul king over Israel. And the LORD said unto Samuel, How long wilt thou mourn for Saul, seeing I have rejected him from reigning over Israel? fill thine horn with oil, and go, I will send thee to Jesse the Bethlehemite: for I have provided me a king among his sons" (1 Samuel 15:35–16:1, KJV).

In the previous chapter, we had the good stuff—dinner and dessert. It was the blessed hope, something near and dear to the heart of Adventists. But in a few places, you might have sensed some unusual and subtle flavors. How did the cook do it, and why?

So let's head for the kitchen, and yes, even venture into the garden, to find out what really happened for dinner and dessert.

We'll start with a touch of honesty: when it comes to religion, almost nothing divides the human family as quickly as discussions of last things, *eschatology,* to use the technical word. It also has the potential for dividing liberals and conservatives among Adventists too.

But before we panic, let's remind ourselves—as many times as necessary—of two things, reminders that we must take seriously if we are going to live and hope together as liberals and conservatives in Adventism.

Two reminders

1. Anyone who believes that Jesus is coming again is a conservative Christian, very conservative. In the world outside Adventism, liberals either believe that this world is all there is (when we die, we return to the food chain) or that our immortal souls go to their reward immediately at death. In short, "out there," liberals don't think they need a Second Coming; even Roman Catholics and many other orthodox Christians who don't merit the label "liberal," also place very little emphasis on the Second Coming. For many of them, belief in the immortal soul dramatically diminishes the importance of the Second Coming.

2. A potentially complex topic is based on a very simple truth: Jesus promised to come again and take us with Him to His kingdom. In the upper room, Jesus gave a promise: "I'm going to prepare a place for you," He said to His disciples. "And I will come again and take you home with Me, so that wherever I am, you can be there too."[1] The angelic visitors who stood by the disciples at Jesus' ascension reminded them of this promise: "This Jesus, who has been taken up from you into heaven, will come in the same way as you saw him go into heaven."[2] Our conviction, as believers, is that Jesus will come again and take us to a better world. That idea of a future restored world is what separated Old Testament believers from their Canaanite neighbors. For Israel, history was not just an endless natural cycle that repeated itself year after year. It had a goal.

That is still the major division that separates us from those who think this world is all there is. We're not stuck on this brutal world. Then, as now, God's people believe in restoration. Simple. And we will need to remember that simplicity as we turn to some complexities in the world of conservative believers.

Specific questions that divide Adventists

A conviction that is deeply rooted in the souls of devout conservatives is that when God speaks, He gets it right! I believe Adventists need to say with greater clarity that, in the ultimate sense, God does indeed get it right. He will come again. But before He actually comes, we must state more clearly that the events preceding His coming may not follow our timetable and some of the events on our list may not end up on God's list! The two Old Testament stories cited at the beginning of this chapter, the stories of Jonah and King Saul, couldn't be clearer: The Lord can declare a position and then change His mind or "repent," to use KJV language. Nineveh was marked for destruction but then was saved because the people repented. Saul had been appointed king at God's direction but then lost the kingdom. The Lord took it away from him because Saul did not repent—or perhaps we could say more accurately, because he did not re-pent until it was too late.

Can we expect that kind of change in our understanding of events that lead up to the end? The Disappointment experience, when linked with the stories in the Bible, should enable us to say Yes, even if it is not an easy yes. But before we go further, let's spell out some of the questions that Adventists debate when talking about the end:

1. *Sabbath/Sunday.* How will the Sabbath/Sunday conflict play out at the end of time?

2. *Rome.* What will the role of the Church of Rome be in final events?

3. *Protestantism.* What role will apostate Protestantism play in final events?

4. *United States.* What will the role of the United States be in final events?

5. *Islam.* What role does Islam play in final events?

In what follows, I will argue that preserving the traditional Adventist under-standing of the end time, including specifics relating to the questions noted above, is crucial for preserving our understanding of the issues involved in the great controversy. In that sense, I am with the conservatives. But I will also ar-gue that the Disappointment experience opens the way for us to stay current in addressing these issues by allowing us to see other events and other players as current illustrations in the great battle between good and evil. Thus, we can always speak clearly to our age and to our contemporaries, as history moves toward its final climax. I suggest the phrase *applied historicism* as a convenient label for an approach that preserves a both/and approach to final events, a way of preserving a landmark perspective *and* a present truth perspective, to use Adventist jargon.

Liberals are more inclined to recognize the validity of alternate applications simply because the current situation is more visible to their eyes. Conservatives are more likely to defend the traditional. If we force an either/or choice, every-one loses. If we can develop a both/and approach, everyone wins. In short, we need to find ways of preserving both perspectives if we are to be an effective community. In what follows, I hope to show how we can do that.

The delicate task of proving our position

Before we proceed, I want to speak a caution about the use of proofs for faith. The critics out there have often appealed to science, archaeology, and even to the contradictions in Scripture, to "prove" that the Bible could not be the Word of God. In response, we, who are conservatives, have often developed our own "proofs" from science and archaeology and have sought to explain (or explain away) the contradictions in Scripture. I would like to suggest that both sides are off base in important ways.

Speaking as a believer, I want to affirm that my hope is a simple hope. But because it is a hope, it cannot be proven formally—or disproved formally! Nat-urally, I am grateful for every piece of evidence that supports my faith, but both in terms of my relationship to God and my relationships with people, the re-ally important things in life cannot be proven formally. That includes faith, hope, and love. Because faith, hope, and love spring from a relationship to a person, they are even more precious to me. "For in hope we were saved," says the apostle Paul, thus reminding us that formal proof is not an issue. "Hope that is seen is not hope," he declares. "For who hopes for what is seen? But if we hope for what we do not see, we wait for it with patience."[3]

For those of a more rationalist bent, who may find it difficult to believe in the supernatural—perhaps because they have been steeped in a modern scientific world—a line from Kathleen Norris might be helpful. Norris is a literary person who has moved back to faith from a more secular perspective; her husband, David, somewhat hesitantly, has come to faith with her. She quotes him in a chapter entitled "Truth," in her book *Amazing Grace.* Describing him as "an amateur mathematician and part-time computer programmer, passionately committed to that which can be proven by means of reason," she then records his response to a journalist who was pressing him to define his religious beliefs. "He drew himself up," she says, "until he looked a great deal like Lord Tennyson, and declared, 'I am a scientific rationalist who believes in ghosts.' "[4]

It is important to recognize that even very important truths cannot be "proven" in the formal sense. If that feels uneasy, we can remind ourselves that those things that cannot be proven are not easily disproved! I cannot prove my wife's commitment to me, but I know about that commitment in ways that would make it very difficult for anyone or anything to draw us away from each other. Our commitment to each other is one of the most precious things in the world to me. And that is also a model for how I understand my relationship to God.

But now we need to look more specifically at some matters of history, matters that are more important to conservatives than to liberals, though how we deal with them could be crucial in determining whether or not liberals can come on board with the conservatives.

Second Coming: Then and now

In contrast with the liberals "out there" for whom the Second Coming would be mostly a puzzle, conservative Evangelicals fervently believe in the Second Coming (and in hell!), and they think they know exactly what is going to happen at the end of time. The fact that no two of them can readily agree on the details, however, should be an important cautionary note.

But the landscape today doesn't look at all like it did in 1844. A huge shift in beliefs about the Second Coming has swept through Protestantism since then. When William Miller began preaching that Jesus was coming, he became part of a growing (premillennial) movement that was reacting against the popular (postmillennial) view that the world was getting better and better and that Jesus would return to this "improved" world at the end of a thousand years. Miller opposed that optimistic view of history, and we would say he was right. So, even though our 1844 "fathers" and "mothers" were wrong about setting a date, we believe they were reading their Bibles correctly when they announced to the world that things were getting worse and that the world would soon go up in flames at the Second Coming, an event that would take place at the beginning of the thousand years.

The convictions of our Adventist pioneers were rooted in their understanding of the biblical books of Daniel and Revelation. *Historicism,* the technical term for the way Adventists (as well as the Reformers) interpreted these books, recognized that each line of prophecy in the book of Daniel, for example, ended with the Second Coming and restoration. As a list, it looks like this:

Daniel 2	Nebuchadnezzar's vision of the great image—one kingdom follows another until a great stone (the kingdom of God) destroys the human kingdoms represented by the image. The stone grows until it fills the whole earth.
Daniel 7	Four beasts represent four successive kingdoms, but the last one is finally destroyed, and the Son of man receives the kingdom. In the interpretation of the vision, however, the Son of man has become the "Saints of the Most High," an Old Testament pointer to the church as the body of Christ.
Daniel 8; 9	A ram and goat battle each other. The sanctuary is polluted, but is finally cleansed and restored at the end of time.
Daniel 10–12	A great battle in heaven and struggles on earth continue until the end of time when Michael stands up. Then God's people are delivered. The dead are raised— some to eternal life, some to eternal judgment.

In short, each vision takes us through history until God's kingdom is fully established. In all, four panoramic views of history pass before us, each ending in the dramatic restoration of God's kingdom. This approach is called *historicism* because it portrays a grand march through history to the kingdom of God.

But after the Great Disappointment of 1844, the story takes a novel twist. Daniel and Revelation both contain several prophetic time periods.[5] These have been subject to a wide variety of interpretations through the years.[6] But when the longest one, the 2,300 days, came to an end—on October 22, 1844, according to the Adventist understanding—historicism no longer carried the predictive punch it once did. Indeed, all serious Christians who believed in a personal God had to take a long look at their convictions about prophecies of the end time. Those Adventists who believed that God was at work in the 1844 movement took steps toward *conditional historicism,* a position that enables believers to focus less on quantity (charts) and more on the quality of our Christian life and witness and our relationship with Jesus. Those who rejected 1844 moved toward *dispensational futurism,* a position that continues to call for charts of events, but all in the future. Those two options did not become clear immediately, but the die was cast, and much of the common ground disappeared. Let's look more closely at the differences.

Two choices: Conditional historicism or dispensational futurism

According to Whitney R. Cross, a well-known non-Adventist scholar, "All Protestants expected some grand event about 1843, and no critic from the orthodox side took any serious issue on basic principles with Miller's calculations."[7] But all that was before the Disappointment. Understanding what has happened since then is crucial if we are going to be effective in taking the good news of Jesus' return to the world in our day. One of our greatest challenges is that a huge gulf now exists between Adventists and most other conservative Christians who believe in the Second Coming.

While Adventists continue to hold to conditional historicism, dispensational futurism—the Left Behind™ movement[8]—has swept the field as the most popular view of the end times. Like Adventists, these futurists are premillennialists, believing that Jesus will come at the beginning of the thousand years of Revelation 20. But as far as last day events are concerned, these futurists differ dramatically from Adventists and traditional Protestantism in many respects, driven by their futurist conviction that any prophecies and promises to God's people in the Old Testament that were not fulfilled in the Old Testament era, will be fulfilled at the end of time. In short, futurists completely reject the idea of conditional prophecy, that is, the idea that some prophecies are not fulfilled because the conditions were not met. As a result of rejecting the concept of conditional prophecy, dispensational futurists differ dramatically from Adventists in a host of ways, summarized below under three headings:

1. *Secret coming of Jesus (rapture).* Jesus comes secretly (the rapture) seven years before He comes publicly.

2. *Restored Jerusalem temple.* During the seven years between the secret and public comings of Jesus (the seventieth week of Daniel 9), a Roman prince ("the little horn" of Daniel 7 and 8) will arise as antichrist, bringing to an end the sacrifices that are again being offered in a restored Jerusalem temple, built on the site of the Muslim mosque, the Dome of the Rock.

3. *Old Testament practices are resumed during a millennium on this earth.* When Jesus comes publicly at the end of the seven years, He ushers in the thousand years on earth during which all the unfulfilled Old Testament prophecies will be literally fulfilled. Drawing heavily on Isaiah 65 and 66 and Zechariah 14, dispensational futurists believe that during this thousand years there will be childbirth, death, and animal sacrifices; evil will gradually disappear. The New Jerusalem comes to earth at the end of the thousand years. At that point, all evil will be destroyed.

By contrast, Adventists have maintained the traditional Protestant understanding of a public Second Coming at the beginning of the thousand years, just one *public* Second Coming, not a secret one followed by a public one seven years later. But Adventists have taken the almost unique position that the thousand years are spent in heaven. During that time, the earth itself is empty and desolate. At the end of the thousand years, Jesus, God's people, and the New Jerusalem all come to earth for the final judgment and the elimination of evil.

Now a crucial question: if Adventists and dispensational futurists both claim the Bible as God's Word, how can we differ so widely in our understanding of the book? We're not talking here about differences between supernaturalist conservatives who affirm God's personal presence and miraculous activity in the world, and the naturalist liberals who want to overlook the supernatural aspects of Scripture or explain them away. We're talking about two groups of rock-ribbed supernaturalist conservatives, if you please. How did we get so far apart on last day events?

The crucial issue is whether one can actually "see" the conditionalist elements in Scripture. The ability to see conditionalism is a gift that God has given us through the Disappointment experience. Let's look at it more closely.

Conditionalism: The Adventist difference

The clue to the great gulf between futurist dispensationalists and Adventist historicists lies in the qualifying word *conditional,* which Adventists (cautiously) began to add to the word *historicism* when Jesus did not return soon after the Great Disappointment. Thus *conditional historicism* refers to the Adventist conviction that Jesus did not return immediately because His people did not fulfill the conditions necessary for His return. In short, God delayed His return, an idea suggested by a line in the parable of the ten virgins: "The bridegroom was delayed."[9] Adventists believe that human beings play a key role in the unfolding events of the great cosmic conflict between God and Satan. Put bluntly, we make a difference for good or for evil in the great conflict. From such a perspective, even predictions by inspired prophets can be postponed or actually fail because humans do not make the right choices. That is how Adventists explain the shift from literal Israel to spiritual Israel: God's chosen people rejected their Messiah, opening the door to a new people, those who follow Jesus—a kingdom based on choice, not pedigree.

The fact that predictions can turn out otherwise than predicted is already confirmed by the biblical stories of Jonah's preaching to Nineveh and King Saul's loss of the kingdom to David. But dispensational futurists do not make such an application to these stories. And that's where we Adventists part company with them. They reject the idea of conditionalism with reference to God's people Israel. They believe that if God gives promises to His people, those promises must be fulfilled precisely as found in Scripture. God can be trusted not only to know and predict the future but also to bring it to pass. Thus, as far as the Old Testament is concerned, if God gave promises and predictions about Israel that have not been fulfilled—and readers of every theological shape and flavor, both conservatives and liberals, agree that is the case—then, according to dispensational futurists, those promises and predictions must be fulfilled in the future (hence the label, *futurism*).

Perhaps the most startling aspect of that kind of futurism is that it predicts a return to animal sacrifices in a restored Jerusalem temple. These dispensational futurists are devout Christians who believe in the finality of Jesus' sacrifice on the cross. Yet because of their rejection of conditionalism, they are forced to bring everything from the Old Testament into an earthly kingdom after the second coming of Jesus. In this view, instead of moving us toward a perfect world, the Second Coming takes us back to a world that includes animal sacrifices, political conflict, childbirth, and death. All of that lasts for a thousand years. Then the world will be made new.

But all of this begins to point to a very important question: who shapes history—God or human beings? We take up that question next.

Does God shape history or do we?

I know my church well enough to know that even if we might agree in rejecting the futurist approach, not all of us would be enthusiastic about the way I have described the Adventist position above, at least certain features of it. Although I have tried to be honest and evenhanded in describing where the church stands officially, questions of how the human will relates to the divine will defy easy answers. The crucial issue is, Does God shape history or do we? Adventists would love to answer that question simply with a resounding Yes—thus affirming both sides of a paradox that resists a tidy solution. In fact, saying Yes to both sides is basically what we have done as a church. After all, if Scripture affirms both positions, why shouldn't we? It's a simple solution, but a practical one rather than a strictly logical or rational one. It may be as close to the truth as we are able to get. And it is indeed rational to note that Scripture affirms both sides of the question without telling us just how to put them together.

Can we talk further about that? Let's try, and I'll start with a story.

In 1985, at the Springville, Utah, camp meeting—a beautiful Garden of Eden out in the middle of nowhere—I was giving a series of studies on Jeremiah, a book pulsating with conditional elements. I vividly remember the setting at the beginning of day two. It was a gorgeous day; a gentle breeze was rustling the leaves, the sides of the tent were up, and we could hear the birds singing.

"I'd like to start with a summary of what we discussed yesterday," I said. "The first point is that, in some sense, God knows the future."

Immediately, a voice rang out from the back of the tent. "What do you mean, 'in some sense, God knows the future'? God knows the future!"

I started to respond by referring to passages in Jeremiah that we had discussed the day before, but I was interrupted again by the same voice: "I don't care what the Bible says," he said with conviction and a grin, "God knows the future!"

Surprise! I had come face to face with a good Adventist Calvinist!

But now I want to address the two sides of the question from a perspective that I believe will help us understand each other better, indeed, bring us onto common ground. This is only a quick a snapshot; it deserves a whole lot more.

"Let me do it!" (human will) or "Carry me, Daddy!" (divine will)

Human will or divine will? That's the crucial question and the great divide. Many Christians, even very devout ones, would simply shrug and say, "Both, of course. What's the problem?" The problem is that not everyone is able to say "both," at least not with any enthusiasm. Some would argue tenaciously for the priority of the human; others would insist just as tenaciously for the divine. The tussle between the two perspectives has been a huge source of tension throughout history. We'll look at just a small slice of history here so that we can focus on the differences between Adventists and dispensational futurists.

Those who emphasize the human side of the story talk about free will, human freedom, holiness, and human responsibility. In Protestant Christianity, this free will tradition traces its roots to the Dutch theologian Jacobus Arminius (1560–1609) and the Anglican clergyman John Wesley (1703–1791), founder of Methodism. *Arminian* and *Wesleyan* are the labels used to describe this kind of theology. Among Protestants, its primary supporters would be found among the Methodists and Nazarenes. That's Adventism's natural home too.

By contrast, those who emphasize the divine side of the story talk about divine election, divine sovereignty, and divine grace. Total depravity and original sin are also prominent in their vocabulary, ideas that simply go missing in the free will tradition. Among Protestants, this tradition goes back to Martin Luther (1483–1546) and even more to John Calvin (1509–1564). But the great Roman Catholic churchman Augustine of Hippo (354–430) is generally considered the true father of this "grace" tradition. And in Augustine's mind, free will and grace simply did not fit together: "In trying to solve this question," he said, "I made strenuous efforts on behalf of the preservation of the free choice of the human will, but the grace of God defeated me."[10]

Interestingly enough, though Roman Catholics highly revered Augustine, the Catholic tradition, in general, moved in the direction of free will and human responsibility—so much so that it triggered Martin Luther's "by faith alone" rebellion, the Protestant Reformation. Among Protestants, Presbyterians and members of the Christian Reformed Church identify with this Augustinian tradition. Indeed, *Reformed is* the label that distinguishes this emphasis from the Arminian/Wesleyan free will tradition. In America, at least, the term *Evangelical* generally carries a strong Reformed flavor. The popular Christian journal *Christianity Today* is much more Reformed than Arminian.

It must be noted, however, that the free will tradition can also emphasize grace. John Wesley's theology is a good example. But Wesley emphasized the human role so strongly that he and one of his early compatriots, George Whitefield (1714–1770), actually had to part company. Both continued with very effective ministries, but with each going his separate way, Wesley emphasizing the human will, Whitefield the divine.

To give a more earthy flavor to the discussion, I use two quite different phrases that I heard from our two girls when they were growing up. The labels don't really fit anymore now that the girls are grown, but at one point, one was much more inclined to say to her father, "Let me do it!" The other one tended to say, "Carry me, Daddy." Would you believe that those differences are reflected in the world of worship and theology? They are indeed.

Courage, hope, or just plain confusion?

As I was discussing the tension between these two positions with a good friend, I commented that I took courage and hope from the fact that the labels did not appear to be permanent. They could be moved, remodeled, and changed! I'll comment further on that later.

But his response was one of puzzlement. "Why should that give courage and hope?" he asked. "It just sounds like confusion to me!"

So, why do I take courage and hope instead of simply seeing confusion? Because it means that we have a clear mandate to seek ways of shaping the church so that both perspectives can remain strong. The fact that there is a certain fluidity means that many have not yet settled into their natural "home" where they can love God wholeheartedly. Helping people find their "home" is the crucial task facing every parent, teacher, pastor, and, indeed, every believer. Recognizing the diversity in Scripture and in experience means that we dare not zero in on just one answer and try to force everyone into that mold.

In that connection, I must say that based on my own observations, Methodist parents tend to give birth to Calvinist children, and Calvinist parents tend to give birth to Methodist children. But families can also be divided, and communities tend to drift back and forth too. In Moscow, Idaho, for example, a prominent family of ministers has divided along the human will, divine will fault line. As a result, two of the brothers are Reformed ministers while the father and one son have remained free will. Feelings are so strong, in fact, that one of the Reformed brothers has forbidden the members of his church even to talk with the members of his brother's free will church!

The Reformed brother, who decreed the separation between the two churches, has written a book that forcefully presents Reformed theology. The first edition closes with a poem that reveals the deep sense of horror that rushes into a Reformed believer's soul when free will people start to question God. Questions that seem quite innocent to free will people easily sound blasphemous to the conscientious Reformed believer. The last two lines of the poem are revealing:

> So hold your peace, rebellious pot,
> The Lord is God—and you are not.[11]

The fluidity of the two traditions, however, is revealed in more subtle ways. At major conventions, for example, I have heard mutterings from professors on both sides of the divide, complaining about the drift from Reformed to Arminian theology on the one hand, or from Arminian to Reformed theology on the other. And several years ago at a seminar I was holding at a United Methodist Church in Florida, I asked for a show of hands in response to my question, "How many of you have family, friends, or acquaintances who at one time were in the free will tradition but who have moved to the Reformed tradition?" In that group of some forty-five believers, virtually every hand went up.

When I discuss the subject, I make a serious effort to use neutral language as much as possible. That makes it easier for us to fill in the spectrum between the two extremes. On the divine side, for example, *predestinarian Calvinist* is too narrow a term. It's too easy for free will people (the starting point for most Adventists) to dismiss predestination out of hand and not even think about it anymore. It's just too troubling for them, even though the Bible—especially the apostle Paul—uses that language without hesitation.[12] One devout Adventist, for example, obviously a free will supporter, even went into print with the line "The Satanic God of Calvinism."[13] That's strong language to use for a Reformer who merited several pages of laudatory comments in Ellen White's *The Great Controversy*![14]

If we explore the full spectrum of beliefs on the issue, we will discover that some will emphasize the sovereignty of God and divine foreknowledge while avoiding or even rejecting the idea of predestination. But as one moves deeper into free will territory, the idea of divine foreknowledge comes under fire. The "openness of God" theology is an attempt to address that issue by claiming that God knows everything that can be known, but chooses not to know our moral decisions lest such knowledge compromise our freedom to choose.[15] That's a departure from the more traditional position that God knows everything.

Even with qualifications, however, openness theology is likely to horrify true believers in Reformed theology. They quite rightly sense that if one keeps moving far enough toward the free will side, God simply disappears, leaving only the human. The so-called slippery slope will do its deadly work, and belief in God disappears. The result is pure secularism.

One last comment about the labels before we focus again on eschatology:

churches, like their seminaries, can shift their theologies. Several years ago when I was teaching a class in modern denominations, a Presbyterian pastor whom I invited to visit the class sounded almost like an Adventist, even though he was from the Reformed tradition. He certainly was much closer to Adventism than was the pastor from the United Methodist Church, who told the class that "God is not a person, and heaven is not a place." The students were so startled they hardly knew where to begin with their questions.

Finally, one of them asked, "Then, where is God?"

"We swim in God," said the pastor, a reply that would have astonished John Wesley, the founder of Methodism, fully as much as it did us. Clearly the free will tradition had led this particular pastor far afield.

Now what is so tantalizing in this whole discussion is that the Bible gives us wonderful fodder to support both sides. Not surprisingly, however, one side grabs the texts supporting free will, while the other side grabs the texts supporting the priority of the divine will. And both sides find it easy to ignore or reinterpret the other set of passages. So the arguments continue to boil, with neither side actually hearing the other, and neither side taking seriously *all* of Scripture.

What I find to be even more intriguing and challenging are the implications of the generational shift that I noted above: the switch from Methodist to Calvinist and back to Methodist. Those who love both their church and their children are eager for their children to share their deepest hopes and fears. But in an individualist culture like our own, if a church cannot satisfy the spiritual needs of the children, they will be tempted to go in search of one that does.

To spell that out, if children of a free will bent find themselves in a church that doesn't give enough emphasis to human freedom, they could easily be tempted to find a church that stresses the importance of human initiative and freedom.

Similarly, if children who are longing for a clearer sense of divine direction find themselves in a church that stresses human initiative and freedom, they could easily be tempted to find a church that emphasizes divine sovereignty.

I believe Adventism has a wonderful opportunity to meet the needs of both sides. But because the love of human freedom is so deeply rooted in the Adventist soul, we don't always do a very good job of meeting the needs of those who long for a stronger sense of divine direction in their lives. And I am convinced that such an impulse lurks in the hearts of millions of Adventists. I think we can do better.

But now we must turn to some aspects of Adventist history that may help us understand ourselves as well as our futurist friends, and ultimately, help us take all the Bible seriously—not just the texts we happen to like.

The fruit-basket-upset principle

The crucial factor that ultimately opened the eyes of Adventists to the possibility of conditionalism was the Great Disappointment. It was a fruit-basket-upset experience, as a friend pointed out, one that forced us to look more closely at each piece of fruit as we put it back into our basket.

Initially, the Great Disappointment felt like a horrible disgrace and a disaster. But with the passage of time, it became clear that several blessings had come from the experience, a confirmation of Romans 8:28 that God is at work in all things. In particular, I am referring to the intriguing role of what sociologists call "social support," the powerful effect that the people around us have in helping us believe or disbelieve. Social support is a two-edged sword that can cut either way, reinforcing truth or reinforcing error. One sociologist noted rather wryly, "Much of what we consider reasonable is largely the consensus of the people around us." As uncomfortable as that may sound and feel, there is evidence that seems to point in that direction.

In that connection, I like C. S. Lewis's candid admission of vulnerability. Arguing that difficulties with faith may have little to do with intellect and reason, Lewis asks, "How many of the freshmen who come up to Oxford from religious homes and lose their Christianity in the first year have been honestly *argued* out of it? How many of our own sudden temporary losses of faith have a rational basis which would stand examination for a moment?" He goes on to admit that "mere change of scene" tends to "decrease" his faith, at least at first. "God is less credible when I pray in a hotel bedroom than when I am in College. The society of unbelievers makes Faith harder even when they are people whose opinions, on any other subject, are known to be worthless."[16]

Does that same process work on the positive side? Of course, and here we have the testimony of Scripture. The Epistle to the Hebrews admonishes us to "hold fast to the confession of our hope without wavering, for he who has promised is faithful." But hope doesn't just depend on God, argues the inspired author. We have a work to do for each other: "Let us consider how to provoke one another to love and good deeds, not neglecting to meet together as is the habit of some, but encouraging one another and all the more as you see the Day approaching."[17]

Precisely in connection with the Second Coming, I heard a fascinating illustration of how social support made it possible to believe a doctrine that otherwise had seemed impossible. In November 1991, I heard Eta Linnemann tell the powerful story of how she emerged from the thorough-going rationalism of her German university experience into a living personal faith.[18] For her, the key turning point was coming to the conviction that Jesus was not simply a wandering Palestinian prophet, but was, in fact, her Lord and Savior. Every week, she was meeting with a community of devout Christians who had surrounded her in love and were helping her to grow in faith.

When former students heard of her conversion, one of their first questions was, "And do you believe He is coming again?" "Not yet," she had to tell them. She then told us, her audience, that it took several more weeks of meeting with the believers before the doctrine of the Second Coming actually became believable for her.[19]

Often a fruit-basket-upset experience can clear the way for new insights. When we are securely and comfortably rooted in a traditional environment, the Spirit cannot so easily impress us with anything new and dramatic. But when someone or something upsets our fruit basket, we can see all kinds of things we didn't even know existed before.

In Eta Linnemann's case, the fruit basket upset was triggered by a personal crisis. New converts to any community are most likely to come from people who are in transition or who have been in turmoil. In the early years of Adventism, the fruit-basket-upset experience of the Disappointment led to the establishing of the landmarks that are still so essential to Adventist identity. The little flock who came through that experience still believing that God had been at work in those events, were cut off from nonbelieving family members; they were mocked and derided by their detractors. It was no fun at all. But what that painful experience did was to open a window of opportunity for them so that they could take a fresh look at every aspect of their faith. As they grew and discovered things together, they reinforced each other's faith along the way.

Thus, during those difficult months following the Disappointment, our pioneers met together for prayer and serious Bible study. In the late 1840s, these "Sabbath conferences," as they came to be known, brought the believers together in homes, barns, and upper rooms, as they hammered out our essential beliefs. That's when they came to clarity on the mortality of the soul, the seventh-day Sabbath, and the heavenly sanctuary—beliefs that were quite different from anything they had grown up with. The chaos of the Disappointment had opened their minds to new beliefs. They saw Scripture with new eyes, eyes that could now begin to see the implications of conditionalism as it related to the end of time.

And now, prophecy: Moving toward applied historicism

The next step in this process involved the Adventist understanding of prophecy. They had been so sure that Jesus would come again in 1844. How could they explain the delay when the prophecies seemed so very clear? Had God let them down? The most pointed explanation came from the pen of Ellen White in 1883 when she decided to respond to critics who were mocking Adventists for their continuing faith and hope. "The angels of God in their messages to men represent time as very short," she wrote. "Thus it has always been presented to me. It is true that time has continued longer than we expected in the early days of this message. Our Saviour did not appear as soon as we hoped. But has the word of the Lord failed? Never! It should be remembered that the promises and the threatenings of God are alike conditional."[20]

And so it was that the idea of conditionality began to make its way into Adventist thinking. The book of Jonah illustrates this phenomenon in God's gracious response to the repentant sinners of Nineveh. The KJV bluntly describes the events like this: "God saw their works, that they turned from their evil way; and God repented of the evil, that he had said that he would do unto them; and he did it not."[21] Instead of "repented," the NRSV says God "changed his mind."

How does that square with God's response to Samuel when Saul disobeyed God's command to destroy the Amalekites? Again, from the KJV: "The Strength of Israel will not lie nor repent: for he is not a man, that he should repent."[22] The key phrase is "he is not a man." In other words, God does not repent like a man because a man repents because he finally admits that he has done wrong. Interestingly enough, just a few short lines after the declaration that the Strength of

Israel does not repent, Scripture records the statement noted at the beginning of this chapter: "The LORD repented that he had made Saul king over Israel."[23]

A solution to the puzzle of divine repentance can perhaps be glimpsed in the fact that throughout Scripture God consistently responds graciously to repentant sinners. Thus He "repents," if we use the language of Jonah. Indeed, Jonah admits that the reason he ran away in the first place was that he knew that God would forgive the people of Nineveh if they repented. Though he doesn't say so directly, Jonah seems to have been worried about his prophetic reputation. Apparently he didn't realize that from God's perspective, a failed prediction could mean a successful prophecy!

In any event, Jonah did his job well. And he seems to have been the only one to worry about possible negative fallout from his effective preaching. At least the Bible itself records no complaints or mockery from the people of Nineveh.

But the story of Jonah is troubling for predestinarians. Indeed, they have a hard time with all those passages in the Old Testament that speak of God's repentance. And it doesn't help when modern translations, such as the NRSV, say God "changed his mind." Seven times the Old Testament affirms that God does *not* repent.[24] Yet God still repents! In fact, if we simply look at the word *repent* and its close cognates in the Old Testament, based on usage in the KJV, God repents three times more often than all the other "repenters" put together. The actual score is twenty-eight to nine![25]

In the New Testament, not only is repentance much more popular—*repent,* or a related word, appears sixty-four times—but the people also do far more repenting than does God. Only once does the New Testament refer to God's repentance, and that is a quotation from the Old Testament.[26] Thus, in the "contest" over repentance, God wins in the Old Testament by a score of twenty-eight to nine. In the New Testament, the people win by a score of sixty-three to one. We're just playing with words, of course. Modern translations have found other ways of communicating the idea, especially with reference to God, but also with reference to human beings.

But is there common ground between us and our futurist friends? Most likely, we could all agree that God forgives sinners who repent. That's what both Testaments affirm. And that is really the bottom line in the book of Jonah. The challenge for predestinarians is to see how God (apparently) tries every possible method to lead sinners to repentance. How could the great God of the universe experiment? Doesn't He know what will work?

Scripture would answer with a resounding yes! Of course God knows what will work. But at the same time, it reveals a God who tries every possible method to draw sinners back to Him, to repentance and salvation. For Adventists, the great fruit basket upset of the Disappointment pushed us in the direction of accepting the principle of conditionality. And we gradually began to realize that divine foreknowledge does not mean a fixed plan. Thus, we are able to look at Old Testament passages and recognize that some of the features of the end time may not happen in just the way the prophets described them.

Scripture affirms that God knows our hearts: "You discern my thoughts from far away," declares the psalmist. "And are acquainted with all my ways. / Even before a word is on [his] tongue," exclaims the psalmist, "O LORD, you know it completely."[27] But Scripture also affirms that God will try every possible method as if He did not know what would work. Amos chapter 4, for example, ticks off a long list of methods (most of them disasters) by which God tried—unsuccessfully, we could note—to win the hearts of His people.

Jeremiah is another Old Testament book that paradoxically throbs with examples of conditionality, yet opens with the affirmation that God knew Jeremiah while he was still in the womb.[28]

But now let's put the shoe on the other foot for a moment. We may chide our dispensationalist friends for not looking seriously at the texts that teach the Sabbath and the mortality of the soul. We may even chide them for avoiding those passages in which God is said to repent. But let me be blunt: dispensational futurists have dealt much more seriously with some Old Testament eschatological passages than we have. For example, Isaiah chapters 65 and 66 point to a new world in which people die. But only old people die in that new world, not the young. Zechariah 14 is another important chapter, one that suggests a gradual elimination of evil rather than a clean break. An excellent article in volume 4 of *The Seventh-day Adventist Bible Commentary* takes those passages very seriously. But I find that very few Adventists have paid much attention to it, either among pastors or the laity.[29] It's time to look more closely at the principles laid down in that article. Perhaps the idea of applied historicism can help bring the pieces together.

Applied historicism

If we take *all* the Bible seriously, it will point us to the kinds of answers we need in order to be faithful to our heritage, to Scripture, and to our mission. I do not believe that we should abandon historicism, even if virtually everyone else has. Historicism is too clearly taught in the book of Daniel for us to choose any other alternative. But if we can add the word *applied* to *historicism,* we come very close to a simple approach already used in the Bible. Indeed, it is present everywhere in the book of Revelation. Instead of crying, "Rome!" the Bible says, "Babylon!" The application works because everyone back then knew the beastly characteristics that had made Babylon the symbol for everything evil. Thus believers could say "Babylon" but know that it meant "Rome"!

In applied historicism, then, the key players in the historicist drama become symbols for similar behavior elsewhere. With such an approach, we can ask a question that vexes many Adventists these days: where is Islam in biblical prophecy?

Nowhere and everywhere. Scripture appears to be silent about Islam. But wasn't it also silent about ancient Rome? Are we then left speechless? Not at all. If any kingdom, any power, any church, or even any believer, behaves like the beast, we can apply the principles that are so clearly illustrated in Scripture by the historical entities to which the books of Daniel and Revelation point.

But in making the application, we should be very careful not simply to label a particular institution, nation, or church as evil and beastly as if it were evil in some kind of pure sense. We may be thoroughly opposed to the principles on which a particular system functions, but that does not mean that everyone within the system shares the evil characteristics of the system itself. That is true of Catholicism, Islam, Protestantism, even secularism. There are precious people in each of those "isms."

When James and John, for example, asked Jesus for the two highest positions in His kingdom, they obviously assumed that Jesus operated on hierarchical principles. Not so, said Jesus. The Gentiles use authority in that way. But in My kingdom, serving—not ruling—is the key idea. That is clearly demonstrated in the fact that "the Son of Man came not to be served but to serve, and to give his life a ransom for many."[30] Jesus' response strikes right at the heart of hierarchical forms of church governance. That is our fundamental objection to

Roman Catholicism. But within the Catholic community are many beautiful Christians. Within every community, there are beautiful people. We must not attack their institutions, their nations, or their religions in such a way as to drive them away from the truth. In the words of Ellen White, we should not accost others "in a very abrupt manner, and make the truth . . . repulsive to them."[31]

Jesus had strong words for the leaders of His day, yet Nicodemus and Joseph of Arimathea were part of the group that He criticized so strongly. Jesus chose twelve disciples, yet Judas was among them. It may very well be that when we set out to hunt down the beast, we should play closer attention to Jesus' parable of the wheat and the tares. At some points, it is very difficult to tell them apart. But even when the tares are fully evident, pulling them out could destroy the wheat too. "Let both of them grow together until the harvest,"[32] the master says in Jesus' parable.

While we are waiting for the harvest, we should bend every effort to present a positive message, even when we are dealing with unhappy themes and evil people. Ellen White's counsel to A. T. Jones is worth remembering, indeed, worth memorizing: "The Lord wants His people to follow other methods than that of condemning wrong," she wrote, "even though the condemnation be just. He wants us to do something more than to hurl at our adversaries charges that only drive them further from the truth."[33]

Applied historicism: Bringing liberals and conservatives together

Let's be extraordinarily honest now, as to how applied historicism could bring Adventists together on eschatology.

The conservatives know their last-day events. Everything is spelled out in *The Great Controversy.* But they worry that Islam doesn't seem to be present in biblical prophecy, and they worry about Sunday legislation in two ways. First, in the sense that a time of trouble will, in fact, be a time of high stress. None of us would choose voluntarily to go through difficult times. But second, they worry that at a practical level, almost no one pays any attention to Sunday anymore. It has simply become a day for work, shopping, and recreation. After dark, the haunting worry might be that if the Sunday law doesn't come as predicted, then prophecy gets a black eye and God's reputation suffers. What can we trust anymore if we can't trust Bible prophecy?

Understanding conditional prophecy is the best way to address those worries. There is a little bit of Jonah in us all. We want things to stay put. We want prophecies to be fulfilled to the letter. We need to recognize, however, that reading the Bible from the perspective of conditionalism won't make much sense unless you immerse yourself in the Bible *after* you have become convinced of the *possibility* of conditionalism. There is an unhappy little proverb that all of us need to hear, "If I hadn't believed it, I never would have seen it with my own eyes." Ouch! True. But ouch!

While speaking of conservatives, let me add a worry of my own, namely, that Adventist conservatives may not be worrying enough about the "beastly" attitudes reflected in conservative Protestantism. Southern Baptists, for example, our former allies in the battle for religious liberty, have jumped ship and now want to legislate religion and morality in America. They intend to use the ballot box to gain the majority and then force the country to be holy and to be good. We are with these devout people on many aspects of morality. But we should wholeheartedly oppose their view of how authority should be used in the name of God.

Applied historicism works wonderfully here. Sunday legislation may not be obvious on the horizon. It could return, of course, but whether or not it does, the "beastly" attitudes toward authority that Adventists have said would move us toward an enforced Sunday law are everywhere to be seen today. We have reason to be concerned—and to be vocal about our concern!

Now, let's talk about the liberals. Their great danger is that they shrug too easily. They are more in touch with the world than conservatives and will be more deeply affected by secularist impulses. In many cases, they are almost biblically illiterate, never having learned how to build bridges from an ancient sacred Text, the Bible, to a modern world. Conservatives read their Bibles. They may be highly selective in the way they read, but they do read their Bibles. But the hidden fundamentalism among the liberals is revealed in their tendency to ignore the Bible once it is shown to be adapted rather than absolute. Liberals, both out there and within, are most likely to be excited about the Bible when reading it as literature. That's not wrong. But it is not the same as reading the Bible as God's Word.

Liberals need to be aware that the tendency to keep the traditional pieces in place has great value. None of us can read the future. Yet we know from Scripture and history that attitudes toward force and authority tend to be cyclic. Just how those attitudes will manifest themselves in the future no one knows. But keeping all the pieces of the puzzle together will ensure that we preserve what is most important. Conservatives help do that for us. Our dispensational futurist friends keep all the pieces in a way that is very troubling. But they do keep the pieces, including some that we need to look at more carefully from the standpoint of conditionalism. We don't want to throw out the book of Zechariah any more than we want to throw away *The Great Controversy.* All the details in both sources can give us a clearer understanding of how God has dealt with human beings in the past. That is very important as we seek to understand how He will deal with us today.

I have one more concern. It may be the most crucial one of all, and it involves evangelism. The vast majority of people in our world assume that when God speaks, that word applies to all people at all times. In such a view, if God predicted something, it must come to pass. And that is where conditionalism is potentially dangerous. While it is thoroughly biblical and very practical in the end, it can lead to the collapse of faith if not handled with a great deal of care. That's why I believe it is so important for us to keep the solid foundation of historicism in place. Historicism has been a marvelous gift of God to His people. We are on the threshold of the kingdom and don't know when or how the final moments will take place. But holding firm to our historicist heritage can keep us pointed in the right direction. What we have said about Rome, Protestantism, and the United States in prophecy may or may not take place in exactly the way that we have envisioned it. But the story of those great powers illustrates the forces that are at work in the great conflict between good and evil. Understanding those forces is very important for us today.

From a practical point of view, however, whether or not we know exactly what is going to happen should make no difference in our daily lives. Indeed, we should listen more carefully to the words of the angels to the disciples when they expressed their curiosity about the end of time: "It is not for you," the angels told them, "to know the times or periods that the Father has set by his own authority."[34]

Similarly, Paul had good words of counsel to the Thessalonian believers, words that we need to hear today. In his first letter to them, after describing the events connected with the Second Coming, he gives this practical counsel: "I don't need to write you about the time or date when all this will happen. You surely know that the Lord's return will be as a thief coming at night. People will think they are safe and secure. But destruction will suddenly strike them like the pains of a woman about to give birth. And they won't escape."[35]

As helpful as historicism is to God's people, it does tempt us to forget that most important teaching of the New Testament, namely, that the Second Coming will be a surprise. It will be a surprise for everyone, for those who are ready and for those who are not. If we are right with the Lord, it will be a happy surprise. If we are not, it will be the kind of surprise that is no fun at all. Our goal must always be to make sure that as many of God's children as possible will be ready for a happy surprise when the Lord comes.

Finally, let me emphasize the clarity with which Scripture speaks about the end of time. Even in the Old Testament where the idea of a full restoration from the effects of sin does not seem to have been completely present, the idea of a future, restored world is still very clear. And that unerring focus on future restoration is the crucial difference between the religion of Israel and that of her Canaanite neighbors. Theirs was a fertility religion that wasn't going anywhere. Israel looked forward to a new heaven and a new earth. They did not see with the same clarity that we can see in the light of the New Testament. But they still lived in hope.

Today, the contrast is equally sharp. Adventists accept the clear biblical teaching that Jesus is coming again to usher in a new age. His return is the goal of history, the blessed hope for which we have so earnestly longed.

It would be wonderful if Adventists could get serious about Bible study again, liberals and conservatives together, using their respective strengths to shore up each others' weaknesses. It would help us discover those things that really matter, and it would bond us together just as our pioneers were bonded to each other in the Sabbath conferences of the 1840s. That would be good. Very good.

---

1. John 14:1–3, personal paraphrase.

2. Acts 1:11.

3. Romans 8:24, 25.

4. Norris, *Amazing Grace,* 375.

5. In Daniel, for example, one time, two times, and a half (7:25; 12:7); 2,300 days (8:14); 1,290 days (12:11); 1,335 days (12:12). In Revelation, 42 months (11:2; 13:5); 1,260 days (11:3;12:6); time, times, and half a time (12:14).

6. For a history of the interpretation of Daniel, see Francis D. Nichol et al., *The Seventh-day Adventist Bible Commentary,* vol. 4 (Washington, D.C.: Review and Herald®, 1955), 39–78; for a history of the interpretation of Revelation (the Apocalypse), see *The Seventh-day Adventist Bible Commentary,* vol. 7 (Washington, D.C.: Review and Herald®, 1957), 103–132.

7. Whitney R. Cross, *The Burned-Over District: The Social and Intellectual History of Enthusiastic Religion in Western New York, 1800-1850* (New York: Harper & Row, 1965), 321, quoted in Rolf Pöhler, *Continuity and Change,* 23.

8. Popularized through a phenomenally successful series of Left Behind™ novels and a movie by the same name. (Trademark owned by Tyndale House Publishers, Wheaton, Ill.)

9. Matthew 25:5.

10. *Retractationes* ii.1 (addressed to Simplicianus of Milan), quoted in Henry Chadwick, *Augustine* (New York: Oxford University Press, 1986), 117.

11. Douglas Wilson, *Easy Chairs, Hard Words: Conversations on the Liberty of God* (n.p.: Oakcross Publications, 1991), 189. The poem is omitted from a second edition that carries the same 1991 copyright date but is published by Canon Press, PO Box 8741, Moscow, Idaho 83848.

12. E.g., Romans 8:29, 30. Most of Romans 9–11 reflects Paul's struggles to bring the ideas of free choice and God's election into some kind of harmony.

13. Ralph Larson, *The Hellish Torch,* published privately (1998), 6. Larson, a conservative Adventist perfectionist, declares that Calvinism sees God as "arbitrary, cruel, unforgiving, tyrannical."

14. White, *The Great Controversy,* the chapter titled "The French Reformation," especially 219–221, 233–236.

15. Richard Rice is an Adventist author who has contributed significantly to the debate. See his *The Openness of God: The Relationship of Divine Foreknowledge and Human Free Will* (Washington, D.C.: Review and Herald®, 1980); reissued as *God's Foreknowledge and Man's Free Will* (Minneapolis, Minn.: Bethany House, 1985). See also Clark Pinnock et al., *The Openness of God: A Biblical Challenge to the Traditional Understanding of God* (Downers Grove, Ill.: InterVarsity Press, 1994).

16. C. S. Lewis, "Religion: Reality or Substitute?" in *Christian Reflections* (Grand Rapids, Mich.: Eerdmans, 1967), 42.

17. Hebrews 10:23–25.

18. Eta Linnemann told her story at the November 1991 meetings of the Adventist Theological Society in Kansas City, Missouri.

19. Relevant observations on Linnemann's experience are found in the early pages of her *Historical Criticism of the Bible: Methodology or Ideology? Reflections of a Bultmannian Turned Evangelical,* trans. Robert W. Yarbrough (Grand Rapids, Mich.: Baker, 1990), 7–20.

20. White, *Selected Messages,* 1:67.

21. Jonah 3:10.

22. 1 Samuel 15:29.

23. 1 Samuel 15:35, KJV.

24. Numbers 23:19; 1 Samuel 15:29 (two times); Psalm 110:4; Jeremiah 4:28; 20:16 (see KJV); Ezekiel 24:14.

25. According to *Strong's Exhaustive Concordance of the Bible,* the word *repent* or one of its cognates and derivatives appears a total of forty-four times in the Old Testament. Only nine of those speak of human repentance; all the rest refer to God. Of the thirty-five times that the word refers to God, seven are instances in which God does not repent, generally said with emphasis. That still leaves twenty-eight passages in which God does repent.

26. Hebrews 7:21, quoting Psalm 110:4, one of the Old Testament passages affirming that God does not repent.

27. Psalm 139:2–4.

28. Jeremiah 1:5.

29. "The Role of Israel in Old Testament Prophecy," in *The Seventh-day Adventist Bible Commentary,* 4:25–38.

30. Matthew 20:28.

31. White, *Testimonies for the Church,* 4:68.

32. Matthew 13: 30.

33. White, *Testimonies for the Church,* 6:121.

34. Acts 1:7.

35. 1 Thessalonians 5:1–3, CEV.

Part 6

Crucial Issues in Adventism

The five chapters in part 6 address issues of theological diversity in Adventism. They are all closely linked. The first one brings a historical perspective to a crucial tension within Adventism, the tension between landmarks, the unchanging that never moves, and the present truth, the cutting edge that is always changing.

The topics covered here deserve a great deal of exploration, study, and dialogue. They are topics over which we have quarreled. If we can learn to cooperate instead of quarrel, the church will be greatly strengthened.

Chapter 19

Landmarks and Present Truth

Landmarks. Ellen White says, "The passing of the time in 1844 was a period of great events, opening to our astonished eyes the cleansing of the sanctuary transpiring in heaven, and having decided relation to God's people upon the earth, [also] the first and second angels' messages and the third, unfurling the banner on which was inscribed, 'The commandments of God and the faith of Jesus.' One of the landmarks under this message was the temple of God, seen by His truth-loving people in heaven, and the ark containing the law of God. The light of the Sabbath of the fourth commandment flashed its strong rays in the pathway of the transgressors of God's law. The nonimmortality of the wicked is an old landmark. I can call to mind nothing more that can come under the head of the old landmarks."[1]

Present Truth. Ellen White says, "The message 'Go forward' is still to be heard and respected. The varying circumstances taking place in our world call for labor which will meet these peculiar developments. The Lord has need of men who are spiritually sharp and clear-sighted, men worked by the Holy Spirit, who are certainly receiving manna fresh from heaven.

Upon the minds of such, God's Word flashes light, revealing to them more than ever before the safe path. The Holy Spirit works upon mind and heart. The time has come when through God's messengers the scroll is being unrolled to the world. Instructors in our schools should never be bound about by being told that they are to teach only what has been taught hitherto. Away with these restrictions. There is a God to give the message His people shall speak. Let not any minister feel under bonds or be gauged by men's measurement. The gospel must be fulfilled in accordance with the messages God sends. That which God gives His servants to speak today would not perhaps have been present truth twenty years ago, but it is God's message for this time."[2]

In the 1990s, when I discovered how many Adventists were gripped by the KJV-only mind-set, I began listening very hard to try to find out why. After all, New Testament writers were very free in their use of Old Testament translations. Ellen White began using the Revised Version almost as soon as it appeared, and Adventists have contributed significantly to the literature dealing with modern translations. Why, then, are so many Adventists afraid of modern translations?

I decided that a key factor was simply a variant of all-or-nothing thinking— the slippery slope. The fear is that if a key passage of Scripture goes missing, everything seems to be at risk. If that kind of thinking affects either you or those close to you, I would urge you to go back and re-read the first three chapters of this book—"Anchor 1: The Landmarks," "Anchor 2: The Law of Love," and "Anchor 3: Jesus." It is also very helpful to associate with believers who are not afflicted with the same fears. Hebrews speaks a powerful truth when it says that we should not be "neglecting to meet together, as is the habit of some, but encouraging one another."[3]

In this chapter I want to explore the meaning of landmarks and the present truth in the context of the 1888 crisis, a time when the Adventist Church was in turmoil. Many were haunted by fears that our landmarks were at risk. Ellen

White had much to say at that time. Her very practical comments can provide stability for us.

To gain perspective, we need to go back to James White's response to a Seventh Day Baptist in 1853. Noting that Adventists held "different views on some subjects," White declared that we were united on the "mighty platform" of the Sabbath. He summed up the "great subjects" that united us as the Second Advent, the commandments of God, and the faith of Jesus.[4]

The same simplicity marked the covenant that bound Adventists together in the 1860s, when we organized formally as a church: "We, the undersigned, hereby associate ourselves together, as a church, taking the name, Seventh-day Adventists, covenanting to keep the commandments of God, and the faith of Jesus Christ."[5]

By the 1880s, however, leading brethren had slipped into an all-or-nothing view that turned everything into a landmark and made differences of opinion almost impossible. The General Conference president, G. I. Butler, for example, said that Adventists had "never taken a stand upon Bible exegesis [interpretation] which they have been compelled to surrender."[6]

Was he right? Shouldn't we Adventists know what we believe and stick by it?

Only if we hold to the landmarks themselves—not to all the arguments we have used to support them. And that was Butler's problem, for he was debating with Jones and Waggoner over the meaning of *law* (the "schoolmaster," verse 25, KJV) in Galatians 3. Resisting their view that this passage was referring to the moral law of the Ten Commandments, Butler was calling the traditional view—that the law in Galatians 3 was the ceremonial law—a landmark. Interestingly enough, by 1896, Ellen White had concluded that the term in Galatians 3 referred to both the moral *and* the ceremonial laws, but "especially" to the moral law.[7]

At the 1888 General Conference Session itself, where the issue was bitterly debated, Ellen White expressed alarm when a brother exclaimed, "If our views of Galatians are not correct, then we have not the third angel's message, and our position goes by the board; there is nothing to our faith."

"Not true," she said, calling the statement "extravagant, exaggerated."[8] She herself felt so secure with the landmarks that she could actually question Waggoner's interpretations of Scripture while affirming his right to "honestly" hold "some views of Scripture differing" from hers or those of the leading brethren.[9]

In 1892, Ellen White stated her position even more clearly, arguing that "the unity of the church" did not consist "in viewing every text of Scripture in the very same light."[10] The basis for unity is love for God and love for each other. In short, the landmarks are a small cluster of beliefs connected with the three angels' messages (sanctuary, commandments, faith of Jesus), plus the mortality of the soul.[11]

I believe we need to return to the simplicity of historic Adventism, a simplicity that preserves the central landmarks but allows for "different views on some subjects," as James White put it. Rooted in the "commandments of God and the faith of Jesus," we can be secure and free instead of frightened.

To help us find our way back to our heritage, let me describe how I think we got away from it. It has to do with the Sabbath. Waving the banner "not under law, but under grace," the Reformers unintentionally began to loosen the binding claims of the Decalogue and the Sabbath. Eventually, some abandoned law completely. Dispensationalists, for example, apply law only to the Old Testament past and the millennial future.

But with the Decalogue gone, Protestant believers discovered they had no sure anchor when critics attacked the Bible in the name of science. So, in the early twentieth century, many believers took refuge in the psychological all-or-nothing arguments of fundamentalism, claiming precise scientific accuracy for every word in the Bible, instead of recognizing the Bible's practical value in a wide variety of circumstances. Vivid rhetoric ("One error, and you can toss the whole Bible out!") even made Bible study frightening. Such all-or-nothing thinking can be a special burden for Adventists, because the writings of Ellen White generally are included in the "all."

But today is our day of opportunity as more and more Protestants sense that the Bible is a Book about life and that grace does not silence God's law. So let's leave the dangerous all-or-nothing thinking to others and reclaim our Adventist advantage. Indeed, "the Sabbath is a mighty platform on which we can all stand united." The solid foundation of the Decalogue, the law of love and liberty, gives us the security we need so that we can get on with the business of loving God and each other while we await His return. That will make it safe to rediscover the Bible and use different versions—maybe even hold "different views" on some things!

In 1888, when frightened Adventists expressed alarm at the possible loss of the landmarks, Ellen White was blunt. "There was much talk about standing by the old landmarks," she wrote. "But there was evidence they knew not what the old landmarks were." Some had actually "sealed" their minds "against the entrance of light, because they had decided it was a dangerous error removing the 'old landmarks' when it was not moving a peg of the old landmarks." They simply had "perverted ideas of what constituted the old landmarks."[12]

If one is secure in the *real* landmarks, then one can afford to be excited about "present truth," the phrase our pioneers used to refer to fresh, cutting-edge applications of truth.

The exciting possibilities of present truth can be glimpsed in the Ellen White quotation cited at the beginning of this chapter, even though the quotation comes in the form of a rebuke to G. I. Butler, then General Conference president. Butler could not attend the 1888 General Conference Session because of illness, but he remained involved, sending a telegram that urged the delegates to "stand by the landmarks."[13]

That's when Ellen White rose to the occasion. "The time has come when through God's messengers the scroll is being unrolled to the world," she exclaimed. Then, referring to the attempt by some to prohibit teachers from teaching anything new—an action targeting A. T. Jones, who was under appointment to go as a teacher to Battle Creek College—she continued, "Instructors in our schools should never be bound about by being told that they are to teach only what has been taught hitherto. Away with these restrictions."

A final line in that paragraph is one that should forever keep Adventism alive if we will but listen: "That which God gives His servants to speak today would not perhaps have been present truth twenty years ago, but it is God's message for this time."[14]

Summary

"Landmarks" and "Present Truth" will always stand in a creative tension in the church. Conservatives love "Landmarks"; liberals love "Present Truth." By God's grace we can keep the church strong by nurturing both.

1. White, *Counsels to Writers and Editors,* 30, 31.

2. White, *The Ellen G. White 1888 Materials,* 1:133.

3. Hebrews 10:25.

4. James White, "Resolution of the Seventh-day Baptist Central Association," *Review and Herald,* August 11, 1853. Cited in "Doctrinal Statements, Seventh-day Adventist," in *SDA Encyclopedia* (1996), 464.

5. Original church covenant used to organize Adventist churches when organization first began to happen in 1861. Published in "Doings of the Battle Creek Conference, Oct. 5& 6, 1861," *Review and Herald,* October 8, 1861. See "Covenant, Church," in *SDA Encyclopedia* (1996), 416.

6. Quoted in Knight, *Angry Saints,* 15.

7. Ellen White, *Selected Messages,* 1:234.

8. Ellen White, *The Ellen G. White 1888 Materials,* 1:220.

9. Ellen White, *The Ellen G. White 1888 Materials,* 1:164.

10. Ellen White, *The Ellen G. White 1888 Materials,* 3:1092, 1093.

11. Ellen White, *Counsels to Writers and Editors,* 30, 31. The full quotation is at the beginning of the chapter.

12. Ibid., 30.

13. Ellen White, *The Ellen G. White 1888 Materials,* 1:133, footnote.

14. Ibid., 133.

Chapter 20

The Adventist Church at Corinth[1]

The Bible says, "It has been reported to me by Chloe's people that there are quarrels among you, my brothers and sisters. What I mean is that each of you says, 'I belong to Paul,' or 'I belong to Apollos,' or 'I belong to Cephas,' or 'I belong to Christ.' Has Christ been divided? Was Paul crucified for you? Or were you baptized in the name of Paul?"[2]

The Bible says, "What then is Apollos? What is Paul? Servants through whom you came to believe, as the Lord assigned to each. I planted, Apollos watered, but God gave the growth. So neither the one who plants nor the one who waters is anything, but only God who gives the growth."[3]

Whenever the church desires status in the world, worries about looking good before our upscale friends, plans for attractive new buildings that are properly representative, then the sporadic scandals, the inevitable antics of human beings who are members of the church cause us acute embarrassment. We cry out to ourselves, if not to each other, "Oh, that our church could always look nice so that nice people would want to belong!"

That's when it is particularly helpful to turn to Scripture and remind ourselves that God's people seldom have had their act together for more than a few minutes at a time. Dip your finger into Scripture anywhere and ask the question: how were God's people doing? Whether from the Old Testament or New, the answer is likely to be grim.

That could be discouraging. But in a strange backdoor sort of way, discovering that all God's people have their troubles, even the ones we thought were perfect, actually can be encouraging. I still vividly remember an occasion in the School of Theology when one of our senior colleagues, whom we all admired, was not just late for a departmental appointment, he plumb forgot. He was never late. Students were not late to his classes, nor did they turn in late papers. *On time* was always the watchword. I think the rest of us were a bit startled at our almost unrestrained glee when he slipped. The proof was in! He was human just like the rest of us! It was not an angry, so-there, I-told-you-so kind of reaction. Rather, a certain sense of relief that swept over us, bonding us even closer to a colleague we had long revered.

When I leaf through Psalms, I discover a record of unrelenting trouble. And I wonder why we memorized only the nice things when we were kids: "For he shall give his angels charge over thee, to keep thee in all thy ways. They shall bear thee up in their hands, lest thou dash thy foot against a stone."[4] "The angel of the LORD encampeth round about them that fear him, and delivereth them."[5]

But just as prominent in the Psalms, if not more so, is the solemn cry: "Thou didst leave me in the lurch, O Lord." Why did we not memorize more words like these? "Have mercy upon me, O LORD, for I am in trouble: mine eye is consumed with grief, yea, my soul and my belly. For my life is spent with grief, and my years with sighing: my strength faileth because of mine iniquity, and my bones are consumed."[6] Or from another psalm: "My God, my God, why hast thou forsaken me? why art thou so far from helping me, and from the words of my roaring? O my God, I cry in the daytime, but thou hearest not; and in the night season, and am not silent."[7] That was not just Jesus' prayer, it was the prayer of a real, live, struggling saint in the Old Testament. To be sure, the psalmists almost always move on to faith. But they do spend a chunk of time talking about their troubles.

And isn't that more typical of our lives? Think of the people close to you—your family and friends. Think of this past week, this past month, or this past year. Do you not see more than enough pain, sorrow, uncertainty, and discouragement?

Given this seething cauldron of a world in which we find ourselves, the church is God's gift to us, a community where we may find help, healing, and understanding. Yet, is it not curious that this healing community is the source of so much strife?

Maybe it is because we see the church as the guarantor of truth. And, of course, we are easily convinced that *our* view of truth is the one the church must preserve, and we act accordingly. Though we are drawn by the presence of the divine, all too often, we are driven away by the presence of the human. It is easy to hurt others in the name of the truth.

But if our community is a troubled one, God has given us the story of other troubled communities from which we can learn. One of the most instructive for us, I believe, is the church at Corinth.

Drawing its membership from people with very checkered backgrounds, the Corinthian church was checkered still. Paul reminded the saints that not many of them had been wise, powerful, or of noble birth when God had called them.[8] He ticks off a list of violent offenders against God and the human race, adding, "And this is what some of you used to be."[9] But he goes on to say, "You were washed, you were sanctified, you were justified in the name of the Lord Jesus Christ and in the Spirit of our God."

Washed and sanctified? Not completely. Judging by Paul's correspondence, the Corinthians believers were still struggling with just about every category of sin known to humankind. Perhaps most alarming of all, they were choosing up sides behind their favorite preachers.

And yet, right at that point, Paul and the church at Corinth have something important to tell us, for the three favorite preachers at Corinth—Paul, Cephas (Peter), and Apollos—can serve as convenient types of three different perspectives in Adventism, three different ways of relating to God and the world. These same three perspectives can be found in Christianity in general, but they have come to stand out rather vividly in Adventism in recent years because charismatic spokespersons for each tradition have wanted to say, "This is the way, walk ye in it."

Paul, however, wants to argue that each of the three traditions, each of the three preachers, has a proper place in the church. You can't choose just one. You need all three. The church, as the body of Christ or as the temple of God, can be complete only when all three parts are there. That is the point of this chapter.

Now I must caution you that I am taking some liberties with the text of 1 Corinthians, a risky thing to do in the presence of numerous competent New Testament scholars. But since the New Testament is that part of the Bible that tells us most clearly about the priesthood of all the believers,[10] perhaps they will allow an Old Testament student to tread carefully upon their sacred turf.

So let us focus on some important sections of Paul's first letter to the church at Corinth.

1 Corinthians 1:10–17. Here Paul identifies the three key spokespersons: Peter, Apollos, and himself. Later in the same letter, he comments briefly on Apollos but says nothing further about Peter. So if we are to use these three names as types of three different perspectives, we will have to fill in the picture from elsewhere in the New Testament. Actually, if we were to identify the three perspectives by means of their favorite New Testament literature, we would put Peter with Matthew and James, and Apollos with John. More about that below. But first we must look more carefully at the chapter in which Paul describes the relationship between himself and Apollos and how each serves the larger church in a particular way.

1 Corinthians 3. Chapter 3 begins with a food model: milk is for babies; solid food is for adults.[11] Any congregation is likely to have both.

The next picture is agricultural: Paul sows, Apollos waters, but God gives the increase.[12] In short, the work assignments are different.

The next picture is a building that uses different materials, all of which are important for God's temple, the church.[13] All these contribute to our understanding of a robust biblical pluralism. For my purposes, the truly crucial verses are verses 5 through 7, where Paul describes himself as the one who sows and Apollos as the one who waters. In other words, Paul is the frontline evangelist; Apollos is the pastor and nurturer. The language of verses 16 and 17 drives home Paul's argument. "All of you are God's temple," he argues. "God will destroy anyone who destroys His temple, and you," he tells the Corinthians, "are that temple." In other words, if you drive out Paul, Peter, or Apollos from the church—any one of the three—and thereby weaken the church, you are in deep trouble with God. The temple of God needs all three to be strong and whole.

But now let's live dangerously and make the application to the Adventist Church. I could mention a goodly number of prominent Adventists in each category. That would make for interesting reading. But I have resisted the temptation. In very brief form, however, the following characterizations of what it means to obey can get us started:

- Peter and company say that you *must* obey and *can* obey. The perfectionist element is strong here.

- Paul and company say you must *try* to obey, but you never really can. Jesus pays the price for you. Grace and substitution are particularly strong here.

- Apollos and company say the important thing is to *try*. Love is what matters, and the heart is won by a picture of the Father's love.

We can flesh the picture out a bit more:

Peter. Optimistic, practical, and tends to think in concrete terms rather than abstract. He likes Proverbs in the Old Testament, Matthew and James in the new. Peter tells us to make a list of what needs to be done and then do it. Peter can claim to be a perfectionist because he has reduced the claims of perfection to a list of things to do and a list of things not to do. Action, not motive, is what counts.

Paul. Much more pessimistic, at least about human nature, and much more introspective and sensitive to that simmering cauldron of emotions that shapes our lives. The crucial Pauline letters here are Romans and Galatians. Life is more complex for Paul. He tries his best and still cries out, "Wretched man that I am! Who will rescue me from this body of death? Thanks be to God through Jesus Christ our Lord!"[14] Paul can't do it; he is absolutely dependent on the Lord Jesus Christ. God is the Great Judge of all, and before that Great Judge, Jesus, the Substitute, stands in Paul's place.

Apollos. Optimistic, inquisitive, philosophically oriented, and is especially attracted to the Gospel of John. For Apollos, God is gentle and understanding, more a Father than a Judge. And Jesus is not so much the Sacrifice that satisfies the demands of holiness *up there,* as God's message of love to us *down here.* "Whoever has seen me has seen the Father," said Jesus.[15] That nurtures Apollos's heart and soul.

Another way of characterizing the three positions would be to say that Peter is theocentric—human reason is not as important as obedience to a divine command. Paul is not only theocentric, he is Christocentric. Obedience to a divine command is still terribly important, but it happens in Christ Jesus. Human wisdom and human effort are suspect. God is everything, and He gives it all to us in Christ Jesus. Apollos is more anthropocentric. For him, it is important to understand the truth about God. Human beings are not so much wretched worms, waiting to be saved as they are jewels just waiting to be polished.

But now let's cast all this into a teaching model. The goal in each instance is to effect obedience and reunion with God. How would Peter, Paul, and Apollos go about the task of teaching?

Let's imagine each of them as a piano teacher for a ten-year-old boy. The task: to play a Mozart concerto.

Peter. As a teacher, Peter is happy if the student has no memory lapses and gets the notes right. "Perfect!" he exclaims. But he can speak of perfection only because the standard is a limited one. He does not expect a ten-year-old to reflect all the fine nuances of great music. The danger, here, is that the student may never even attempt to reach the higher standard.

Paul. Paul, as a teacher, is a very sensitive musician. "This is great music," he says. "But you can't possibly master it. Here, I'll play it for you." The substitute takes over. Great music is produced by a master, and the student is captivated. But the danger, here, is that the student may never seriously attempt to bridge the gulf between his own abilities and those of the master.

Apollos. Apollos, as a teacher, is especially concerned that the student's efforts be rewarded. "Good job!" he says when the student tries hard—regardless of how rough the music might sound. The student feels encouraged. But the danger, here, is that he will mistake effort for mastery.

Note the weaknesses of each: With Peter, the student can view as mastery something that actually is less than mastery. With Paul, the student can allow another to attain mastery instead of attempting it himself. With Apollos, the student may be content to allow effort and good intentions to replace mastery.

A master teacher will incorporate the best of all three elements. I well remember sitting in on a music lesson when one of my daughters was just beginning with a new cello teacher. I was absolutely intrigued as I watched this master teacher blend the best from all three worlds: You can do it! (Peter). There is an awesome standard beyond your reach! (Paul). You did your best; that's good! (Apollos).

Most Adventists can—and do—profit from all three perspectives. But our failure to be careful Bible students, distinguishing between the three emphases, makes us very vulnerable if a particular spokesperson for one of the three strands becomes too forthright or too narrow in their public statements.

The differences in people and the differences in our relationship with God at different times in our lives will often determine which emphasis is most helpful at any particular point. Three key aspects from Adventist life and lore can help to illustrate the differences:

Sin. For Peter, sin consists of deeds—a list of things to do and not to do. Paul sees sin more as a twisted nature, a distortion at the very heart of man. Apollos simply sees sin as flawed intention, a lack of love.

Mediator. How does each of the three relate to that troublesome statement from the pen of Ellen White that we "are to stand in the sight of a holy God without a mediator"?[16] Both Peter and Paul would see the absence of a Mediator as a threat. For Peter, however, the threat can be overcome by perfect obedience. Paul would not know how to interpret such a statement, for he sees Christ as the essential Mediator between God and man. Apollos, reflecting the Gospel of John, sees the absence of a Mediator as a promise, not a threat—a promise of a time when we will know God so well that we will come into His presence without fear.

For me, Apollos's view of the Mediator came as a precious insight while I was a ministerial student in the Adventist Theological Seminary at Andrews University. I was asking why I needed a Mediator if the Father loved me. So I embarked on a study of the biblical concept of mediation and discovered John 14–17. In particular, John 16:26, 27 records Jesus' statement: "On that day you will ask in my name. I do *not* say to you that I will ask the Father on your behalf; for the Father himself loves you, because you have loved me and have believed that I came from God" (emphasis added).

The reason for the fundamental difference between Paul and John (Apollos) is that the setting in which each views the Mediator is quite different. For John, the Mediator represents the Father to humanity. For Paul, the Mediator is humanity's representative before the Father. John's view makes more sense in the setting of a family; Paul's view makes more sense in the setting of a courtroom. Both concepts are thoroughly biblical, though some believers will be drawn to one picture more than the other.

Pride. Each of the three traditions is quite capable of reflecting the essence of sin, namely, a wrongful and exclusive pride. The followers of Peter are tempted to claim, "We are the historic Adventists, the only true Adventists." The followers of Paul are tempted to claim, "We are the only ones who preach the true gospel." And the followers of Apollos are tempted to claim, "We are the only ones who really understand the truth about God." In short, each of the three positions is equally vulnerable to the sinful exaltation of self.

My own insights in this matter have come by a long and circuitous route, and my thinking has been sharpened by controversy in the church. When Desmond Ford declared that there was "no biblical way of proving the investigative judgment,"[17] I was upset with him. The investigative judgment, as I understood it, had become an important part of my theology. So I decided to search out the roots of my understanding of the doctrine. To my amazement, I discovered that my view was based on the later writings of Ellen White and was not found at all in her earlier works. Ultimately, my research led to the publication of my Sinai-Golgotha series of articles in the *Adventist Review* in 1981 and 1982.[18] In short, I traced how Ellen White's perspective on God shifted from an emphasis on the power of God and external motivation, to an emphasis on the goodness of God and internal motivation.

In the initial version of the study, which I presented at the West Coast Religion Teachers Conference at Pacific Union College in the spring of 1980, I gave the distinct impression that Ellen White was moving away from one perspective of the atonement (a price paid heavenward) toward another perspective (a message sent earthward). Today, I would say that she was adding the second perspective (that of Apollos and John), while refining the first (that of Paul). But right at the end of that presentation, my teaching colleague, Jon Dybdahl, raised a question that set me to thinking.

"What do I say to a student," he asked, "who says that he has a hard time worshiping a God who insists that human beings stand before the whole universe as a witness to God's goodness? The student told me that he finds it much easier to worship a God who simply gives us salvation as a gift. What do I say to such a student?"

I sensed that I had come close to something very important to Jon. I asked him if we could talk. We did—for two hours, two precious hours. As we shared together, Jon described how the message of Christ's death on his behalf had transformed his life when he was in mission service in Thailand. I described how I had been blessed at the seminary by John's message of the Incarnate Mediator.

Just prior to my conversations with Dybdahl, I had finished reading a book by Robert D. Brinsmead[19] in which he had imposed Paul's courtroom setting on the Gospel of John. So I blurted out, "It's just not fair to do to John what Brinsmead does to John." To which, Dybdahl responded, "And it's just not fair to do to Romans what Graham Maxwell[20] does to Romans." At that point, something like scales fell from both of our eyes, and we realized that I was drawn more to John and he was drawn more to Paul. The perspectives are different, but both are thoroughly biblical. We agreed that we should let John be John, and Paul be Paul. Now we still carry on lively discussions, but don't have to read each other out of the church. It is a great joy and a relief.

Such an approach requires a more careful reading of both John and Paul, rather than a homogenizing of both. We all have to resist the temptation to claim support for our position from passages that may not share our perspective at all.

Is it not possible that such differences can explain why there were three favorite preachers in Corinth instead of just one? The differences are real. And Paul tells us they are legitimate.

Paul emphasizes the great gulf between God and humanity. That message reaches the hearts of those who have been oppressed by too much of Peter. It reaches those who are just awakening to the promptings of the Holy Spirit, those who sense the great chasm between themselves and God. They don't need a gentle God so much as they need a high and powerful One who stands for all that is holy and good—but who sent Jesus Christ to pay the price for human sin. In Christ, such a one can find peace and joy.

But some Adventists, including many who have grown up with good and gentle parents, are very much attracted to Apollos. For them, God is gentle and kind. Yes, Paul sows the seed, and Apollos waters, but they are particularly blessed by Apollos.

I will not attempt to critique all three positions, but given my own natural home in the Apollos perspective, perhaps I can note what I perceive to be a significant weakness in this position that I call home. To be blunt, our anger often comes up short. God smiles a lot. He even ends up smiling when He shouts. But in the world in which we live, Christians must retain the ability to be angry and get angry. When innocent women are gunned down by a man who hates women, is that not a time for great anger, for being ashamed of this race of beings called human? Apollos has a hard time getting angry enough at sin.

What of the future?

Can the church learn to live with the differences between Peter, Paul, and Apollos? I hope so. I sense an increasing mood among us to come together, to pray, to share, to help each other in our difficulties and sorrows, and to try harder to understand each other. And the variety in Scripture is God's way of meeting that very need. To sense the differences between Peter, Paul, and Apollos should not tear down the temple of God, but build it up. And our failure to take Scripture seriously places the church at risk. The study of His Word is the source of our strength, the measure of our unity. And it is Scripture that also sets the limits for our diversity.

To close this chapter, I will cite a passage from the pen of Ellen White. Generally, she is quoted in support of each of the three traditions. And because she wrote so much over such a wide period of time, she can be used to support any of the three perspectives and even to pit one against the other. But in *Counsels to*

Parents, Teachers, and Students, she has a marvelous statement as to why we need a diversity of teachers:

> In our schools the work of teaching the Scriptures to the youth is not to be left wholly with one teacher for a long series of years. The Bible teacher may be well able to present the truth, and yet it is not the best experience for the students that their study of the word of God should be directed by one man only, term after term and year after year. Different teachers should have a part in the work, even though they may not all have so full an understanding of the Scriptures. If several in our larger schools unite in the work of teaching the Scriptures, the students may thus have the benefit of the talents of several.
>
> Why do we need a Matthew, a Mark, a Luke, a John, a Paul, and all the writers who have borne testimony in regard to the life and ministry of the Saviour? Why could not one of the disciples have written a complete record and thus have given us a connected account of Christ's earthly life? Why does one writer bring in points that another does not mention? Why, if these points are essential, did not all these writers mention them? It is because the minds of men differ. Not all comprehend things in exactly the same way. Certain Scripture truths appeal much more strongly to the minds of some than of others.
>
> The same principle applies to speakers. One dwells at considerable length on points that others would pass by quickly or not mention at all. The whole truth is presented more clearly by several than by one. The Gospels differ, but the records of all blend in one harmonious whole.
>
> So today the Lord does not impress all minds in the same way. Often through unusual experiences, under special circumstances, He gives to some Bible students views of truth that others do not grasp. It is possible for the most learned teacher to fall far short of teaching all that should be taught.[21]

My students and my correspondents have had experiences with the Lord that have enriched me greatly. This world is such a complex place that I am convinced we have only begun to fight when it comes to understanding each other and the needs of those around us. One of the most exciting challenges before us is to learn from Scripture how we can better meet the needs of God's children. He wants His church to be the place where wounded, hurting people can come together, to find understanding, hope, and courage, and to remind each other that a better world lies ahead. Until that better world comes, may God grant each of us grace to help build the temple of God so that we may all worship within.

---

1. A revision of a Sabbath sermon preached at the Walla Walla College Church on December 9, 1989.

2. 1 Corinthians 1:11–13.

3. 1 Corinthians 3:5–7.

4. Psalm 91:11, 12, KJV.

5. Psalm 34:7, KJV.

6. Psalm 31:9, 10, KJV.

7. Psalm 22:1, 2, KJV.

8. 1 Corinthians 1:26.

9. 1 Corinthians 6:11.

10. Cf. 1 Peter 2:5, 9.

11. 1 Corinthians 3:1, 2.

12. 1 Corinthians 3:6–9.

13. 1 Corinthians 3:10–17. (In 1 Corinthians 12, in yet another picture, the human body illustrates the diversity of gifts within the church.)

14. Romans 7:24, 25.

15. John 14:9.

16. White, *The Great Controversy*, 425.

17. Desmond Ford, Adventist Forum lecture on the investigative judgment, October 27, 1979, Pacific Union College, Angwin, California.

18. "From Sinai to Golgotha," pt. 1, *Adventist Review*, December 3, 1981, 4–6; "One Law, Two Mountains," pt. 2, *Adventist Review*, December 10, 1981, 8–10; "The Story of a Pilgrimage," pt. 3, *Adventist Review*, December 17, 1981, 7–10; "Ellen White's Pilgrimage to Golgotha," pt. 4, *Adventist Review*, December 24, 1981, 7–9; "The Theology of Ellen White: The Great Controversy Story," pt. 5, *Adventist Review*, December 31, 1981, 12, 13; "Even the Investigative Judgment Can Be Good News," *Westwind* (Walla Walla College alumni journal), Winter 1982, 4–7, 11 (addendum to *Adventist Review* series); "The Prodigal Son Revisited," *Adventist Review*, July 1, 1982, 7–11 (sequel to *Adventist Review* series).

19. Robert D. Brinsmead, *Judged by the Gospel: A Review of Adventism* (Fallbrook, Calif.: Verdict Publications, 1980). In terms of the typology suggested here, Australian Robert Brinsmead moved through all three strands in Adventism. First, he was an angry perfectionist; second, he was an angry antiperfectionist and a supporter of a substitutionary theology; third, he was an angry opponent of substitutionary theology; fourth—and presently—he is none of the above, and is no longer a believer.

20. Graham Maxwell, seen by many as someone who reinterprets the forensic passages in Scripture.

21. White, *Counsels to Parents*, 432, 433.

Chapter 21

A Work in Progress: *Questions on Doctrine* Debate

The Bible says, "Cry aloud, spare not, lift up thy voice like a trumpet, and shew my people their transgression, and the house of Jacob their sins."[1]

The Bible says, "If I say to the wicked, 'You shall surely die,' and you give them no warning, or speak to warn the wicked from their wicked way, in order to save their life, those wicked persons shall die for their iniquity; but their blood I will require at your hand. But if you warn the wicked, and they do not turn from their wickedness, or from their wicked way, they shall die for their iniquity; but you will have saved your life."[2]

The Bible says, "The LORD called to the man clothed in linen, who had the writing case at this side; and said to him, 'Go through the city, through Jerusalem, and put a mark on the foreheads of those who sigh and groan over all the abominations that are committed in it.' To the others he said in my hearing, 'Pass through the city after him, and kill; your eye shall not spare, and you shall show no pity. Cut down old men, young men and young women, little children and women,

240

but touch no one who has the mark. And begin at my sanctuary.' So they began with the elders who were in front of the house."[3]

The Bible says, "Fallen, fallen is Babylon the great!" "Come out of her, my people, so that you do not take part in her sins."[4]

The Bible says, "But I say to you that listen, Love your enemies, do good to those who hate you, bless those who curse you, pray for those who abuse you."[5]

The Bible says, "Through love become slaves to one another. For the whole law is summed up in a single commandment, 'You shall love your neighbor as yourself.' "[6]

Ellen White says, "In laboring in a new field, do not think it your duty to say at once to the people, We are Seventh-day Adventists; we believe that the seventh day is the Sabbath; we believe in the non-immortality of the soul. This would often erect a formidable barrier between you and those you wish to reach. Speak to them, as you have opportunity, upon points of doctrine on which you can agree. Dwell on the necessity of practical godliness. Give them evidence that you are a Christian, desiring peace, and that you love their souls. Let them see that you are conscientious. Thus you will gain their confidence; and there will be time enough for doctrines. Let the heart be won, the soil prepared, and then sow the seed, presenting in love the truth as it is in Jesus."[7]

Ellen White says, "In the advocacy of the truth the bitterest opponents should be treated with respect and deference. . . . The very last work in the controversy may be the enlightenment of those who have not rejected light and evidence, but who have been in midnight darkness and have in ignorance worked against the truth. Therefore treat every man as honest. Speak no word, do no deed, that will confirm any in unbelief."[8]

The Bible says, "The fruit of the Spirit is love, joy, peace, patience, kindness, generosity, faithfulness, gentleness, and self-control. There is no law against such things."[9]

God knows. You need to know that I know. I need to remind myself that they are there. I'm talking about the heavy quotes from the Bible at the beginning of this chapter—from Isaiah, Ezekiel, and John.

Could such quotes undermine everything I have written thus far in this book? Possibly. But I pray not. Liberals typically don't take sin seriously enough. Conservatives can take it so seriously that they destroy themselves as well as others. And it is the hard passages from Isaiah, Ezekiel, and John that have driven conscientious conservatives into strident forms of evangelism. Any thoughtful person is likely to be haunted by Ezekiel 3: If you don't warn the wicked, "their blood I will require at your hand." But in an important sense, the follow-up line is even more deadly, for the prophet says that if I do warn them, I will have saved my own life. That's a sobering truth, to be sure, but from a spiritual perspective, the great danger looms that I will warn others, not for their sake, but for my own. That's raw selfishness, but acted out in the name of God. If the gospel means anything at all, we must seek to share it for the sake of others, not just to save our own necks.

The ideal, of course, is to be so excited about the gospel that we can't keep from sharing the exciting news. Our story will be an echo of the testimony John recorded in his first letter: "What we have heard, what we have seen with our eyes, what we have looked at and touched with our hands, concerning the word of life. . . . We declare to you what we have seen and heard so that you also may have fellowship with us; and truly our fellowship is with the Father and with his Son Jesus Christ." And the textual variant that concludes that testimony always intrigues me: "We are writing these things so that *our* joy may be complete," says the NRSV. But the footnote states that it could also be "so that *your* joy may be complete."[10] What a joyful dilemma! To be so excited about the story of Jesus that I can't sort out whether it is for my benefit or for yours!

All that is part of this story. But perhaps most important of all is the realization that has come home to me from looking at the conservative side of myself, namely, how damaging it would be for me—and no doubt for others—if I were to take the strong words from Isaiah, Ezekiel, and John and run with them. I have discovered to my horror that when I am preoccupied with the shortcomings of others, the fruits of the Spirit simply wither and die within me.

I want to be like Jesus. I want to spend eternity with Him. And that means that I greatly covet the fruits of His Spirit: love, joy, peace, patience, kindness, etc.

All that is simply a preamble to the *Questions on Doctrine* debate, a debate that is terribly important for Adventism, even if you don't know anything about it. The reason it is terribly important is that devout conservatives are gripped by the issues. And right here I want to enter a plea to the liberals to stay on board. Those of us who are conservative need your more detached coolness to keep us from doing anything rash.

But this will be a short piece, because the line at the beginning of the chapter title is very true: "A work in progress." I don't know what will happen in the *Questions on Doctrine* debate. It is far too early to tell. I know what I hope will happen. That will become clear, even in my brief comments here.

The amazing event that triggered this chapter took place on October 24–27, 2007, at Andrews University—the *Questions on Doctrine* Conference. And from that conference came a picture that still leaves me nearly speechless, a picture of three Adventists standing side by side at a Communion table: Ángel Rodríguez, head of the General Conference Biblical Research Institute; George R. Knight, Adventist historian; and Colin Standish, president of Hartland Institute, an independent Adventist organization noted for its sharp critique of the organized church.

For two reasons that picture is amazing: First, that these men were side by side at all; second, that they were standing together at a Communion table.

Organized by three young scholars—Julius Nam, Jerry Moon, and Michael Campbell—the conference marked the fiftieth anniversary of the 1957 book, *Seventh-day Adventists Answer Questions on Doctrine.*[11] That book was the culmination of conversations between leading Adventists and prominent Evangelicals in America. The Adventists were eager to identify more fully with the Evangelical understanding of the nature Christ and His saving work. But that meant taking a fresh look at our history, not a happy task for some.

All this raises crucial questions, each deserving a book-length exploration: Can our understanding of truth and of the Bible change? Is there more than one way of looking at truth? How should we relate to the surrounding culture? On what basis can we work with those we once opposed?

I will simply make three points, each—like the questions above—deserve fuller treatment, and each echo parts of this book. But because this is a work in progress, I am intentionally brief.

First, we have solid grounds for shifting our emphasis from confrontation to cooperation, preserving confrontation as an option when needed. Jesus points the way. While claiming the Old Testament God as His own, indeed, claiming *to be* the Old Testament God, Jesus nevertheless demonstrated that when God took human flesh, He dramatically shifted away from the violent confrontational methods that mark so much of God's activity in the Old Testament. Jesus never killed anyone, never struck anyone. He could get angry, but His anger was against evil. And when He attacked evil, the children and the weak came running to Him even when He was angry. Check out Jesus' cleansing of the temple in Matthew 21:12–16. It's amazing.

Second, a positive approach inspires hope and courage in people who might otherwise sink into oblivion. "Neither do I condemn you," Jesus told the adulteress. "Go your way, and from now on do not sin again."[12]

In Adventist history, Ellen White could urge a brother heading to Africa to speak with other Christians on "points of doctrine on which you can agree." To the contentious A. T. Jones, she declared, "The Lord wants His people to follow other methods than that of condemning wrong, even though the condemnation be just. . . . Treat every [person] as honest," she urged. "Speak no word, do no deed, that will confirm any in unbelief."[13]

Once, after I had shared that last quote in class, a student wrote me a note at the end of the term. "My sister and I were on the outs," she said. "But now we're the best of buddies just because I decided to treat her as honest. Thank you for the quote."

My final point is that an opportunity like the one provided by the *Questions on Doctrine* Conference is rare. Such moments usually last no more than a few minutes. The quarreling of Acts 5 too easily overwhelms the Pentecostal beauty of Acts 2. We must work quickly while the window is open. Adventists who have used strong language against the church and against all efforts to work with Evangelicals have become friends with their opponents. "New friends," said one, "even one whose paper appalled me." "Excellent fellowship with Evangelical presenters," he commented.

That's the kind of stuff of which the kingdom is made. And it happened because some young Adventist scholars decided we really should treat each other as honest.

---

1. Isaiah 58:1, KJV.

2. Ezekiel 3:18, 19.

3. Ezekiel 9:3–6.

4. Revelation 14:8; 18:4.

5. Luke 6:27, 28.

6. Galatians 5:13, 14.

7. White, *Gospel Workers,* 119, 120; cf. Ellen White to Elder Boyd, "Letter to a Minister and His Wife Bound for Africa," June 25, 1887, Letter 12, in *Testimonies to Southern Africa* (Washington, D.C.: Ellen G. White Estate, 1974), 14–20. This letter is an almost verbatim original of the quote in *Gospel Workers.*

8. White, *Testimonies for the Church,* 6:122.

9. Galatians 5:22, 23.

10. 1 John 1:1–4; emphasis added.

11. Prepared by a representative group of Seventh-day Adventist leaders, Bible teachers, and editors, *Seventh-day Adventists Answer Questions on Doctrine: An Explanation of Certain Major Aspects of Seventh-day Adventist Belief* (Washington, D.C.: Review and Herald®, 1957). Under the editorship of George R. Knight, an annotated edition was published in 2003. George R. Knight, ed., *Seventh-day Adventists Answer Questions on Doctrine,* annotated ed. (Berrien Springs, Mich.: Andrews University Press, 2003). The Evangelical response also appeared in book form: Walter R. Martin, *The Truth About Seventh-day Adventism* (Grand Rapids, Mich.: Zondervan Publishing, 1960).

12. John 8:11.

13. White, *Testimonies for the Church,* 6:121, 122.

Chapter 22

A Work in Progress: Cross and Atonement

The Bible says, "When I came to you, brothers and sisters, I did not come proclaiming the mystery of God to you in lofty words or wisdom. For I decided to know nothing among you except Jesus Christ, and him crucified."[1]

The Bible says, "For our sake he made him to be sin who knew no sin, so that in him we might become the righteousness of God."[2]

The Bible says, "There is therefore now no condemnation for those who are in Christ Jesus."[3]

The Bible says, "Have I been with you all this time, Philip, and you still do not know me? Whoever has seen me has seen the Father."[4]

Ellen White says, "God's people are tempted and tried because they cannot see the spirit of consecration and self-sacrifice to God in all who manage important interests, and many act as though Jesus were buried in Joseph's new tomb, and a great stone rolled before the door. I wish to proclaim with voice and pen, Jesus has risen! he has risen!"[5]

Others say, "The earliest converts were converted by a single historical fact (the Resurrection) and a single theological doctrine (the Redemption) operating on a sense of sin which they already had—and sin, not against some new fancy-dress law produced as a novelty by a 'great man,' but against the old, platitudinous, universal moral law which they had been taught by their nurses and mothers. The 'Gospels' come later and were written not to make Christians but to edify Christians already made."[6]—C. S. Lewis

This will be another brief chapter. But it might be the most important one in the book. But because the discussion is a work in progress, I am intentionally brief.

The chapter is crucial because Adventists differ in their understanding of what the Cross means. But we can't just dump the Cross or even avoid it. Without the Cross, there would be no resurrection; without the Cross, there could be no crown. If we live in hope, it is only because of the life, death, and resurrection of Jesus.

So why did Jesus have to die? The question is crucial but yields two dramatically different, yet complementary answers. Those who are gripped by one answer are easily alarmed by those who are gripped by the other. And it works both ways. Most Christians find both answers meaningful and will no doubt be puzzled by the intensity of the debate engendered by those who are intense. But this is another case where we do not choose our battles. So we have to take all sides seriously.

What are the answers? Both declare that Jesus died to save us, but then the difference emerges. One answer points the Cross heavenward and sees the death of Jesus as a Sacrifice that satisfies the demands of divine justice: sin requires death. This view can be called the *objective atonement,* indicating that Jesus' death satisfies some kind of objective demand apart from the experience of the believer. It can be the demands of the law; it can also be seen as satisfying divine wrath. Thus the words *substitution* and/or *satisfaction* are also linked with this view. Those who hold this view are strongly attracted by Paul's writings, especially Romans and Galatians.

The other answer points the Cross earthward and sees the death of Jesus as a powerful revelation of God and His love for fallen creatures. This view is called the *subjective atonement* because it focuses on human experience. Thus it is part of Jesus' answer to Philip: "Whoever has seen me has seen the Father."[7] Those who hold this view are strongly attracted by John's Gospel, especially John 14–17.

But then the battle begins. Those who are gripped by the objective atonement are inclined to argue that the other view is weak on the doctrines of sin and salvation. Without a real sacrifice pointed heavenward, they argue, the sin problem hasn't really been solved.

On the other side, those who are gripped by the subjective atonement argue that the other view gives the impression that God demands a pound of flesh before He will save human beings. The more extreme rhetoric is likely to call the substitutionary atonement an immature view that should be outgrown.

Outside of Adventism, and from Christian history, both views bring along unwanted baggage. The subjective view has been called the "moral influence" theory, because the Cross is sometimes seen as only influencing the moral nature of humanity. As sometimes held by the more liberal Protestant churches, the subjective atonement can indeed undervalue the power of sin and the need for salvation.

The objective view also carries baggage. As held by Christians outside of Adventism, the objective atonement can be linked with a narrow view of salvation that excludes those who do not explicitly accept the sacrifice of Jesus. Thus the good heathen, the good Buddhist, or the good Muslim cannot be part of God's kingdom. The strong language, especially among Calvinists, can also be problematic. The term *penal substitution,* for example, tends to trigger the pound-of-flesh objection noted above. The rhetoric of satisfying divine wrath has a similar effect.

In Adventism, two developments that can be documented in the experience and writings of Ellen White are worth noting. First, in her later writings, she stepped back from her earlier emphasis on satisfying the "wrath of an offended deity," speaking rather of satisfying the "demands of the law." Second, chapter 70 in *The Desire of Ages* has bequeathed to Adventism the conviction that the ignorant, but honest, heathen can be saved. Commenting on the sheep and goats in Matthew 25, she speaks persuasively of "heathen . . . who worship God ignorantly, those to whom the light is never brought by human instrumentality, yet they will not perish."[8]

Drawing on the previous two chapters in this book, I must note a tension in the church. While the subjective or revelatory view of the cross is thoroughly biblical (see for example John 14–17) and is very much appreciated by many Adventists, other Adventists view this perspective with alarm and tend to treat those who hold it as second-class Adventists. The Johannine, or subjective, atonement perspective has not been part of the *Questions on Doctrine* debate. That discussion is mostly between the perfectionist theology of Peter and the substitutionary theology of Paul, to borrow the labels I suggested in chapter 19.

I believe it is time to address the atonement issue honestly and in good faith. My own experience has been immeasurably enriched by my discovery of my incarnate Lord in John 14–17. As I have frequently noted, however, I did not discover that wonderful news until I was in my second year at seminary. For all kinds of reasons, discovering that Jesus was God on earth and continues to be God in the present may always be a late discovery in a Christian's life. But it is central to Scripture and crucial for Adventist theology.

If the two sides are going to work together, however, we must recognize that not all the Bible writers give the same emphasis. If both sides can recognize the other's position as being fully Christian and fully Adventist, it will greatly enhance the work of the church. But the demeaning rhetoric will have to stop. It is not appropriate, in my view, to characterize the Johannine perspective as a non-Christian deviation that is destructive to the gospel. Nor is it appropriate to describe the Pauline perspective view as an immature theology in which God is seen to be demanding a pound of flesh.

But changing our views of the other side cannot simply happen by flipping a switch. Our impressions are often deeply rooted and inflamed by inappropriate rhetoric from the other side.

I do, however, have two suggestions that I have found helpful personally. If others, on both sides, would be willing to explore them with me, I suspect we could make good progress. I will spell them out rather pointedly.

1. Memorize Bible passages that the other side finds meaningful. Here it is crucial to try and hear Scripture from the other person's perspective, not simply to underscore our own. That does not happen easily or immediately. In my case, I elected to memorize Romans 8 and 2 Corinthians 5:14–21. In that connection, I should mention that a general truth or rule about memorization that I had already found applicable elsewhere proved to be true here too. In brief, because it takes me a long time to memorize a passage of Scripture, about the ninety-seventh time through I begin to see truths that I hadn't seen before and am blessed by them.

And that has certainly been the case with the substitutionary passages in Scripture that I have set out to memorize. My understanding of the Cross has deepened and been enriched. I no longer feel that I have to reinterpret every passage of Scripture to meet my favorite perspective. I can let Paul be Paul, James be James, and Peter be Peter. And I think that means that I can also let God be God.

Now, when I go to *The Desire of Ages* and read the chapter "It Is Finished,"[9] for example, I can honestly admit that it is almost entirely substitutionary in its view of the Cross. I am grateful that I don't have to reinterpret it or avoid it. I am grateful that I can be blessed, instead of troubled. My solution won't work for everyone; indeed, probably no one else will be blessed in just the same way I have been. But by sharing our various perspectives honestly with each other, we can walk together toward the kingdom.

In this connection, I note the observation of a colleague, one for whom Paul's theology is especially precious, a colleague who has helped nurture my appreciation for substitutionary theology. He observed that the trajectory of my experience appeared to be quite different from his. His deepening appreciation for the things of God began with a keen awareness of human sinfulness—his own sinfulness. Now he is gaining a deepening appreciation of the goodness of God.

By contrast, he observed, my experience seems to have started with a deep appreciation for God's goodness, and I am now gaining a deeper understanding of human sinfulness. I think he is right. Our experiences will never be exactly alike. But it has been an enriching experience for us both as we have joined our minds and hearts together in the search for the good things of God.

2. Recognize that God did not demand a Sacrifice for His benefit, but gave a

Sacrifice for our benefit. In my case, discovering that Jesus was God in the flesh banished forever the haunting specter of a reluctant deity. If God Himself took human flesh and came to earth to save me, He really must want me in His kingdom after all! God wasn't just letting Jesus sneak me in the side door as some kind of concession. No! My salvation was no concession. God came to earth because He really wanted me in His kingdom.

I decided that one of the mental pictures suggested by certain biblical passages had led me astray. In particular, the picture of Jesus pleading His blood to the Father had given me the impression that Jesus was my Friend, but that the Father still needed to be convinced. Admittedly, protection from a holy deity can be a terrifying necessity. In his early years, for example, Martin Luther was just as frightened of the Son as he was of the Father. For him, the only safe approach to God was through the gentle virgin Mary!

In that connection, John 16:26, 27 has played a crucial role in my thinking. Not only has that passage enabled me to transform from a threat into a promise that scary Adventist line that we "are to stand in the sight of a holy God without a mediator,"[10] it has also helped me see that as long as I need a Mediator, I have one. If the passage is truly a promise, then God is not about to pull the rug out from under us. He cares for our needs.

That same passage may also be helpful in addressing what I consider to be an erroneous impression that it is God who demands a sacrifice. Is it not possible that the need for an atoning sacrifice is driven by perceptions engendered by our twisted minds? As I see it, the belief in a pound-of-flesh God is the deadly result of sin. As the effects of sin and guilt gnawed away at the human mind, the "gods" became more and more demanding, more and more violent. The end result of that kind of thinking was the conviction that the gods demanded every firstborn among humans. God recognized that devastating logic and commanded Israel to provide an animal substitute. "Every firstborn male among your children you shall redeem," says Scripture.[11] That same psychology is reflected in Micah 6:6–8. Moving up the ladder of potential sacrificial gifts, the prophet ends with, "Shall I give my firstborn for my transgression, / the fruit of my body for the sin of my soul?" (verse 7).

The prophet's response implies that God is demanding no such thing. Indeed, the Good News Bible makes the *no* explicit at the beginning of the climactic verse 8. But the story of Jesus, indeed, the death of Jesus, brings to an end, once and for all, any human thought of earning God's favor through a sacrifice. Jesus really did pay it all.

With such an approach, one could speak of a psychological and governmental necessity for the death of Christ. Such language would have distinct advantages over the absolute necessity implied by more extreme forms of Calvinist theology. Such an approach would also put to an end any thought that God was demanding a pound of flesh, but it would recognize that God gave a pound of flesh, so to speak, because diseased human minds thought it was the only way to find peace. We do not serve a vindictive or vengeful God. But we do serve a God who is willing to pay whatever price our twisted minds may demand. And that's what we see on the Cross.

So let's put our heads and hearts together, seek God's presence, and study His Word so that Gift of God can be the kind of good news He intends it to be. By God's grace, whether we find John or Paul more helpful, we can all rejoice when any of God's children discovers that God has made it possible for them to be in His kingdom. That should be wonderful news for us all.

---

1. 1 Corinthians 2:1, 2.
2. 2 Corinthians 5:21.
3. Romans 8:1.
4. John 14:9.
5. Ellen White, "An Appeal to Our Ministers and Conference Committees," *Special Testimonies Series A,* November 1890, 29.
6. Lewis, *The Screwtape Letters,* 126.
7. John 14:9.
8. White, *The Desire of Ages,* 638.
9. White, *The Desire of Ages,* 758–764.
10. White, *The Great Controversy,* 425.
11. Exodus 13:13; see verses 11–16.

Chapter 23

A Visit to the Eye Doctor

The Bible says, "In everything do to others as you would have them do to you; for this is the law and the prophets."[1]

Ellen White says, "Every association of life calls for the exercise of self-control, forbearance, and sympathy. We differ so widely in disposition, habits, education, that our ways of looking at things vary. We judge differently. Our understanding of truth, our ideas in regard to the conduct of life, are not in all respects the same. There are no two whose experience is alike in every particular. The trials of one are not the trials of another. The duties that one finds light are to another most difficult and perplexing.

So frail, so ignorant, so liable to misconception is human nature, that each [of us] should be careful in the estimate [we] place upon another. We little know the bearing of our acts upon the experience of others. What we do or say may seem to us of little moment, when, could our eyes be opened, we should see that upon it depended the most important results for good or for evil."[2]

She knew she needed glasses, but wasn't happy about the prospect. She slipped into the doctor's chair and waited.

When the doctor arrived the questions began: Is it clearer this way, with John, or this way, with Paul?

What does a touch of Matthew do? Help or hinder?

How about a little bit of Proverbs? Better or worse?

Lamentations? Too much Lamentations?

Philippians?

How about a psalm? Does that help?

She was delighted with her new glasses. She could see! And she was grateful the doctor had not used all his lenses just for her. Some of them would be more helpful for him.

Their eyes were different. Their glasses too.

But each could see more clearly because the lenses matched their particular needs.

Sometimes, they would switch glasses—not in order to see more clearly, but to remind each other that their eyes really were quite different.

Then they would both be grateful for their own. And with very different glasses they would gaze together at the distant mountains, rejoicing that they could both see them so clearly.

---

1. Matthew 7:12.
2. Ellen White, *The Ministry of Healing*, 483.

If you have appreciated this book, you'll want to read these also.

Chosen by Grace
Stuart Tyner

Is the biblical doctrine of the end-time remnant all about you and me? Or is it about God? Is it about our determined attempts to obey and overcome and somehow become "safe to save"? Or is it about God's active, zealous commitment to give us the gift of salvation? Over and over again, God has singled out a small group of ordinary people and given them an extraordinary mission—to draw attention to His everlasting love and long-suffering faithfulness.

ISBN 10: 0-8163-2309-7

Getting Back to the Heart of Adventism
Robert S. Folkenberg Jr.

The General Conference Session of 1903 faced a financial crisis. The church was on the brink of bankruptcy. Its flagship institutions lay in a crumpled heap of ashes. But the delegates spent the first two days of the session recommitting themselves to the mission of the church. They focused on the proclamation of the three angels' messages. In times like these, shouldn't we?

ISBN 10: 0-8163-2347-X

The Promise of Peace
Charles Scriven

Too many Adventists have settled into a mind-numbing routine centering on an inherited lifestyle rather than on our Lord. Charles Scriven declares the Adventist vision in a manner at once practical and brief. Your life mission goes beyond family, church, and job. God's mission takes you on a path from common places to uncommon ones. Here you may live by the promise of peace. And blessed you will be.

ISBN 10: 0-8163-2350-X

Three ways to order:

1 Local	**Adventist Book Center®**	
2 Call	**1-800-765-6955**	
3 Shop	**AdventistBookCenter.com**	 Pacific Press®